N

Palestine
Transjordan

Hadhramaut
Aden
Pr.

Br.Somaliland

Kenya
Tanganyika
Zanzibar

Seychelles

Mauritius

India

Burma

Hong Kong

PACIFIC OCEAN

INDIAN OCEAN

Ceylon

Malaya

Brunei
Sarawak

Singapore

Br.North Borneo

Christmas I.

Cocos I.

Papua
New Guinea

Gilbert Is.

Solomon Is.

Ellice Is.

New
Hebrides
(Br.& Fr.)

Fiji
Is.

Western
Samoa

Tonga

Norfolk I.

Australia

Tasmania

New Zealand
Antipodes I.

Macquarie I.

ERN OCEAN

Weihaiwei

WHO KILLED THE BRITISH EMPIRE?

WHO KILLED THE BRITISH EMPIRE?

AN INQUEST

GEORGE WOODCOCK

JONATHAN CAPE
THIRTY BEDFORD SQUARE LONDON

FIRST PUBLISHED 1974
© 1974 BY GEORGE WOODCOCK
JONATHAN CAPE LTD, 30 BEDFORD SQUARE, LONDON WCI

ISBN 0 224 01012 3

SET IN 11 PT GARAMOND 1 PT LEADED

PRINTED AND BOUND IN GREAT BRITAIN BY
COX & WYMAN LTD, LONDON, FAKENHAM AND READING

Contents

Introduction

No empire in the history of the world has ever died from a single cause, much less from the initiative of a single person. The title of this book has therefore to be regarded as largely figurative, for one answer to the question it contains would be 'No one' and another would be 'Mankind'. Thus, when I ask 'Who Killed the British Empire?', my intention is far from suggesting that any one identifiable executioner performed the stupendous function of eliminating an imperial complex that less than thirty years ago embraced a quarter of the world's land surface and ruled a quarter of the world's population. I mean rather to draw attention to a web of circumstances, to a conspiracy in which not all the members were identifiable human beings, or necessarily human beings at all. Some of them in fact were social forces of which it is hard to give any clear and visible image except in terms of the changing behaviour of the people they affected. Others were even less personifiable: economic forces, for example, that seem to have moved outside either individual or collective wills.

One fact is clearly certain. Never has the will or the action of a subject people, however heroic or persistent, been alone sufficient to destroy an imperial power. 'A society', said D. C. Somervell, 'does not ever die "from natural causes", but always dies from suicide or murder—and nearly always from the former.' Arnold Toynbee's *A Study of History*, in the introduction to whose first abridged version this sentence appears, is in fact largely devoted to an impressive charting of such cultural suicides and the causes that precipitated them, and it would not seem excessively Nietzschean to write a political history of the world in terms of will and its erosion.

I suggest, then, that when empires, as distinct from less ambitious cultures, expire, one almost always finds a combination of four factors contributing to their downfall: (1) the will of the oppressed peoples, often provoked by the desire to imitate and eventually to supplant the alien rulers; (2) the threat of external enemies and especially of rival empires (e.g. Rome against Carthage, or Holland against Portugal, or, in a less obviously belligerent way, the United States against Britain in the 1940s); (3) the decline of the will and ability of the imperial people to rule, a development linked closely with the erosion of their collective image of themselves as a master race; (4) the faceless power of economic circumstances which, despite all the plans of politicians and financiers, can transform an empire from a crown of diamonds to a crown of thorns, and can make the imperialist's burden so intolerable that he prefers to shed it, as the British so hurriedly shed the remaining fragments of their Empire in the years that followed the Suez crisis of 1956.

Of all these factors, it is obviously the third—the loss of confidence by imperial rulers in their own masterliness—that is crucial to the demise of all empires, though it is usually modified and often precipitated by the other factors, and particularly by the fourth—economic pressures sometimes complicated by the demands of imperial administration and defence. But, as is shown by the case of Portugal, a minor power that now ironically operates the world's leading conventional imperial system, an empire can endure a great deal of economic difficulty as well as internal insurrection and international hostility and still survive, so long as its rulers remain convinced of the viability and the rectitude of their dominion.

If the Romans had remained as willing to rule (and as able to maintain a sufficient army) as they had been in the days of Augustus, the barbarians would not have eroded the crumbling dikes of their empire and swept through the gaps. If the Spaniards had remained as certain of divine approval of their mission of colonization as they were in the reign of Ferdinand and Isabella, the rebellion of their American colonies in the early nineteenth century would not have succeeded; it would not even have occurred. If in the 1940s, instead of feeling so morally exhausted by the second of two great wars that they could not face the effort needed to assure the Empire a generation of renewed existence, the British had been able to draw upon the resolution and ruthlessness with which they suppressed the Mutiny a century before, India would not have become free. And without India free, there would have been no dismantling of the chain of dependencies and protectorates in Africa, the Middle East and the China Seas which formed the core of the colonial empire (as distinct from the white dominions) and which acted as the peripheral defences of India and of the sea routes to the trading empire on the China coast.

The resolution of the rulers was not merely modified by the other factors in the equation of empire. In turn, it modified them, and one of the most interesting problems that will have to be considered in tracing the fate of the British Empire is the interplay between imperial and anti-imperial forces and feelings— whereby the British taught rebellion to their subjects, and established such a rapport with those who sought to destroy their power that a sensitive internal opponent of British colonial rule like Gandhi and a shrewd external opponent like Franklin D. Roosevelt would both apply their greatest pressures when they sensed that the will by which the Empire was sustained had begun to weaken. One can even show that the decline in the imperial resolution resulted in shifts of financial priorities among the rulers in Westminster, so that the maintenance of the Empire may in fact have been more viable than it appeared during the 1940s to British rulers who yielded hastily to economic pressures that with resolution might have been resisted.

Inevitably, there is a degree of arbitrary arrangement in the way I have chosen to proceed with this inquest into the causes of the death of the British Empire, and its rebirth as that enigmatic international phoenix, the Commonwealth of Nations. To begin, since I am concerned with the British Empire as a declining factor in twentieth-century history, I have chosen to deal almost entirely with the New or Second Empire, as it is variously called, the complex of colonies, protectorates, protected states and self-governing territories that later became dominions that developed after the dismemberment of the Old or First Empire at the Treaty of Paris in 1783.

But the First Empire did not actually die. It was merely pruned of its heaviest boughs, and its remnants—the old Caribbean colonies, Canada, Newfoundland, the beach-heads already acquired in India and a few less important territories—formed the nucleus of the Second Empire, which the chances of war, the demands of

Indian defence, and the demographic forces that led to emigration and settlement, gradually filled out. One cannot therefore
claim with any truth that the British—as some historians seem to
suggest—actually performed a feat that would have been unique
among master races; to start afresh with the building of a new
empire after the first has perished. Rather, there is a long historical
process by which the First Empire merged into the Second,
shedding the American colonies on the way, and the Second
Empire merged into the Commonwealth of Nations, shedding
Ireland, Egypt, Iraq, Burma and South Africa, but still retaining
within its now largely symbolic embrace many of the territories,
such as Newfoundland, Bermuda and the Caribbean islands, that
were there from the beginning more than three hundred years ago.

For this reason alone it will be impossible entirely to ignore the
First Empire and the lessons of its fate. Indeed, a case might be
made (though I would not respond to it) for devoting a chapter
to the events of 1783 and the conflict that led up to them. For one
could extract from the American War of Independence a scenario
for the end of empire whose basic elements were in fact repeated
and fulfilled in the much longer and more gradual process of
transformation that led to the series of surrenders, from India and
1947 onwards, that have been the twentieth-century equivalent of
the events of 1783.

The insurgent colonial people was there, and so, supporting it
in 1783 for their own imperial reasons, were the rival external
powers—in that age France and Spain, anxious to regain some of
their own lost colonies and to halt the growth of British sea
power. The economic element was certainly present, since the cost
of maintaining, reinforcing and supplying an army, consisting
largely of German mercenaries, three thousand miles across a sea
that had to be effectively patrolled by British ships, was considerably more than that of providing a similar army for service on
the European continent.

If the British had been resolute in their intention to retain the
insurgent colonies, the economic cost would have been accepted,
as it was accepted not many years later in the Napoleonic Wars. In
political terms the internal American divisions between rebels
and loyalists, and between colonies with often opposed interests,
could have been more intensively exploited. With even slightly
better military co-ordination, the rebellion might have been de-

feated in the field and, if victory had been followed by a generous
settlement, the First Empire might have remained intact, with the
North American colonies gaining their liberties within the Empire
as Canada and the other dominions were to do in the following
century.

But the imperial rulers did not have the will to victory. The
American war was conducted with less conviction than any other
major war the British fought, not excepting the Boer War. Normally efficient generals made blunders which must be attributed
less to lack of competence than to the lack of vision that comes
with the failure of intent. For it was not merely a war against
people of their own stock that they were fighting; it was a war in
defence of imperial concepts that the forces of economic change
and social reform were already making obsolete in Britain itself. It
was one occasion when, in relative terms, the worst lacked all conviction while the best 'were full of passionate intensity', and the
best opposed war against their brethren when it was fought to
sustain an outdated mercantilism.

Here, then, already in 1783 we have all the factors—insurgent
subjects, external enemies, economic difficulties and the lapse of
conviction among the rulers—that were to emerge again as the
Second Empire declined. But there is one essential difference between the situation created by the withdrawal of the future
United States from the First Empire and the complete liquidation
of the Second Empire—as an empire—which took place in the
mid twentieth century.

The loss of the North American colonies, though it deprived
Britain of its most important possessions at that time, created only
a brief interruption in the imperial progress. The conquest of
India during the next half-century provided an alternative imperial power base, while the development of the white dominions
in Canada, South Africa and Australasia assured the spread of
British institutions and the protection of British interests in widely
scattered areas of the world. The conquest of sea power and the
pioneering development of a manufacturing industry shaped for
overseas trade enabled Britain to gain and to hold for decades the
economic hegemony of the world, a hegemony which it protected
by the acquisition of the colonies that defended its most important
sea routes. Indeed, it might be argued that the loss of the American
colonies actually stimulated the British to recognize opportunities,

in India and elsewhere, which before they had virtually ignored, and in this way to build up an effective empire in Asia, Africa and the South Pacific.

Thus, from imperial defeat in 1783, Britain rose to become the most dominant naval power the world has known, and to assemble an Empire that in size and population dwarfed any of its predecessors or contemporaries. With its fleet and its Empire, Britain — whose army was negligible by the standards of continental Europe — became a major power and, for most of the nineteenth century, the world's exemplar and leader, whose achievements other nations emulated and whose aura of strength and self-confidence was so intimidating that its real power was rarely even tested.

The most dramatic consequence of the collapse of the Second Empire was that the process of imperial growth, which continued into the 1920s, appeared to go into sudden reverse a quarter of a century later, and, like a realization of Shelley's lines from *Hellas*, where 'faiths and empires gleam, Like wrecks of a dissolving dream', Britain's greatness faded from the world's eyes. Once India with its resources of manpower and its strategically important territory was gone, Britain could not remain a power in Asia, and, though the imperial frame of mind lingered for a while after the end of the Raj, the main reasons for retaining the remaining colonies as imperial possessions had vanished. There were no longer any sea routes left which Britain had an urgent need to protect, and in any case Britain's sea power, so shaken in the Second World War, was no longer an instrument of domination in a world where the grander strategies were determined by the nuclear armaments of the two countries that had emerged strengthened from that war – the United States and Russia.

Furthermore, in 1783, when nationalism was still only emerging, great areas of the world were open to the territorial imperialist, and many remained so until the great scramble for Africa and the islands of the South Pacific in the late nineteenth century. Today the world is closed to territorial conquest, and the possibility no longer exists — and is not likely to recur in a foreseeable future — of creating an empire of the kind the British and their European rivals ruled up to the 1940s. This is not to say that imperialism is dead; it has merely been transformed into a pattern of spheres of continental or subcontinental influence dominated by territorially and industrially massive powers rather than a pattern of distant and scattered possessions linked by navies and trade routes. The possibility of a small group of Atlantic islands or any other territorially minor country dominating as much of the world as the British did in 1930 was visibly terminated in 1947.

Rudyard Kipling, the laureate of Empire, was also its threnodist; in the lines that cast their vatic shadow over the imperial holiday of Queen Victoria's Diamond Jubilee, he had foreseen the process.

> Far called, our navies melt away;
> On dune and headland sinks the fire:
> Lo, all our pomp of yesterday
> Is one with Nineveh and Tyre!

These lines were deeply prophetic, and why they were is the subject of this book. I am concerned with the death of the British Empire, not primarily with its growth, but in historical no more than in biological processes can death and growth be divided, and it was by growth and maturing that the Empire's death was made inevitable and also unique. Thus a weaving together of complementary strands of development and decay is inevitable when one traces, for example, the emergence of responsible institutions within the dominions in response to British parliamentary traditions, and the consequent detachment of these dominions from Britain itself; it is equally inevitable when one considers how Indians and Africans proceeded towards liberation largely by discarding their own traditional political concepts and substituting those of their conquerors.

Essential to this line of reasoning is, of course, the perception that, unlike the rulers of classical and baroque empires, the British were never single-minded in their desire to rule or in their sense of having been elected to do so. Undoubtedly it appeared to many ordinary English people—as it appeared to me as a schoolboy in England during the 1920s—that in a temporal as well as in a spatial sense the sun would not set on the British Empire in any conceivable future, for such people then accepted without question that in the nature of things an Englishman was superior to a man of any other race. The British ruling class was more realistic. Its members rarely saw themselves—as their counterparts in the Roman or Chinese or Ottoman Empires had done—as ministers of an eternal realm; men like Rhodes and Chamberlain, with a passionate sense of imperial destiny, were unusual at any time in Britain.

It is significant that only in India—where the Moghul tradition retained a useful charismatic appeal—and then only as late as 1876, did the British monarch assume the Roman title of Imperator, which at that time the rulers of no less than three European States—Russia, Germany and Austria—maintained, and which France had only recently abandoned. In the rest of the Empire— the dominions, colonies and protectorates—the imperial title was never formally assumed; the ruler was not Rex Imperator but merely Rex, the *primus inter pares* of a feudal aristocracy which democracy had drained of substance.

From the beginning of the Second Empire, and even in the last days of the First, the idea of a realm held in trust was constantly present in British minds, and if this was paternalism, the idea of fatherhood implies that the son will one day grow up. In this sense the British Empire was different from the French; the British assumed that the subject peoples would eventually—at however distant a day—be brought to the level of education and responsibility when they could choose their own political destinies; the French assumed that there was no better destiny for any people than to become citizens of the French Republic.

If the doctrinaire centralism of the Jacobin tradition, reinforced by Napoleon's vision of a continental empire, affected French imperial notions almost to the end, the pragmatic gradualism which gave the British Empire its peculiar character was largely a product of the extreme variety of the possessions administered mainly by those two sedate departments of His Majesty's Government, the India Office and the Colonial Office. In India Britain was the successor to an empire established by Turkish-Mongol invaders over a population consisting largely of Hindus and speaking more than a dozen major languages and several hundred dialects. Most Indians were related ethnically to the peoples of Europe, but this was not the case in the West Indies, where the descendants of Africans populated some of the oldest British colonies, or in Africa, where the interests of Victorian merchants and Edwardian planters helped to shape the administration of multi-tribal black peoples, or in Burma, which the accidents of history had made a province of a country—India—with which its people had few common traditions. In Ireland the subject people, a mixture of Iberians, Celts, Norsemen, Scots and Anglo-Normans, were hard to distinguish from their rulers across the narrow channel that divided them from Great Britain, particularly as their native Erse had been almost entirely submerged by an eloquent local English. The vestiges of independent Irish political institutions had been destroyed by immersion in the imperial Parliament before the end of the eighteenth century; by contrast there were parts of the Empire—notably the Indian principalities and the sultanates of Malaya—where ancient native absolute monarchies were allowed to flourish almost untouched by the paramount rule of the British Crown; there were desert sultanates on the verges of Arabia where the suzerainty of Westminster consisted of little more than treaty subsidies and military protection. A fair proportion of the British domains—varying in size and importance from Ascension Island to Egypt and in mutual remoteness from Gibraltar to the Falklands—were occupied mainly for their importance as strategic bastions or as coaling and supply stations on the long communication-lines of empire. Of all these varied territories, the situation of Egypt was perhaps the strangest of all; since 1922, when the British protectorate officially ended, Egypt was nominally an independent State, but British troops remained in occupation until 1954, so important was the Suez Canal regarded as a lifeline to India.

But next to India the most important components of the Empire were those settlements in temperate climates which later coalesced into the dominions of Canada, Australia, New Zealand and South Africa. These were colonies in the classical sense, for all of them had large European populations whose ancestors at least had come as immigrants. In Australia and New Zealand, where the immigrant populations were almost entirely Anglo-Celtic, and in Canada, where there was a large French-speaking group anxious to retain its traditional rights and customs, the indigenous peoples had been reduced to negligible minorities. In South Africa the Bantus and other black races remained in the majority, and if the British and Boer settlers differed bitterly enough to go to war on more than one occasion, they were united in the aim of keeping the native population in subjection.

While in India and the Crown colonies the British were a small military, administrative and trading caste, superimposed on native peoples allowed to retain almost undisturbed their customary social organizations, the Europeans in the self-governing colonies that became dominions set about creating homogeneous white societies. Like the Pilgrim Fathers, they were inclined to see their settlements as new worlds in the literal sense of being free of oppressive links with the old. The French Canadian, habituated to autocracy, was perhaps in the beginning an exception, but even before the conquest of 1760 the temptations of the free life of the forests had made it difficult to build in Canada a replica of France's caste-ridden *ancien régime*, and after the conquest it needed only a brief introduction to parliamentary practices to make the *canadien* as fervent in his desire for political responsibility as any British colonist. After the experience of the American rebellion, the autonomist inclinations that appeared among settlers in British North America and in the colonies of the South Pacific inevitably modified the policies of the imperial Government in Westminster, and thus it was that Canada, even more than Ireland, acted as a pioneer in initiating the long chain of modifications in status among the British possessions that led to the final liquidation of the Second Empire.

I have chosen to centre my study of that Empire not on 1783, when its phoenix progress began, nor on 1947, the most dramatic of all the dates in its falling flight, but rather on what historians may eventually decide was the most potent in its effects of all the Empire's critical years: 1930. To those who were not reading the signs it seemed a very ordinary year in the history of the British Empire. As a result of the Second World War and the acquisition of former German territories in Africa and Oceania, granted as mandates but administered as Crown colonies, the Empire had reached its broadest extent. The establishment of suzerainty over certain South Arabian sultanates during the 1920s had put the final touches to this largest of all the world's empires. It had such an imposing air of permanence and power that even its enemies— with the possible exception of Japan—did not imagine how fragile was the structure that held it together: a geodesic dome of prestige rather than a citadel of power. No one then envisaged that before the end of the 1960s it would virtually have ceased to exist. Yet in that year of 1930, for those who chose to observe them, the strains that the Empire had endured from its beginning at last showed themselves in irrevocable structural flaws that were manifested in three crucial incidents in which fateful and irreversible decisions presaged the approaching failure of resolution in all the imperial directions—in India, in the colonies, in the dominions.

It was, in India, the year of Gandhi's most imaginative manoeuvre in his fight for independence, the great salt march, which dramatically epitomized the popular opposition to British rule and which ended in an event hitherto unparalleled in the history of any empire, when Gandhi visited the Viceroy of India at the latter's request and the two men reached an informal agreement— the first of many steps on the English path of surrender to nationalist pressure.

In the same year, the British abandoned Weihaiwei to the Chinese. Unlike Shanghai, Weihaiwei was not a treaty port that remained under at least nominal Chinese rule; the territory was actually leased to Britain and, like Hong Kong, had been administered as a colony. This was the first abandonment of territory by the British (except for the special European cases of Heligoland and the Ionian Islands) since the adjustments that followed the Napoleonic Wars; it was significant because it represented less a recognition of growing nationalism in China than a surrender to moral pressure from Japan and the United States, the powers which later played the most active external roles in the fall of the Empire.

Finally, it was in 1930 that a conference of dominion and British representatives met in Whitehall to draft a series of resolutions embodying the individual sovereignty under a Common Crown of the self-governing territories of the Empire. With the Statute of Westminster which in 1931 gave legal standing to these resolutions the Empire first began to merge into the Commonwealth.

Part I of this book, then, will survey the Empire at its point of greatest territorial extension. Part II will be concerned with the developments from 1783 to 1930 that led up to that year's points of crisis: the shifts in British policies in accordance with the imperatives of imperial government, the initiatives that came from the colonies, the influence of international events and the pressures of imperial rivals. These developments will be seen as creating an evolutionary process that worked within the Empire and whose inevitable destination—once the creation of dominions out of colonies had begun—was the end of imperial rule. Nationalist activities in Ireland; the influence of alien European minorities like the Boers and French Canadians; the effects of the First World War, whose illusory gains masked a weakening of British strength both absolutely and in relation to other world powers: such facets of a century and a half of imperial growth and change will find their places in this part of the book, but the centre of attention will be held by the progression of the dominions to that point when the existence of virtually independent nations within the opening structure of the Empire was explicitly recognized.

In Part III, which takes its start from Gandhi's triumph in 1930, attention will shift away from the white dominions to India and the events leading to the granting of independence by a British Labour Government in 1947 to the two countries that emerged out of a partitioned Raj. Part IV will move to the Middle East and Africa, where the final stages of the Empire were luridly illuminated by the last and most disastrous of all imperial ventures: the Anglo-French intervention in Egypt over the issue of the Suez Canal in 1956. It will lead to an analysis of the series of decisions that led the British to dismantle the Empire so rapidly once India had been given independence. It was a process remarkably different from the obstinacy with which the Romans and the Chinese, even in decline, defended their crumbling classic Empires. The British, in some degree, actually willed the end of their role as empire builders, setting an example which, reluctantly and after attempting to suppress post-war movements for colonial liberation, their most important imperial rivals—the French and the Dutch—followed. This is a situation sufficiently unprecedented to be worth analysis. How far was it due to a failure of morale after the disaster of the Suez adventure? How far was it due to the survival of those idealistic dreams of a better world to come that were fostered during the Second World War? How far was it due to a growing sense of the primacy of European interests, already in evidence as early as 1914?

What remains of the Empire, in spirit and in fact, is one of the questions which Part IV will ask. How far does the Commonwealth carry on identifiable traditions of the Empire, and how durable have been the cultural and political contributions which the Empire made to the countries that have become its successor States?

Finally, the crucial question: what conspirators killed the

Empire? Who, among its subjects, its rivals, its rulers, played the fatal roles? How far must mere individuals be named in the indictment? How far must we lay the blame, as Tolstoy might have done, on the impersonal social, political and economic forces we often call History?

The tumult and the shouting have died; the Captains and the Kings, as Kipling foretold, have departed. Already a generation is growing up to which the Empire is not even a memory. It is time to walk in the ruins and listen to their silent voices.

Part I
The Great Routes of Empire

I Sea Power, Settlement and Trade

In the decline of the British Empire, as in its formation, the central geographic fact is that of Britain as a group of islands without a continental hinterland. It faces on to the Atlantic, like all the modern European nations that acquired maritime empires, with the sole exception of Italy, last-coming and least successful. Yet only at the end of the fifteenth century did Britain begin to pursue its seaward destiny. During the late Middle Ages, before the revolutionary changes in shipbuilding and navigational techniques that made ocean-voyaging possible in the Tudor age, England had attempted to ignore its surrounding oceans and, making use of what was essentially a coastal navy, to create a land-based continental Empire across the narrow channels that divided it from France and Ireland. This Empire, which in the days of the Black Prince included most of France, survived in fragmentary form on the continent of Europe until Calais was finally surrendered in the reign of Mary Tudor. Ireland was annexed as part of the same medieval attempt to create an Anglo-European Empire, and was held until the twentieth century because, while sea power remained a key to world power, an Ireland ruled from anywhere but London would be a perpetual threat; better an unruly subject realm, so long as it screened the western seaports of England, than a country free to form perilous alliances.

By the time Calais was lost in 1558, the first voyages that led to the establishment of a maritime British Empire, distinct from but associated with the vestiges of the old medieval domain of Ireland, the Channel Islands and the Isle of Man, had already been undertaken, for Cabot had discovered Newfoundland before the death of Henry VII. On Newfoundland in 1583 the first British settlement beyond the ocean was attempted; to this day, as a province of Canada, the island remains a part of the

Commonwealth. In the following year the first abortive expedi
tion sailed to Virginia. From this time onwards the building up
of the Empire continued steadily, with the one major setback of
1783, until the point of maximum territorial expansion between
the two World Wars.

In this development of the Empire, which in all lasted more than
four centuries, the factors of sea power and sea transport were
essential. Having failed to maintain its foothold on the continent
of Europe, the strongly centralized England which was formed
and consolidated under the Tudor monarchy could find ways to
national prosperity and national greatness only by turning to
advantage the very sea that constricted its powers of immediate
territorial expansion.

The sea was already a source of food, for until the middle of the
present century cheap fish was an important part of the diet of the
English masses; fish was also a source of trade, in terms of salt
cod sold on the markets of continental Europe, and an inducement to exploration. By the end of the fifteenth century fishermen
from Bristol were joining the Bretons and Portuguese who had
begun to exploit the Grand Banks of the north Atlantic with their
abundant supplies of cod. Indeed, the existence of Newfoundland
may have been known to European fishermen—and kept a secret
—before it was sighted by Cabot. It was mainly in this oceanic
fishing industry that the West of England seamen so active in the
early development of the Empire were raised and trained.

But it was only in the reign of Elizabeth, with the concurrent
development of European ocean-going fleets and of trade beyond
Europe (resulting from Portuguese ventures which by 1487 had
reached the tip of Africa and revealed the existence of the Indian
Ocean), that the development of sea power became important,
first to protect England itself and then to protect and extend its
activities as a trading power. The development by Devon captains of small mobile fighting ships and of the broadside firing
of naval cannon not only saved England from invasion by the
Spanish Armada, at a time when the Elizabethan militia would
have been virtually powerless against well-trained Spanish infantry. It also laid the foundation of England's maritime prosperity,
by piracy first and then by trade.

Like the Homeric heroes who created the ancient sea kingdoms
of the Aegean, the sixteenth-century rulers of England had little

compunction about sharing the proceeds of piracy. Such gains were used largely to finance the trading companies which not only provided a market for the English textile industry, whose growth was being encouraged in Tudor times by a primitive capitalism and a pre-mechanical factory system, but also brought to England the products of trade in the form of bullion or exotic goods which could either be conspicuously consumed at home or traded in Europe by such enterprises as the Merchant Adventurers.

The Muscovy Company, earliest of the great English overseas trading corporations, founded in 1552 and still in existence, was created with the aim of discovering a north-east passage around Siberia to China, that Mecca of Renaissance explorations, but this intent was quickly abandoned, as were attempts to establish a route through Turkestan to Persia, and the Company settled down to a trade by way of Archangel which resulted in no British territorial gains and fell away after the mid seventeenth century. With the power of Sweden and the growing power of Russia, there was little room for British imperialist ventures towards the north-east. Indeed, the only possession the British ever acquired in that direction was Heligoland, a strategically valuable North Sea island seized from the Danes in 1814 and used as a North Sea outpost for the Royal Navy until in 1890 it was traded with Germany for an acknowledgement of British rights over Zanzibar, an exchange to be quickly regretted, since Germany turned Heligoland into a naval base which complicated operations during the First World War.

Other Companies, however, established themselves on what soon became the highways of empire. It had long been the idea of merchants and statesmen to find the short route to China, and when interest in the north-east passage beyond Archangel diminished, the dream of a north-west passage continued to inspire voyagers until it was finally sailed by Amundsen in 1903. For more than a century before this it had been recognized that the passage would have no commercial value, and the interest in finding it had become almost purely scientific, but the dream of a trade route had lasted long into the eighteenth century, and as one of the by-products of north-west explorations the Hudson's Bay Company built its fur-trading posts on a sheet of salt water that bit deeply from the north into the continent of America. In

this way, by seventeenth-century charter and subsequent occupation, it established a British claim to the land between Lake
Superior and the Rockies which later became the central provinces
of Canada; after the conquest of New France in 1760 the North-
west Company, with which the Hudson's Bay Company eventually
united, extended the tenuous British occupation as far as the
Pacific. The Hudson's Bay Company owed its survival and that of
British claims in Rupert's Land to its ability to sustain maritime
communications through the northern seas.

Suzerainty like that so cavalierly granted by English monarchs
over land in North America inhabited by hunting Indians was not
feasible where there were established governments representing
long-developed and sophisticated if decaying civilizations. Thus,
the companies that traded to the east were slow to acquire territory, and the important imperial role of a Middle East trading
combine like the sixteenth-century Levant Company was to
establish a political interest in the eastern Mediterranean. This
later blossomed in the British support of Greek independence,
which led to the destruction of Turkish naval power at the battle
of Navarino in 1827; eventually, when the authorities in Whitehall
and Calcutta began to regard the Russian drive towards Constantinople as a potential threat to India, it involved a support
for the tottering Ottoman Empire that led Britain into its one
European conflict in the hundred years between Waterloo and
1914. This was the expensively inconclusive Crimean War of
1854–6, which, for Britain, was an imperial rather than a European war, aimed at safeguarding the routes to its Asian possessions and spheres of trade. This interest in the Middle East,
initiated by the merchants of the Levant Company, was not translated into territorial terms (except for the occupation of the
Ionian Islands) until the late nineteenth century, when Cyprus
was acquired and Egypt occupied.

It was a later and more modest Company, beginning in 1591
with an expedition that failed completely, that eventually established not only the trade routes, but also the motives, for the
greatest extension of the Empire outside the white dominions of
Canada and Australia. Starting with insecure little trading posts
on the coast of India, growing by treaties with the Moghuls and
lesser Indian princes, expanding by conquest, the East India
Company developed from a humble trading corporation at the

end of the seventeenth century to the leading power on the subcontinent of India a hundred years later.

But the ambitions of the East India Company extended, as its
name suggested, beyond the Indian subcontinent. India, in fact,
had been a second choice as the centre of its activities, for it had
begun by competing with the Dutch for the spice trade of the East
Indies, and only in the later seventeenth century, after two generations of commercial mayhem—like the slaughter of the British
traders by their Dutch rivals on Amboyna in 1623—had the
Netherlands East India Company finally succeeded in pushing its
British counterpart to the periphery of the Indonesian archipelago.
Even then—though seventeenth-century trading ventures in Siam
and Tonking and even as far away as Japan failed because of the
hostility of local rulers—the Company maintained from 1685 a
stubborn beach-head at Bencoolen on Sumatra, and outlasted
Dutch expansiveness. Attempts to undermine the Portuguese
monopoly of the China trade were eventually successful in 1757
when Canton was opened to commerce; after the Opium Wars
of 1840–2, the treaty port system spread from Canton to every
important centre on the China Coast, and a commercial empire
that existed parallel to the territorial British Empire down to the
1940s was created on the peripheries of a nominally independent
State, the Empire of the Manchu Sons of Heaven, whose own
imperial myths maintained the fiction that their suzerainty embraced the whole world. It was also to further the trading interests
of the East India Company, and to protect the trade route through
the Strait of Malacca to China, that the first British footholds in
Malaya were acquired at Penang in 1786 and Singapore in 1819.

In the east, certainly, it was the flag—in the sense of the actual
British Raj—that followed trade, for not until after the Mutiny
was the empire of the East India Company dissolved, when
Whitehall began to rule its Asian domains, not indirectly through
the Board of Control which since 1784 had exercised a parliamentary supervision over the Company's activities, but directly through
the India Office established in 1858.

Throughout these years the link between sea power and commercial power was vital. If it had not been for the Royal Navy,
supporting the East India Company's own private marine, possession of India would often have been endangered by French
squadrons based on Mauritius, and later on Batavia, and the

China trade would have been destroyed; this in turn would have adversely affected the standard of living in a Britain that had already become dependent for its prosperity on extensive foreign trade. The link between sea power, trade and the welfare of the nation as well as of the Empire was later to be dramatically demonstrated in the two World Wars of the present century, when famine was prevented in the British Isles only by the existence of a merchant navy so numerous that, despite immense losses from submarine activity, commerce could survive with the dominions, and with that successor State to the First Empire, linked to the Second by ties of tradition that both sides have been reluctant to admit: the United States.

The industrial revolution contributed notably to this pattern of sea power and seaborne trade. Britain pioneered the technology that led to a large surplus of manufactured goods for which there was a demand abroad, and it also fostered on the Clyde and the Tyne the world's largest shipbuilding industry. From the time when the Portuguese developed the caravels which took their explorers down the coast of Africa—perhaps even from the time when the Phoenicians developed the first stormproof galley— developments in shipbuilding have been crucial to the spread of maritime empires. The eighteenth-century East Indiamen, the largest merchant ships of their age, heavily armed and slow-moving, served admirably while the Company held its monopoly in the Far East, but as soon as its exclusive trading rights came to an end, the competition between the merchants of the Chinese treaty ports demanded swift and light ships, and from the opium clippers of the 1830s (which had to be fast enough to evade the Chinese coastal patrols) developed the fine-lined tea clippers of the 1860s that sailed from the China coast around the Cape of Good Hope to London in a hundred days.

Early in Queen Victoria's reign, with the advent of the steam-ship and the rise of commercial shipping lines (the P. & O. ships began their historic run down the Red Sea from Suez to India in 1840), the British began to develop a merchant marine which until 1914 was larger than the combination of all its rivals. Not only did this merchant marine carry British manufactured goods all over the world, and return with the raw materials and food needed to sustain a country where agriculture had become subordinate to industry. By providing shipping services for customers from other countries the merchant marine also created the invisible exports which enabled Britain to live for generations beyond its apparent means, selling abroad less than it ever bought. Above all, it kept open the great shipping routes which were the vital lifelines of empire.

They were vital to more than trade, for the reasons for imperial development were always more complex than the merely economic factors by which left-wing critics like Lenin were accustomed to describe, explain and condemn the European maritime empires. Trade may explain both the origins and the continued existence of some British colonies, and it was certainly the strong motive in the evolution of the commercial empire that flourished for a few decades on the China coast. But the preponderance of trade was a feature principally of those possessions or spheres of influence where the climate was too rigorous or the native population too numerous for Europeans to become a significant element in the working population. In Canada and South Africa, in Australia and New Zealand, even in Kenya, settlement quickly became the leading factor in imperial development and also—as we shall later see—in imperial dissolution. In such colonies trade and settlement tended to exist in conflict rather than in harmony.

Settlement had been an important element from the early beginnings of British imperialism; it was even a feature of the medieval protoempire, oriented towards Europe, that developed under the Plantagenets. Conquest and partitioning of new land was vital to the early expansive phases of a feudal society. The Norman conquest of England allowed landless and enterprising men to win estates and acquire gentility in the process; and the system of property-holding developed by the new, crude Norman aristocracy, with its emphasis on entail and primogeniture, meant that there were always younger sons seeking estates in the marcher lands and over the seas. Such men not only followed the Crusades with an eye to the main chance of spoil in Byzantium or baronies in the Holy Land; they also provided the leaders of the Anglo-Norman invasions of Wales and later of Ireland. If legend is to be believed, such English adventurers in search of land left the narrow world of Europe and the Levant even before the end of the Middle Ages; the first abortive settlement of Madeira is said to have been attempted in 1371 by Robert Machin of Bristol, eloping with the heiress Ann D'Arfet. But the first settlements that have any real significance in terms of the global British Empires belong to the late years of Elizabeth I and the succeeding Jacobean era, when the virtual unification of Great Britain took place through James VI of Scotland assuming the crown of England; the Union of 1701 was merely the formal confirmation of a process of integration which—whatever twentieth-century Scottish Nationalists may argue—included the Scots as partners from the seventeenth century onwards in the development of the British Empire.

The process of Tudor and Jacobean settlement did not begin in the territories of North America to which the monarchs of Britain and France laid claim in defiance of the Papal grant to Spain of all newly discovered land west of a line 370 leagues west of the Cape Verde Islands. The first post-Renaissance British settlements were made in Ireland, where the attempt to subdue that country by the immigration of English and Scots Protestants began in the reign of Elizabeth and continued in that of James I, so that to the earlier Anglo-Norman landowners was added a class of plebeian settlers, ancestors of the Protestant Orangemen who today form the larger of the two embattled sections of the population of Northern Ireland.

Those who started the early British settlements in North America—in Newfoundland, Virginia and New England, in Bermuda and Barbados—did not face the Irish problem of subduing another people closely related to themselves in language and culture, if not in religion. They might encounter rival imperialists—Spaniards in the Caribbean, Dutch on the Hudson River, French in Acadia and Quebec—and fight with them over land or the fur trade. But the native peoples were little interested in possessing land for settlement; they were hunters who might occasionally, like the Iroquois, practise a primitive and shifting mode of agriculture, but who remained largely nomadic and withdrew into the wilderness as the European immigrants advanced, to emerge for trade or guerrilla warfare. The white men treated them as enemies or as unreliable auxiliaries in their wars with rival European empires. In the more northerly settlements a pattern of small proprietorship was encouraged by the democratic tendencies of dissenting religion. Something very close to a feudal pattern, on the other hand, was attempted in several of the southern colonies—such as Maryland and the Carolinas, which were granted to English noblemen and gentry, as was New Jersey—and even, when the Scots first claimed it, in the bleaker outpost of Nova Scotia.

Yet even in these almost baronial concessions the land was quickly divided; the elaborately graded society of feudal Europe was transplanted no more successfully to the Thirteen Colonies than to New France, where relations between the habitants on their strip farms beside the St Lawrence and the *seigneurs* who served as their nominal overlords remained far simpler and freer than relations in Old France between the overlords and the peasants.

But even though there was a simplification of the social structure both in the English colonies and in the French settlements that joined them after the conquest of Quebec, a planter aristocracy of a new kind, built on the labour of convicts and of slaves, nevertheless emerged in the southern colonies of North America and also in the sugar-growing islands of the Caribbean. In North America this resulted in political differences of orientation between the various colonies which—long after the declaration of American Independence and the death of the First British Empire in 1783—reached a point of climax during the Civil War, and even now are incompletely resolved.

As I have already remarked, the history of the Thirteen Colonies is relevant to the present narrative only in so far as it is reflected in the subsequent history of the Second Empire. In that history too we observe a double pattern of settlement, part neofeudal and part popular, in both cases related to the maintenance of sea power and the development of maritime transport.

In the early settlements, ocean transport was perilous and uncomfortable; those likely to find their way to the colonies were either impoverished gentlemen and their adherents, who combined a sense of adventure with some special inducement such as land grants; lesser people who went against their will, such as convicts and soldiers; or those driven by some special necessity, like the dissenters who went in search of places to practise their beliefs in freedom or the Scottish crofters and landless English and Irish labourers who went because there was nothing left for them —often not even food—at home. As the volume of shipping across the Atlantic increased after the Napoleonic Wars, and especially after the development of steamboats, the volume of immigration increased correspondingly, and the preponderance of popular over gentlemenly immigrants changed the social make-up of Canada and the later-developing white dominions, and effectively frustrated the attempts to re-create a class society of the kind that flourished in Britain. Inevitably, the emergence of a way of life at once more populist and more pluralist (because of the variety of immigrant stocks) than that of the First Empire was to play its part in the process of dissolution which we shall be observing at work in the Second Empire. Throughout the present century, even after the Empire had merged into the Commonwealth, the streams of immigrants brought by the old imperial sea routes steadily changed the character of the societies and cultures of the dominions.

The great sea-borne elements—trade and settlement—that created both British Empires inevitably came into conflict. The so-called mercantilist system that governed imperial relations until the triumph of free trade at the end of the eighteenth century was not a consciously elaborated system, nor was even the word mercantilism known to those who operated this pattern of economic relationships until—towards the very end of its reign—Adam Smith invented its name and transformed it into a concept. Nevertheless, in all European empires until the nineteenth century the trading interest was at first in the ascendant.

In the system of colonization developed by the ancient Greeks, cities, rather like amoebae, would divide into separate entities as they grew too populous for good or economic government; and many States that became Mediterranean powers in their own rights, such as Byzantium and Syracuse, Tarentum and Cyrene, began as instantly independent colonies founded by expeditions sailing from the cities of the Greek heartland.

This was far from either the aim or the methods of early British imperialists. Not only did the great licensed companies which traded to the civilized Asian countries expect and enforce a monopoly of commerce against all rivals, whether English or foreign, but the laws by which the imperial Parliament regulated the actual colonies of the First Empire were framed to favour English ship-owners, merchants and manufacturers. The colonies most cherished by Whitehall and by the mercantile interests of London and Bristol were the islands that were purely plantation colonies, with small white populations and large slave-labour forces, which manufactured nothing and exported raw or partly processed materials in English ships to English ports. The real settlement colonies, where European and primarily English immigrants formed a majority of the population, presented difficulties that proved insoluble until after 1783, when the 'mercantilist' methods were gradually abandoned. Though the dissenting origins of the New England colonies in particular should have suggested caution, English Parliaments for two centuries sought to rule the colonies exclusively in order to further English trading interests. Seventeenth-century laws decreed that goods could only be carried between England and the colonies by English ships. Trade between the colonies and countries outside the Empire was strictly limited, and trade between New England and New France before 1760, though it went on, was in point of law illegal. As late as 1750 the English manufacturers were triumphant in their attempts to frustrate the development of factories in the colonies; in that year the Iron Act forbade the construction in the colonies of rolling mills, forges and other plants connected with the making and processing of iron. Such attempts to restrict trade and manufacture contributed as greatly to the American Revolution as the issue of taxation without representation.

Even after 1783 the British imperial administration was not entirely freed from 'mercantilist' attitudes. The East India Company still ruled India largely as a source of profits for English shareholders, and while in the Second Empire little attempt was made by the British Government to interfere with trade and manufactures in the white colonies of Canada and Australasia, restrictive laws in India continued until after the First World War to frustrate the development of local manufactures, and created an issue around which nationalist sentiment could crystallize.*

But trade and settlement, separately or in competition, were

---

* The public burning of British-made cloth became an emotionally potent ritual of the movement for Swaraj or independence, and the re-establishment of a native handweaving industry to replace that destroyed by the competition of Lancashire looms became one of Gandhi's objectives. It acquired such an aura of sacredness in Indian eyes that even today, long after the British have departed, and long after an independent India has become dedicated to the goal of technological transformation, considerable funds are still expended by a financially hard-pressed Government on subsidizing a completely uneconomic *khadi* or handwoven cloth industry.

not the only reasons why imperial possessions were gained or kept. There was little trade to be won, and no space for settlement, in places like Gibraltar and St Helena. But as fortresses to protect the trade routes, as bases for the naval squadrons that maintained British supremacy in every sea except such closely landlocked waters as the Baltic and the Black and White Seas, and as coaling stations during the century, haunted by the now extinct slave figure of the stoker, between the decline of sail and the appearance of oil-driven ships, these were essential units of a maritime empire, indispensable valves of the great machine. There were also large colonies, like those of East Africa, which were acquired to prevent potentially hostile powers controlling coastlines that might endanger one or other of the great routes of empire. Often such colonies had secondary attractions, such as the cool highlands of Kenya, admirable for European settlement, and the spice gardens of Zanzibar, but others, like Somaliland, would have been useless as well as expensive to maintain if it had not been for their strategically important position—in the case of Somaliland at the base of the Red Sea opposite to Aden.

Of course the reasons for acquiring possessions were not always the same as those for retaining them. Quite a number of colonies that became vital in the pattern of empire were acquired by war or other historical accident with little thought of their uses in the future. Hong Kong, which seemed so useless to the British in 1841 that Captain Charles Elliott was reprimanded and dismissed for having annexed it, became and remains—more than 130 years after its acquisition—one of the great *entrepôts* of the Far East. The fever-stricken island of Bombay, which seemed the whitest of Indian elephants when Charles II received it as part of the dowry of his Portuguese queen, became in the hands of the East India Company one of the main centres of British trade and power in India. And Rupert's Land, that careless gift which the same King Charles made to his warrior uncle, embraced the great prairie lands that transformed Canada from the small confederation of Atlantic colonies which it was in 1867 into the world's second largest country.

There were other, less tangible and more volatile motives for the retention of imperial possessions. Britain became a world power, because of the circumstances that allowed her to acquire the largest of the maritime empires. Once the greatness and power had been achieved, they were enjoyed for their own sakes. Adam Smith, who believed Britain would be far better off without her colonies, concluded in 1776 that there was no likelihood of a willing relinquishment of empire; his remarks—which represent an early stage of the conventional liberal-radical wisdom about imperialism—are worth remembering, since up to the mid twentieth century they seemed to define fairly accurately the practice of most British rulers and the sentiments of a large segment of the British population.

> No nation ever voluntarily gave up the dominion of any province, how troublesome soever it might be to govern it, and how small soever the revenue which it afforded might be in proportion to the expense which it occasioned. Such sacrifices, though they might frequently be agreeable to the interest, are always mortifying to the pride of every nation, and what is perhaps of still greater consequence, they are always contrary to the private interest of the governing part of it, who would thereby be deprived of the disposal of many places of trust and profit, of many opportunities of acquiring wealth and distinction, which the possession of the most turbulent, and, to the great body of the people, the most unprofitable province seldom fails to afford. The most visionary enthusiast would scarce be capable of proposing such a measure, with any serious hopes at least of its ever being adopted.

Adam Smith was correct in his opinion of the power of national pride and private interest, but the objects of both pride and interest changed significantly during the twentieth century. What had once been a matter of collective pride began to look like a reason for collective shame. The very classes that had once sent their sons to govern the colonies and the India Raj now found other directions in which to satisfy their needs for action and also to serve their material interests. As soon as the Empire reached maximum dimensions for the very prosaic reason that the shrinking of unclaimed regions precluded any possibility of further growth, the elan of success began to abate, and the opposing forces within the British nation began to gain strength.

But this metamorphosis had only just begun to become evident in 1930, and the bastions of empire—the dominions and India, and the scattered colonial fortresses—were still there in their complete-ness, more populous, more extensive than any past had seen them. All these places were able to fulfil their dramatic and changing roles because they were sustained and guarded by the great imperial sea routes, and these routes enable one to trace and classify the hundred-odd dominions, colonies, dependencies, pro-tectorates, protected states and treaty ports (not to forget those more nebulous domains known as 'spheres of influence') that combined to form the territorial and commercial empires of Britain in the springtide year of 1930. In that year His Majesty's gunboats sailed unchallenged up the rivers of China and His Majesty's representatives ruled *de jure* or *de facto* over the lands of the Pharaoh and the Great Moghul, over Jerusalem and Babylon and Baghdad, over the Rockies and the Himalayas and the Mountains of the Moon, over tropical jungles in four continents and frozen wastes in the Arctic and the Antarctic, over Rajput princes claiming the ancestry of the sun and Cypriot heirs of the glory that was Greece and palaeolithic hunters wandering the deserts of Africa and Australia.

In 1930 one could trace five great routes of British dominion, each as vital to imperial survival as the massive stone roads that laced through Europe and the Andes and sustained the empires of the Romans and the Incas. The route used longest by European voyagers ran down the west coast of Africa, following the explora-tions of Cão and Dias in the fifteenth century, and up the east coast of the continent as Vasco da Gama had followed it, into the Indian Ocean and across to the Malabar Coast. It continued as the great imperial route to the end of the eighteenth century. Then it was largely superseded by the route through the Mediter-ranean and the Red Sea which was already becoming a prime imperial highway even before the Suez Canal was cut through the sleeve of desert uniting Africa and Asia. This route led overland and later by canal across the isthmus of Suez to the Red Sea, and down past the coasts of Arabia to India and a final destination at Bombay or Calcutta. From India two further routes branched out, with Ceylon as their pivot. One led eastward to Singapore and the China Seas. The other went south-eastward to Australia, New Zealand and the Oceanic Islands.

Finally there was the western route, first charted by the seekers after the north-west passage, and leading across the Atlantic to

Newfoundland and Canada. A branch ran southward to touch
Bermuda in mid Atlantic and reach the West Indian islands and
the small mainland possessions on the coasts of Central and South
America. An even more southerly branch of the western route
touched the Falkland Islands with their dependent territories,
defending the pre-Panamanian way by Cape Horn to British
Columbia and the Polynesian archipelagos.

As I trace these routes in the remainder of this first part of my
book, I shall tell of the acquisition and eventual role of each possession, so that the chapters will be a series of historically oriented
ruttiers which will not only transmit a sense of the cultural and
economic variety of the Empire at its height, but will illuminate
its growth as a prelude to the later chapters, which will trace the
course of its decline.

II The Grand Route of Empire

The passenger who travelled in 1930 on the grand route of empire was left in little doubt, from the moment he boarded his liner, of the main destination to which it was sailing. He would certainly travel, if he hoped to become an imperial somebody, on one of the Peninsular and Orient Steamship Company's mailboats. The P. & O. made up for the modest tonnage of its vessels by its historic repute (it was founded in 1834 to carry the mails to Spain and made its first sailings from Suez to India in 1840, and to Singapore and Hong Kong in 1845), by the romantic allure of the places it served, and by the peculiar social life that was fostered between its decks. Each mailboat that sailed through Suez was a microcosm of the Empire in all its Indian grandiosity; the neophyte experienced his first encounter with the rigidities of protocol into which British Indian social behaviour had long ossified, while the Old India Hand, who had found himself of disappointingly little account on leave, could experience again, as soon as he set foot on shipboard, the deference paid to a status acquired by his special kind of merit.

The structure of Indian society—in 1930 no society counted in India but that of the British conquerors and a few favoured native princes—was, indeed, as passengers travelling through Suez soon discovered, significantly different from that of the European aristocratic world. Neither inherited title nor military rank gained the greatest deference. Those spare and sallow men who were treated more respectfully every day that the shores of Britain receded into the past and the distance were in fact civil servants, for India had become rather like classical China in the sense that power and prestige were vested in a mandarinate chosen by examination and trained in a tradition of dedicated service first to the Raj and afterwards to the Indian people, a tradition that British officials in India sustained on the whole conscientiously, stinting neither time nor effort and often at great risk to health and life.

Only the Viceroy—the Empire's leading proconsul, who wielded more autocratic authority than the King–Emperor would dare to claim in Whitehall—stood apart from and above the oligarchs of the Indian Civil Service; he was always a member of the House of Lords (and usually an aristocrat by descent), since only through a titled nobleman could the royalty implied in his powers be properly symbolized. But it was rare to find a member of the hereditary aristocracy in the Indian Civil Service, which consisted mainly of upper-middle-class young men who had proved themselves as classical scholars at public school and university. From among the Civilians, as they were generally called, the high officials who actually ruled India were chosen. The Indian Civil Service was as exclusive and carefully chosen a body as Plato's Guardians, on whom it may to an extent have been modelled; it comprised usually between 1,000 and 1,200 members.

Even the Indian Army ranked below the Civil Service, and provincial bureaucrats, together with members of such services as the Indian Imperial Police, the education and forest services, and so on, ranked even lower. Below the officials ranked all Europeans, no matter how wealthy, who held non-governmental positions, whether as missionaries or men of business—the despised box-wallahs. Even among box-wallahs there were levels of acceptability. Wholesale trade might pass, but retail trade was barely respectable, and even the equality said to prevail inside the walls of a British club in India, as in an army mess, could be strained if a box-wallah presumed to drink without invitation at the end of the bar tacitly reserved for the leaders of the local British community; few did in fact presume. The attitude towards commerce that crystallized in India after the Mutiny may seem curious in a country where British penetration was pioneered by merchants. But the worst decades of the East India Company's reign were the period of the nabobs, those merchant adventurers who extorted fortunes from Indians and returned home to use them in corrupting the unreformed electorate. When Pitt established the Board of Control in 1786 it was to curb the excesses of those who thought of India in terms of amassing wealth, and as the Company shed its exclusive trading privileges first in India

(1813) and then on the China coast (1833), the distinction widened between the merchants—unattached traders now in an ambiance of free competition—and the civil servants. In the later years of Company rule these were entirely detached from commercial activities and occupied with collecting taxes, administering justice, and carrying out tasks of general government among peoples now regarded, in the light of Victorian humanitarianism, less as conquered subjects than as imperial wards. Thus the merchants ceased to wield by proxy, as they had done in Clive's time, the power of the Moghuls; they returned to their original aim of making profits. The tradition of imperial rule, receding beyond the Moghuls to the Hindu empire of the Guptas and to Ashoka and his fellow Mauryas before the beginning of the Christian era, fell into the hands of the Civilians. When the Mutiny was finally defeated, they would achieve the ambition that had eluded Muslim and Hindu imperialists alike, and establish the unified India embodied in the Vedic tradition of the Chakravartin, the universal Wheel-King. Few Civilians saw their role in such exalted terms, but all of them felt and most displayed a sense of moral as well as political superiority over those who came to India for reasons other than to rule it.

Already, as the P. & O. mailboat sailed west along the Channel, the molecules of this hierarchic society—so different from anything that survived in Britain itself after 1914—reassembled in proper order; the neophyte who, by the time he reached Bombay or Calcutta, had not learnt his place and how to behave in it was more insensitive than most middle-class Englishmen half a century before to the nuances of social behaviour. Anglo-Indian society in its complex rigidity was in fact a model for all those exotic and protocol-ridden offshoots of the British world that flourished wherever the colonial empire (as distinct from the dominions) existed.

In 1930 the Empire span on an axis that stretched, not from London to Ottawa or Canberra, and even less from London to Pretoria, but from London to Delhi in the bright brisk months of winter and from London to Simla in the summer months, when the plains of Hindustan were parched and dusty, or melting under the torrents of the monsoons. From that summer of 1798 when Napoleon sailed for Egypt with the intent of destroying the British lines of communication to Calcutta, only to be foiled by the brilliant tactics of Nelson at Aboukir Bay and Sidney Smith at Acre, the Governments of both Britain and India had lost no opportunity of protecting the sea routes, and almost every territory and outpost of the Empire which the neophyte India hand passed as he sailed the Red Sea route between London and Bombay had been retained, even if it had not been acquired, for the purpose.

The Channel Islands

Indeed, the only possession of the British Crown on this route that did not fall into this category was the first one passed before leaving the English Channel for the storms of the Bay of Biscay. In fact, the Indian traveller would not even catch sight of the Channel Islands, for they lay well out of British territorial waters on the French side of the Channel, at the entrance to the Gulf of St Malo. The French call them Les Îles anglo-normandes, and this gives a better clue to their significance than the English name, for they are the last relics of a history which antedates even the earliest of British imperial ventures. Modern Britain, as a political entity, dated from the conquest of England in 1066 by William of Normandy, and it was by virtue of his devious descent from this Norman duke that George V still held the Channel Islands. The islands were attached directly to the Crown and were governed by their own medieval assemblies, or States. By the twentieth century they had lost any strategic importance they might once have had, for the era of wars with France had ended, and the group lay too far south of the shipping ways through the Channel to be useful as a protection or noticeable as a threat to British sea power. They had become a garden of England, growing early flowers and vegetables, rearing celebrated breeds of cattle, providing a mildly exotic holiday spot for English people too timid to venture into completely foreign lands. Their population, originally a mixture of Breton and Norman, had long been adulterated by English immigration; yet a Norman-French patois lingered which had vanished in France; it symbolized the anachronistic character of this oldest of the British royal dependencies, a memento of origins rather than a manifestation of present realities. When the Germans invaded the Channel Islands in 1940 the British Government in fact regarded the group as dispensable, attempting neither to defend nor to recover it until after the end of the war in 1945.

Gibraltar

Gibraltar, the next Imperial possession on the way to India, was treated quite differently and resolutely defended, as it had been in every British war since its capture from Spain in 1704. Gibraltar was in some ways an unimpressive possession: its area—just over two square miles—was less than a thirtieth that of the Channel Islands, and its civilian population in 1930 about a fifth. It was a rocky promontory jutting from the coast of Spain, with no hinterland, no room for little farms or herds of prize cattle, no room even for holiday-makers to lounge at leisure. Its importance lay solely in the fact that it commanded the entrance to the Mediterranean.

In classical antiquity Gibraltar was one of the Pillars of Hercules, the natural coastmarks which defined the region of safe navigation. Beyond it lay the River of Ocean, the vast unknown sea on which only strange men defiant of the Gods, like the Phoenicians, would venture. In modern times it had become important as a fortress, not as a boundary point, and it was used as such by the Moors and by the Hapsburg kings of Spain. Whoever held Gibraltar controlled the sea route from northern and western Europe to north Africa, Alexandria and the Levant.

By 1930 Gibraltar had been in British hands for more than two centuries. Its retention, if not its acquisition, rested on dubious grounds even by the standards of international relations accepted in the imperial era. It was captured in 1704 by a joint force of British and Dutch soldiers acting nominally on behalf of the Archduke Charles of Austria, claimant to the Spanish throne. Then, in secret negotiations with the French, concealed from the Dutch and Spaniards, the Rock was ceded to Britain; the cession was confirmed in the Treaty of Utrecht in 1713. The Spaniards besieged Gibraltar in 1726, and again, with more serious intent and French assistance, in the great siege from 1779 to 1783; when peace was signed in the latter year the Thirteen Colonies were lost but Gibraltar remained to play its vital role in the Second Empire. Napoleon's expedition to Egypt, with India as its distant aim, emphasized the importance of retaining this strongpoint

which assured the Royal Navy access to the Middle Sea; after
the Suez Canal was opened the abandonment of Gibraltar was
unthinkable.

Gibraltar was one of the few British possessions governed as a
fortress. In theory it had been a Crown colony since 1830; in
practice the military authorities were in control, for the commander of the garrison was also the Governor and ruled entirely
through his nominated Executive Council. There was no Legislative Council, and the people of Gibraltar had no say in con-
ducting their own affairs. Yet they were—and still are—among
the least troublesome of imperial subjects, mainly because they
have always dreaded more than British rule the prospect of becoming subjects of Spain. Before 1704 the Rock was inhabited by
Spaniards, with perhaps some mingled Moorish ancestry, but
most of these departed early in the British occupation to live on
the mainland around Algeciras, and Gibraltar's subsequent human
population, like its celebrated Barbary apes, was imported from
various parts of the Mediterranean and had no common loyalty
except to Britain. By Mediterranean standards the Gibraltarians
were prosperous; the garrison and the naval base provided employment, and a multitude of small traders was sustained by the
visits of Orient-bound liners and Mediterranean cruise boats.
Thus, even down to the character of its population, Gibraltar had
been shaped more than any of the other British colonies to fit its
function as a key point on the imperial sea routes.

Tangier

The possession of Gibraltar was not the only evidence of British
intent to prevent alien control of the vital channel between the
Pillars of Hercules. The passenger entering the Strait of Gibraltar
would undoubtedly see, on an average clear day, the white buildings of Tangier on its African shore. It was one of the few possessions which, in 1930, the British would admit to having held
and abandoned, for in general they stuck to Queen Victoria's
maxim; 'Giving up what one has is always a bad thing.'*

Like Bombay, Tangier came into the hands of Charles II in

* She showed her sound imperial instinct when she made this remark to Salisbury
at the time when Heligoland was being exchanged with Germany for Zanzibar. Had
her advice been followed, and had Heligoland remained a British ocean outpost,
the naval history of the First World War might have been very different.

1661 as part of the dowry of Catharine of Braganza. The British accepted it with zeal, since they regarded the fortress as admirably placed to protect the trade developed in the Mediterranean by the Levant Company. They strengthened the defences, built a mole to protect shipping in the bay, and sent expeditions against the Barbary pirates. But the occupation proved costly in money and men alike, and the hostility of the Moors was so persistent that in 1684 the British withdrew; twenty years later Gibraltar was captured.

Yet even possessing Gibraltar, Britain had no intention of allowing Tangier to be occupied by another European power. In the mid nineteenth century the Foreign Office cultivated its influence in Morocco, and when the Spaniards invaded that country in 1860, Britain warned them against any attempt to occupy permanently either Tangier or its neighbouring coast; since Palmerston was in power the warning was heeded. The same policy was maintained towards the French, and in 1904, at the time of the Entente Cordiale, an agreement was reached by which Tangier became a neutral and international territory, governed by a commission of which, in 1930, Britain was a leading member. Thus, even without the possession of Tangier, the main object of British policy, the protection of the route to India, had been maintained.

Minorca

Sailing beyond Gibraltar into the Mediterranean, the Orient traveller passed, out of sight to the north, other territories which had belonged briefly to the Empire and played their part in the naval domination over the inland sea. The first was Minorca in the Balearic Islands. Seized during the War of Spanish Succession for its great harbour at Port Mahon, it was held by Britain from 1708 to 1756, when the French captured it. In 1763 it was restored to Britain, and remained a part of the First Empire until 1782; then, unlike Gibraltar, it did not prove strong enough to withstand a Spanish siege. It passed out of British possession, but not without leaving a picturesque legacy in the English Georgian villas that still grace the outskirts of Port Mahon.

It is significant of the shift in imperial aims after 1783 that during the Napoleonic wars the British made no attempt to recover Minorca. The Western Mediterranean strategy based on the axis of Gibraltar and Minorca was linked with the polarization of the First Empire between Britain and North America. The main external threat to that system was an alliance of France and Spain, whose combined American dominions, extending in an arc from the St Lawrence through the Great Lakes and the Mississippi valley to the Caribbean and Central America, encircled the Thirteen Colonies. Guarding the approaches to both Barcelona and Toulon and shielded by Gibraltar, Minorca was an ideal base to threaten the Bourbon alliance from the rear and to divert Franco-Spanish naval power from the Americas. Thus the loss of Minorca in 1756 was considered disastrous enough to justify the court martial and shooting of Admiral Byng, who had failed to defend it, but by 1782, when Minorca was lost a second time, the fall of Yorktown had already sealed the fate of the First Empire, there was no point in continuing a strategy aimed at the defence of the Thirteen Colonies and no effort was made either diplomatically or militarily to repossess the island. The British had not yet acquired the retentiveness which later made them regard the loss of almost any fragment of territory as a dishonour to be avoided. That came when they assumed the mantle of the Moghuls, preoccupied with the question of face so vital to the power of an Asian ruler.

British imperial policy in the Mediterranean during the Napoleonic wars was based on two complementary strategic aims. The first was the continental defeat of France, for which purpose it was the Iberian mainland rather than the peripheral islands that the British aimed in alliance with local patriots to capture and hold. The second aim, which gained increasing importance after Napoleon's Egyptian venture in 1798, was to prevent the creation of a strong hostile base in the Middle East. This concern preoccupied British policy-makers until late in the 1950s, and the desire to control the naval routes in the central Mediterranean led the British between 1794 and 1815 into a series of imperial ventures that brought such unlikely places as Corsica and Sicily under the aegis of the Second Empire, established the long British rule over the Ionian Islands, and turned Malta into a fortress even more formidable than Gibraltar.

All these places were islands and therefore easily captured and defended by a country with a strong navy and a small professional army. All were suitably placed to intercept possible French incursions into the Levant. And all were inhabited by peoples who appeared at the time to prefer British presence and protection to the rule of either the French or—in the case of the Ionian Islands —the Turks.

Corsica

The Corsican incident was the strangest and the briefest. Britain had encouraged Corsican rebellions in the early eighteenth century against the Genoese, and had given tacit approval to the flamboyant German adventurer Von Neuhoff, who persuaded the islanders to crown him King Theodore I; Theodore ruled briefly, fled to London, and, after two unsuccessful attempts to re-establish his rule with covert British help, found his way into an English debtor's prison and was buried in the churchyard of St Anne's, Soho. In 1793, under their patriot leader Pasquale Paoli, the Corsicans called on the British to protect them against the French, who had acquired Corsica from the Genoese in 1768. In 1794 Corsica was constituted a monarchy, with George III as king, but the Corsicans showed themselves unappreciative of the honour, and by 1796 it was clear that they were as ungovernable by the British as by anyone else. The imperial Government decided to withdraw from a land where the difficulties of administration seemed to exceed any possible strategic gain, and Corsica played no part in the brilliant naval manoeuvres by which Nelson foiled Napoleon's Egyptian venture. Bastia was captured again in 1814, but more as a personal gesture against Napoleon than for any military reason, and it was abandoned without regret after Waterloo.

Sicily

A similar problem of dealing with a violent and volatile population brought an end to the rather longer British occupation of Sicily. The nominal reason for the British landing on the island in 1806 was to support Ferdinand III, who had been chased to the island when the French imperial armies drove him from Naples. Commanding both the direct sea route to Alexandria and the alternative route through the Straits of Messina, Sicily was of great strategic value to the British, who treated it for a decade as a virtual protectorate. The ambassador from the Court of St James carried out the same duties as the Resident in a tributary Indian state, and Lord William Bentinck, who in his later role as Governor-General of India was responsible for such dramatic reforms as the suppression of suttee and thuggee, occupied himself in Palermo formulating a new constitution for the Sicilians with a bicameral parliament on the British model. It aroused little local enthusiasm, and when the Bourbons were restored in 1815 this imitation of Westminster was abolished without apparent opposition. Yet, as Bentinck must have heard with ironic pleasure, in 1820 it was to demand a restoration of his constitution that the capricious Sicilians rose in rebellion.

Malta

But by this time Sicily no longer interested the British, who had chosen as the pivot of their command of the Mediterranean the little group of islands scattered between Sicily and the African continent and known as Malta. Long an important link between Europe and Africa, a great megalithic ceremonial and trading centre, an outpost of the Phoenicians, Malta commanded the widest and most used channel between the western and eastern lobes of the Mediterranean. Experience had also proved—most dramatically when the Knights Hospitallers defended it against the assaults of Suleiman the Magnificent in 1565 and thus saved Italy from a massive Turkish invasion—that Malta was a natural strongpoint and with proper fortifications and a capable commander was virtually impregnable.

Having been ruled by the Knights Hospitallers in a way that left them much local autonomy, the people of Malta had no tradition of subjection to a neighbouring kingdom (though the rulers of Naples and Sicily had nebulous reversionary rights should the Knights abandon control) and certainly they showed no wish to accept French domination after Napoleon abolished in 1798 the rights of the Order. Instead, they launched a formidable guerrilla uprising, using the network of boundary walls on the islands as an improvised defence system, and called for British aid. When Nelson blockaded the island and eventually expelled the French, the Maltese elected his deputy, Captain Alexander Bell, president

of their provisional Government. The Treaty of Amiens restored
the islands to the Knights Hospitallers, but the Maltese protested
that only the British could defend them against the hated French,
and, like the Corsicans, they invited George III to become their
king. The British temporized, leaving Bell as Civil Commissioner
—and virtual governor—until, in 1813, they assumed sovereignty.

Long before the strains of Verdi at the Khedive's command
celebrated the opening of the Suez Canal in 1869, the vulnerable
importance of the Mediterranean as a route to the east had been
brought home to the British not only by Napoleon's expedition
to the Nile (in which his capture of Malta had been an incident)
but also by the steady Russian pressure through the Balkans
towards Constantinople and Asia Minor. At no time after 1798
did the British doubt that command of the eastern Mediterranean
was in fact essential if they were to sustain the Indian Raj, and
Malta proved an excellent instrument for furthering that aim. The
great harbour of Valletta was impregnable as a naval sanctuary
before the evolution of air warfare, and became the headquarters
of the Mediterranean Fleet, sustained by the Royal Dockyard
built there during the nineteenth century. Too crowded (at the
rate of about 2,000 to every one of their 120 square miles of land)
to live by the intensive agriculture they practised, the Maltese
were bound to Britain by economic self-interest, since the Royal
Navy provided most of them with a direct or an indirect living.
Like the Gibraltarians, they were a mixed race of Italians, Arabs,
Greeks and Phoenicians, with their own Maltese dialect which in
1934 they were to elevate to the status of an official language, and
they had no wish to transfer their allegiance from Britain to Italy,
the only other candidate for sovereignty.

Malta was almost as closely ruled in the interests of imperial
defence as Gibraltar. After rioting in Valletta, a dyarchical constitution had been set up in 1921. The Governor ruled with a ministry of Maltese, chosen from among the elected representatives,
who controlled the local affairs of the island, but the decisive
power lay with the Nominated Council, in which the commanders
of the British armed forces formed a majority. Any popular
movement that seemed a threat to British control over this vital
anchor of sea power was automatically repressed, and in 1930 the
constitution was suspended. It was to be restored and suspended
again in 1932 and finally revoked in 1936, when the islands were

returned to Crown colony government in which the British officials sustained a virtually complete control.

Beyond Malta, in the eastern Mediterranean, the Greek islands had always impressed British rulers with their strategic possibilities. Britain dabbled in the affairs of Crete, as other powers did, during the late nineteenth century, and both the Ionian islands and the island of Cyprus played more direct roles in the imperial pattern.

The Ionian Islands

By 1930 the Ionian Islands had long been abandoned, but for more than fifty years in the nineteenth century they seemed indispensable to the international manoeuvres of Britain. Including Odysseus's Ithaca and Aphrodite's sacred Cythera, the group forms a screen along the Adriatic coast of Greece from the marches of Albania to the Peloponnese. As with Sicily and Malta, prior French interference gave Britain an excuse for occupation. The group was apportioned to France in the great sharing out of Europe and Asia between Napoleon and Alexander of Russia at the Treaty of Tilsit in 1807, but with the final defeat of Napoleon the powers acknowledged that the 'United States of the Ionian Islands' should become a British protectorate. As such, the islands played their part in Britain's support of the Greeks during their struggle for independence in the 1820s, but, despite their Hellenistic sympathies, the British did not transfer the archipelago to the new Greek State founded in 1831. Prudently retained, the Ionian Islands had their value in countering the efforts of Russia to destroy Turkey and to control the eastern Mediterranean by the occupation of Constantinople. Greek involvement on the Russian side during the Crimean War made the maintenance of British domination doubly necessary, and as late as 1861 even Gladstone (who had briefly ruled the islands as High Commissioner) claimed that 'it would be no less than a crime against the safety of Europe' to cede the islands to Greece. Greeks, including the islanders themselves, thought otherwise, and after they had deposed their Russophile King Otto in 1862 and replaced him by the Danish prince who became King George of the Hellenes, their wish was finally granted; six months before King George was elected, his sister Alexandra had married Edward, Prince of Wales, and

Greece was accepted by Lord Palmerston as a reliable friend of Britain. In 1864 the British troops and warships left the fortress capital of Corfu for good. The abandonment of the Ionian Islands did not go unlamented by British strategists; as late as 1900 Admiral William Fisher, who modernized the British navy, regretted the loss of Corfu, a 'splendid place for the fleet and of enormous importance in case of war', adding sardonically, 'The epitaph of England will be: "What was won by the sword was given up by the pen."'

Cyprus

Only fourteen years after withdrawing from Corfu the British were again exercising their authority over a Greek population and over a land even more closely linked with the cult of Aphrodite than Cythera; this was Cyprus, off whose beach at Paphos she is said to have been born out of the sea foam. Cyprus lies in the great angle of sea between Anatolia and Syria. Myceneans and Egyptians, Assyrians and Phoenicians, Persians and Macedonians and Romans, all had possessed the island as strangers possessed the priestesses of the temple of Paphos. As long ago as 1191 it became for the first time a dependency of the British Crown, conquered from the Byzantine Empire by Richard Cœur de Lion, who bestowed it on Guy de Lusignan when the Saracens expelled him from his Crusader kingdom of Jerusalem. Cyprus became a minor Levantine power under Guy's descendants, thanks to its position on the trade routes between the Muslim realms of the Middle East and the Christian kingdoms of Europe; commerce sustained the Crusader kingdom until the end of the fifteenth century, when the Venetians seized the island, to be expelled in their turn by the Ottoman Sultans in 1571.

Cyprus was still under Turkish rule when Disraeli gained control of it in 1878 with the exertion of a little diplomatic pressure. The date of British occupation is significant. It took place on June 4th. A war in the Balkans had recently ended in the defeat of Turkey by the Russians, who were supporting the insurgent Slavic peoples of the Ottoman empire. At the Treaty of San Stefano, signed on March 3rd, 1878, the Russians forced the Turks to accept the creation of a larger Bulgarian State, which gave the Tsarist army a bastion within striking distance of Constantinople.

Austria-Hungary, anxious to discourage the creation of large Slav States which might encourage discontent in the Hapsburgs' own multi-racial domains, opposed the treaty, while Disraeli and his Foreign Minister, Lord Salisbury (one of the great unwilling architects of the British Empire), rejected any settlement that would threaten the stability of the Sublime Porte and bring Russia nearer to the route Alexander had taken to the confines of India. Disinclined to re-enact the Pyrrhic victories of Crimea, the British did not become involved in the Balkan war, but the possibility of giving naval aid to Turkey in the event of further Russian aggression had to be faced, and it was obviously in the interests of Whitehall, and of Vienna, to diminish the Tsarist triumph. At the same time, Bismarck was pleased to enhance the prestige of the recently united German Empire by offering Berlin as the site of a congress to reassess the Treaty of San Stefano.

The Congress, which began on June 13th, 1878, was a triumph for Disraeli since it resulted in the abandonment of greater Bulgaria. The British occupation of Cyprus, which not only shielded the approaches to Anatolia and Syria, but also commanded the route from the Russian Black Sea ports to Sinai and Alexandria, took place nine days beforehand, and served as a warning to the Russians that the British would not stand aside if they advanced farther in the Levant. It was accepted by the Turks on the tacit understanding that in return Britain would protect Asia Minor from future invasion. To avoid discussion at the Congress of Berlin, which determined the fate and status of Turkey's European dependencies, Cyprus remained nominally under the sovereignty of the Sublime Porte, and until 1914 Britain occupied Cyprus as a tributary of Turkey, to which it made a small annual payment of cash and salt. When Turkey entered the First World War on the German side, Cyprus was immediately annexed to the Empire.

Little was done in fact to turn Cyprus into the fortress for defending British interests in the Middle East which Disraeli had envisaged. The harbours were not deepened to take large warships, and garrisons remained small. During the First World War the British Government even offered Cyprus to Greece as a bribe to take up hostilities against Germany; it was not accepted, and the idea of uniting Cyprus with the Hellenic mainland was restricted to a small local *enosis* movement which acquired neither influence nor prominence until after the Second World War.

With the break-up of the Turkish Empire, the usefulness of Cyprus seemed to have ended; for Britain gained territories that appeared to offer more immediate protection to Suez. Cyprus was retained, partly because the British did not like to hand over its Turkish minority to Greek rule, and partly because the idea of abandoning territory was difficult for the Colonial Office to accept. In later years the possibility of creating a major naval base would be revived, but in 1930 Cyprus was regarded as one of the less interesting British possessions and much more attention was paid to the region known as the Holy Land, which Britain now controlled under League of Nations mandate. This was divided into the two territories of Palestine and Transjordan. Transjordan was administered as a protectorate; the Emir, Abdullah, was a Hashemite prince, but his army, the Arab Legion, was commanded by British officers. The High Commissioner of Palestine controlled affairs in Transjordan almost as closely as he did in Palestine, which was ruled as a crown colony, with no popular representation and with executive power in the hands of British officials.

Palestine

The Holy Land had held a special fascination for the Victorian English, with their evangelically tinged Anglicanism; the visit to Palestine was a staple theme for travel memoirists, and the country's arid landscape and Biblical-looking inhabitants appeared in innumerable paintings, from academic events by Holman Hunt down to the daubs and splashes of a legion of amateur water colourists; the tour of the sacred places was a high favourite among the journeys organized by the enterprising Thomas Cook and his successors. During the First World War it seemed to many pious English people that, having by grace divine created an Empire five times as large as that of the Romans, the British race was now elected to succeed where even the Crusaders had failed and to rescue the Holy Sepulchre from the power of the infidel. When General Allenby tramped on foot at the head of his army into Jerusalem on Christmas Day, 1917, there were many throughout the Empire who appreciated his symbolic humility.

Satisfaction at the custodianship of holy ground was compounded by a strong opinion of the strategic importance of
Palestine, an opinion the British had held since 1799, when
the successful defence of Acre had played a crucial part in
foiling Napoleon's plans to dominate the overland route to
India.

There was nothing wrong in such calculations in purely strategic terms, as the Israelis have demonstrated in recent years by
using Palestine as a base to invade the Sinai isthmus and dominate
the Suez Canal.

Yet even if Clausewitz was correct in his celebrated aphorism
that 'War is nothing more than the continuation of politics by
other means,' war is useless unless its political basis is sound.
In acquiring Palestine the British had introduced a political
factor that would frustrate all their military calculations. This
was Lord Balfour's vague but portentous declaration in 1917
favouring the opening of Palestine as the Jewish national home
– a declaration which the Zionists took to mean support for
what would become, territorially as well as figuratively, a Jewish
nation.

During the years between 1918 and 1930 there was a small,
steady migration of Jews into Palestine, mainly from the pogrom-
ridden lands of eastern Europe. The first of the kibbutzim had
been founded; the first truly Jewish city since the Diaspora—Tel
Aviv—had risen on the outskirts of Jaffa. Yet in 1930 the Jews
were still a small though quickly growing minority: less than
200,000 out of a population that, counting the nomadic and
frontier-despising Bedouin, came to nearly a million. The Arabs
still outnumbered them four to one.

At first there had been little resentment between the two communities, since the Jews began by buying unoccupied land from
absentee owners, and their presence brought a slight but perceptible increase in prosperity to a poor country depleted by centuries of war followed by centuries of misgovernment. Through
most of the 1920s, under the tactful, soldierly administration of
Lord Plumer, communal peace was maintained, but 1930 was a
restless year, the beginning of a restless decade, with the Jews
forming an underground protective force called the Haganah, and
Arabs tempted to accept the leadership of the fanatically anti-
Semitic Mufti of Jerusalem. Trouble had begun in 1928 in minor

clashes because of the crowding in Jerusalem of holy sites belonging to three world religions. Almost imperceptibly the tension
tightened, until an insignificant incident—an Arab's protests when
a Jewish boy threw a ball into his garden—led to riots throughout
Palestine in which Jews and Arabs died and British troops were
brought from Egypt. Sidney Webb, the old Fabian imperialist who,
as Lord Passfield, had become Colonial Secretary in the Labour
Government of 1929, decided that the simplest way out was to
win Arab confidence by restricting Jewish immigration; in doing
so at the end of 1930 he raised a worldwide storm among Zionist
sympathizers which frightened the Government into withdrawing
the restriction. Palestine was opened to a stream of newcomers
which increased as the European future of the Jews closed in upon
them with the rise of Nazi fortunes; in the process Arab confidence was quickly lost.

By 1930, however, the situation in Palestine had not reached the
point of irremediable crisis, though an Arab attempt on the life
of the Attorney-General in Jerusalem foreshadowed a time when
the region would become as unsafe for Britons as it already was
for Arabs and Jews. Some British administrators found consola-
tion in the old doctrine embalmed in public-school Latin, *Divide
et impera*. It was a doctrine that had success under the guise of
'indirect rule' in tribal countries like Nigeria, and it was to be
disastrously tempting in British India, with its Muslim–Hindu
rivalries. The difficulty in Palestine was that not only the subject
peoples but also the British were divided. There were pro-
Zionists among them and also pro-Arabs, especially among military men whose vision was clouded by images of martial Bedouin
and who had as little understanding of the urban Arab and his
frustrations as the pro-Zionists had of the desperate passions
developing in the hearts of members of the Palestinian Zionist
community—like Vladimir Jabotinsky, who was already preaching violence as necessary for survival of the Jews in what they
regarded as their ancestral homeland. Even so, 1930 ended with no
more than a few riots which had required for their suppression a
show of force less than that needed to suppress a hundred
imperial bushfires of the Victorian era, and until the actual Nazi per-
secution of the Jews in Germany made the situation acute after
1935, imperial strategists could still reasonably regard Palestine
as an effective reserve bastion in the Levant.

Egypt

It was to Egypt, represented by the untypical nest of commerce and chicanery known as Port Said, that the voyager to India came after his liner left Malta or steamed on a more northerly course through the Strait of Messina, with the smoking peak of Etna to starboard as the last view of Europe. Cyprus and Palestine, like the earlier British possessions of Minorca and Corsica, had passed in the distance, out of sight over the broad Mediterranean horizons, and the passenger's view of the Levant, after he left Port Said, would be the arid desert of Sinai, through which the ship sailed in daylight, its great superstructure gliding among the sands like some moving palace, until at Suez it finally entered the humid heat of the Red Sea, suffocating and barely endurable in an age before air-conditioning became a commonplace of ocean travel.

To defend this seaway through a waste inhabited mainly by wandering Bedouin, an ancient country had been subjected to British rule, and though by 1930 Egypt was nominally a sovereign State, it was still occupied by a British army reported to have a strength of 11,420 men, second only (in the overseas Empire) to the British forces in India. King Fuad of Egypt — a Balkan like Cleopatra, for he came of an Albanian line—performed the motions of ruling with his own cabinet and, when he chose to summon it, an elected parliament. But even his Egyptian army and his ports were controlled by British officers, a British financial adviser overlooked the budget of his kingdom on behalf of foreign creditors, and the British High Commissioner maintained an overall supervision of Egyptian affairs. Britain had proclaimed as recently as 1922 her own Middle Eastern version of the Monroe Doctrine when she warned the other powers that though Egypt was 'independent', in the sense that she had at last shed the nominal suzerainty of Turkey, no interference by a third party in British–Egyptian relations would be tolerated. Not until 1936 would a treaty finally be signed by which the High Commissioner in Cairo was transformed into an Ambassador and the British troops withdrew to their primary task of defending the Suez Canal, the lifeline to India. Even then, as events within three years were to prove, British recognition of Egyptian independence would be conditional on the safety of the Empire, for at the outbreak of the Second World War the whole country was reoccupied to hold off the German–Italian threat to Suez. Real Egyptian independence would have to wait for the 1950s.

Yet in a formal sense Egypt was never a part of the Empire; it was not the Union Jack, but the green flag of the kingdom, spattered with stars and crescent, that the visitor saw flying over its buildings; the white marble statues of Queen Victoria that glowered over almost every *maidan* in India were absent from Egyptian cities. British officials were either nominally in the employ of the Egyptian Government, wearing fezzes like their native counterparts as they supervised the police and administered taxation, or they were representatives, not of the Colonial Office but of the Foreign Office. Until 1914 Egypt, like Cyprus, had actually remained under the suzerainty of Turkey. When Turkey became Germany's ally in 1914, the British ended the relationship and declared Egypt a British protectorate, as it remained in fact if not in law despite the declaration of its independence in 1922. The leading British official, formerly combining the power of a proconsul with the humble title of Agent and Consul-General, was raised to the status of High Commissioner, but respect for traditional French interests in Egypt prevented Whitehall from following the customary practice by which a protectorate was usually transferred within a couple of years or so from the care of the Foreign Office to that of the Colonial Office.

It was not Egypt itself that in the last resort interested Britain, though imperial prestige was inflated by the fact that British arms, if not the British flag, stood guard over the Pyramids and the Valley of Kings and the great Hellenistic city haunted by the ghosts of Alexander and Mark Anthony. There was also, while the Lancashire textile industry still flourished at its late Victorian level of productivity, some economic benefit from controlling the cotton fields of the Nile delta and ensuring that they were properly irrigated; but by the 1920s the rise of an Indian cotton industry had sharply reduced Lancashire's markets and its need for raw cotton. And there were the loans whose safeguarding had given Britain the excuse to occupy Egypt in 1882 and to hold it in the face of general European disapproval. But an excuse it was, masking the real reasons for the action. For Gladstone ordered the occupation with the same ultimate end in mind as Disraeli had envisaged when he bought out the Egyptian Government's interest in the Suez Canal in 1875: the protection of the short route to India. The point was put succinctly in a letter written by Lord Cairns in January 1876 which Robert Blake quotes in his biography of Disraeli. 'It is now the *Canal and India*; there is no such thing now to us as India alone. India is any number of cyphers; but the Canal is the unit that makes these cyphers valuable.'

It has been observed that, however divided so-called imperialists and anti-imperialists in the Victorian age may have appeared to be in questions relating to the dominions and the dependent colonies, they were astonishingly united in their recognition of the need to maintain British rule over India. Even the most extreme Liberal Free Trader suspected uneasily that the ability of English manufactures to compete in world markets depended largely on Britain's position as a world power, and that the retention of India—like the naval control of the world's sea routes—was necessary to maintain that position. The Suez Canal was the point at which the twin British obsessions regarding India and sea power came together; this fact made inevitable Gladstone's occupation of Egypt as soon as Arabi Pasha appeared as the prototype of Egyptian nationalism and raised the threat that Egypt might fall into unfriendly hands. Wolseley's prompt defeat of Arabi at the battle of Tel el Kebir was in fact a remote victory in the perpetual war to defend the frontiers of India.

The association between Egypt and Britain, necessary as it may have seemed, was never happy, and all the reserves of stern dutifulness that the imperialists could muster were needed to sustain it. There was none of the strange love–hatred that developed between the British and the Indians, exemplified most astonishingly in the deeply personal relationships between Gandhi and the Viceroys. The Egyptians wholeheartedly resented the British presence, and the British reciprocated with so low an opinion of the Egyptians that to 'gyp' (in other words, to act like an Egyptian) is still slang for to swindle. But in spite of this enduring mutual dislike, the impulse to create order out of existing disorder which inspired the British proconsuls (especially exemplified in Lord Cromer, who was a member of the banking dynasty of the Barings) resulted in the evolution in Egypt of the framework on which a modern nation could later be built. The police and the army were reorganized on European lines; courts were set up throughout the country where for the first time in centuries—perhaps the first time in Egyptian history—a poor man might expect to win justice against a rich man; a railway system was established, and regular steamship services plied the Nile; Alexandria was transformed into a modern seaport and Cairo into a reasonably efficient capital city; the irrigation system was overhauled so that it became a means of storing as well as distributing water. Perhaps most important, in the light of later events, Western education was encouraged, breeding the literate malcontents who would modernize the aims of Arabi and whose new forms of nationalism were already, by the 1929s, provoking unrest and disorder in Egyptian cities.

In 1924 nationalist militancy was manifested dramatically in the assassination of Sir Lee Stack, the British Sirdar or Commander-in-Chief of the Egyptian Army (and ex-officio Governor-General of the Sudan); this had brought British reprisals and a series of Egyptian political crises ending in absolute government by King Fuad. The king had his own ambitions for an independent Egypt but was too weak to stand without British support, while in British eyes his ascendancy was preferable to that of the radical nationalists, so that in 1930 Egypt was enjoying an interlude of uneasy truce. The traveller who passed through the Canal, perhaps taking a side trip to Alexandria or Cairo while the ship fuelled, or breaking his journey for a steamer trip up the Nile to the Cyclopean ruins of Karnak, would be imperilled by no enemies more formidable than the touts who sprang up everywhere he went, and would go on his way confirmed in his opinion of the durability of the Empire and in his conviction that the British were patiently bringing a backward and ungrateful people out of medieval darkness into the light of progress.

His passage beyond Suez down the Red Sea would do little to lessen his sense of imperial power, for, despite the presence on its eastern shore of the Yemen, and of the kingdom of Hejaz whose port of Jeddah—dangerous territory for Christians—was the landing place for pilgrims who went to Mecca from the British domains of farther Asia, this almost landlocked water was virtually a British lake. Its western shores were Egyptian and Sudanese, firmly under the control of forces commanded by the British Sirdar in Cairo. The island of Perim occupied the centre of the narrow exit from the Red Sea, and not far beyond, on the south-western corner of Arabia, stood the well-garrisoned fortress and coaling station of Aden; both had been British since the mid nineteenth century. The whole African shore of the Gulf of Aden, facing the port and the entrance to the Red Sea, was a desert known as British Somaliland, over which a protectorate had been declared in 1888.

All of these places were possessions so politically troublesome that the very obstinacy with which the British insisted on possessing them was an illustration of the importance imperialists attached to a territory if it did no more than help secure the safety of one of the great sea routes. Aden, Perim and Somaliland had been occupied on orders, not from Whitehall but from Calcutta, for the Government of India was even more urgently concerned than that of Britain to protect the steamship routes that were fed until 1869 by the overland route to Suez and afterwards by traffic through the Canal. An informal understanding between the India Office and the Colonial Office marked off the Red Sea as an Indian sphere of influence, and at no time did the rulers of the Raj neglect to safeguard it.

Aden

The urgency of their concern was demonstrated emphatically by the fact that the first P. & O. steamer sailed from Suez to Bombay in 1840, while Aden, then an ancient but decayed Arabian seaport with vague legendary links with the Queen of Sheba, was captured from the Sultan of Lahej in 1839 by an expedition led by Captain Haines of the Bombay Marine. As the nineteenth century went on, Aden prospered as a coaling station, renowned as the dirtiest port of Asia, and revived as a centre attracting the commerce of southern Arabia. The traveller in 1930 who landed at Steamer Point for his day in Aden, and fought his way through the local touts and beggars to take a dilapidated cab over the arid pass into the town of Crater (whose name accurately described its site), would be less aware of the presence of the garrison than of the interesting fact that, if trade indeed followed the flag, it was Indian rather than British trade; for here, as everywhere along the shores of the Arabian Sea and the Indian Ocean where the Union Jack was raised, it flapped its benisons over the merchants

from Gujerat, who arrived close behind the soldiers and sometimes before them, and who—whatever trials other Indians might
endure under the Raj—were among the leading beneficiaries of
the spread of empire.

Somaliland

The garrison at Aden was needed to protect it as much from the
predatory tribes of the Yemen and the Hadhramaut as from rival
imperialists, and while Somaliland was occupied to save it from
the French or Italians, both of whom had already encroached in
this area, the actual fighting there (except for the Second World
War, when the Italians occupied the territory in 1940 and were
driven out in 1941) was with the people of the country. The So-
malis were led in a *jihad* or holy war against the British intruders
by Sheikh Mohammad bin Abdullah Hassan. From 1899 this religious leader, whom the British called 'the Mad Mullah', led his
dervishes in a guerrilla war that survived four major British
offensives; he was finally defeated in 1920 when the British combined the traditional desert tactics of a specially created Camel
Corps with the use of aircraft. Somaliland had only its strategic
value to recommend it to imperialists; otherwise it was a torrid
desert over which 300,000 nomad herdsmen wandered in an area
as large as England. Its products, as a colonial handbook for 1930
laconically lists them, were 'cattle, sheep, goats, hides, skins and
gum', which it exported in 1929 to the value of £238,000; most
of this was livestock shipped to feed the garrison on Aden's
arid rocks.

Arabia

Somaliland had been administered by the Colonial Office since
1905, but Aden and Perim were still under the control of the
Indian Government, which sent out Political Residents. The Political Service also administered the bizarre collection of treaties by
which the British had bound to friendship the rulers of every
desert realm along the southern coast of Arabia and round into the
Persian Gulf, where in Kuwait the zone of protection joined the
mandated territory of Iraq; linking with Transjordan, Iraq completed the circle of British power surrounding Arabia. Some of the

sultans of the Hadhramaut, persuaded by the ardent explorer and British agent St John Philby, had pledged their friendship as late as the 1920s; they formed the Protectorate of South Arabia.

The little realms of the Persian Gulf, of which Bahrein, Kuwait, Qutar, and Muscat and Oman were the most important, were ruled by Bedouin sheikhs of fierce Islamic orthodoxy and predatory inclinations whom many British wanderers found temperamentally congenial. The most wayward were the eight little tribal states on the southern shore of the Gulf, ruled by petty corsairs addicted to slave trading and piracy. Until the British imposed peace by gunboat, this was actually called the Pirate Coast; after that it became the Trucial Coast. The link with the ancient sultanate of Muscat and Oman was one of the oldest British connections in the Gulf; the first treaty, hastily concluded in 1799 at the time of French activity on the Nile, bound the sultan and King George III to a friendship that would last 'to the end of time and till the sun and moon have ended their revolving career'. The little archipelago of Bahrein, with its pearl divers, its elegant breed of white donkeys much sought in Arabia, and its busy dhow-building yards, was the most prosperous of these Arab sultanates until oil was found in Kuwait. It was also, because of the surrounding water, the most salubrious, and for this reason it was the centre of British power, where the senior Political Resident for the Gulf maintained his establishment.

The Persian Gulf

After leaving Aden the South Arabian coastline of dunes receding into stony desert would be visible to the India-bound traveller, but unless the first port of call happened—and this was somewhat unusual—to be Karachi, his liner would swing out of sight of land somewhere near the headland of R'as Fartak, whence the ancient Greek mariners had struck across the Arabian Sea towards the Malabar Coast. Rarely did any British boat larger than a freighter or gunboat creep into the torrid waters of the Persian Gulf, unless it were some decrepit passenger ship like that which Lord Jim deserted, worn out on the Far Eastern runs and living out the days before break-up as a pilgrim ship.

Yet the Persian Gulf had been a focus of British activity ever since trade with the Far East began to interest London merchants.

First it was seen as a stage on the way to India. Since the sea voyage around Africa was long and beset by armed Portuguese vessels, and the Suez route jealously guarded by Egyptians, who sought to sustain their position as middlemen in the trade between Arabia and Venice, the route which the pioneer English traders took to the Far East—making the great journey in 1583 that took Ralph Fitch wandering beyond India into Burma and Siam—lay through Aleppo in Syria, down the Euphrates valley to Baghdad and Basra, and thence by sea from Ormuz on the Gulf to Goa in India. Even this was a perilous route, since the Portuguese controlled the sea traffic in the Gulf as well as in the Arabian Sea.

Years later, after Fitch returned with his tales of the Moghul court and the Golden Chersonese, and the East India Company was founded as a result, the English returned to the Gulf because the only way to secure the beach-heads they had established in western India was to destroy Portuguese power in the Arabian Sea. Fortunately for the English, the Portuguese had behaved so arrogantly that the great Shah of Persia, Abbas I, welcomed the East India merchants and allowed them to trade at Jank. This was in 1616; six years later the Company's ships collaborated with the Persians in expelling the Portuguese from their stronghold of Ormuz, and in 1622 English merchants were allowed to move their headquarters to Bandar Abbas and to set up a subsidiary factory in the splendid capital Abbas had built at Isfahan.

Even in the enclosed waters of the Persian Gulf, the British could not escape the intrusive presence of the Dutch, who had already expelled them from the East Indies and now out-traded them at Bandar Abbas. The East India Company moved temporarily into Mesopotamia and in 1643 established its factory at Basra, which in the eighteenth century became an important centre of British power in the Middle East. It was only about 1750 that the Dutch in the Persian Gulf effectively declined and Britain became the dominant European power. In 1763 the East India Company set up its Persian headquarters at Bushire, with virtually exclusive trading rights and an agent recognized by the Shah as 'the Governor-General of the English nation in the Persian Gulf'. By the early nineteenth century the British position was so assured that the Company established a regular postal service down the Euphrates to the Persian Gulf and thence by sea to India, which halved the time taken by letters sent to Calcutta around the Cape.

Iraq

As, after 1783, India became the main focus of British imperial interest, it was natural that the British should seek to extend their power beyond the Persian Gulf and bring the larger neighbouring territories into their sphere of influence. During the nineteenth century British commercial interests entered the valley of the Euphrates, British consuls advised the local boys, and the rough infrastructure of a modern society—river boats, telegraphs and a postal service—was introduced.

In 1914 the opportunity offered by the Turkish alliance with Germany was eagerly seized; units of the Indian Army moved into Mesopotamia and, supported by British and Anzac units with some help from the Arabs, finally defeated the Turks in 1918. After two years of intense political disorder, Mesopotamia was awarded to Britain by the League of Nations in 1920 as a Class A mandate, which meant that the country would remain under British tutelage until its people were regarded as politically sophisticated enough to rule themselves. The British established Emir Faisal of the Hashemite dynasty of Arabia as a puppet king of the new State, which was renamed Iraq, and by 1930, though the mandate was still in operation, its end was already visible; in the summer of that year a treaty was signed between the British and King Faisal's Government providing for the end of direct British rule by 1932. However, the treaty of 1930 provided not merely for the maintenance of a British military airport, but also for the transport of British troops through Iraq in the event of emergency. In the Second World War these rights—exacted with a view not only to the defence of India but also to the protection of British interests in the newly discovered Iraq oilfields—would be used to carry out a second occupation of Iraq to save it from falling into German hands. Until the middle of the 1950s Iraq would remain a political client of Britain, outside the Empire, but less free than the dominions which stayed within it.

Persia and Afghanistan

It was mainly the fear of Russia that prompted British adventures in Persia and Afghanistan. They became the chief battlegrounds in that long war of intrigue which was celebrated by Kipling as the Great Game; it began at the end of the eighteenth century when Lord Wellesley, as Viceroy of India, sent John Malcolm to Teheran to conclude a political treaty with the Shah, it produced its own special heroes like Bokhara Burnes, and it ended only when the British finally left India in 1947.

Through the century after the British annexation of the Sikh kingdom of Punjab in 1849, which brought the frontiers of India to the confines of Afghanistan, the idea of turning the latter country into a protectorate, and even of establishing a protectorate over Persia, was frequently advocated by those who favoured a 'forward' policy of aggressive frontier action as the best way of ensuring the security of India, both internal and external. But the actual results of British military interventions in Afghanistan between 1838 and 1919 ranged from complete disaster to ignominious stalemate; the campaigns were marked by political and military blunders relieved only rarely by feats of generalship like Roberts's famous march on Kandahar, which had no influence on the final outcome of the wars they embellished. At best, after vainly attempting in 1879 to impose a protectorate, the British succeeded in extracting from the Afghans an undertaking not to enter into close relations with any other power, but even this they surrendered after the inconclusive war of 1919, when the Government of India finally recognized the complete independence of Afghanistan.

In fact, though this result was far less than the expansionists who advocated the 'forward' policy had hoped, it served the original purposes of intervention; the Russians were kept out, a buffer state was sustained on the north-west frontier of India, and Britain did not have to face the cost of garrisoning a country celebrated for its guerrilla warriors since the age of Alexander. The record of failure by the Indian army in this region showed the inferiority of the military as compared with the naval arm of British power as a means of expansion beyond easily fortified natural frontiers. Small places on the routes of empire were acquired easily from the sea, and lands thinly populated by primitive peoples, like western Canada, Australia and much of Africa, could be won and occupied without great difficulty, but—as South Africa showed just as vividly as Afghanistan—a determined and resourceful foe in possession of a difficult terrain could be defeated only at great effort and then not permanently.

Military limitations certainly explain why British attempts to intervene in Persia were even less extensive and less determined than in Afghanistan. The only region where the territories of Persia and the British Raj came together was that frightful desert on the borders of Baluchistan where thousands of Alexander's men had died of thirst and exhaustion on the retreat from the Indus; even among the incompetents who staffed the Indian Army for long periods in the nineteenth century, there were no generals rash enough to attempt a re-enactment of that ancient folly. Therefore the only way of attacking Persia was by sea through the Gulf, and even then an invading army must march through the southern deserts and the Zagros mountains to reach the vital centres of Persia, situated on the Iranian plateau.

The only serious British–Persian war illustrated the limited possibilities which such a situation imposed on an invader with less than a large and very well-equipped army. In 1856 the Persians seized Herat in northwestern Afghanistan. The British were sensitive to any threat but their own to the integrity of Afghanistan, but quailed before the difficulties of a military expedition to its most distant frontier. Accordingly, a diversionary expedition under Sir James Outram sailed from Sind into the Gulf and seized Bushire. The mixed force of British and Indian regiments then marched inland, defeated a Persian army, and penetrated far enough into the interior for the officers to leave their signatures on the ancient sculptures of Persepolis. But, as anyone who has flown over Persia will know, a great desert divides Persepolis from Isfahan, and another vast barrier of sandy waste and tortured mountains lies between Isfahan and the nineteenth-century Persian capital of Teheran. For a small expeditionary force to advance deeper into this geographically and politically hostile land would have been military suicide, and Outram decided to withdraw undefeated to the coast and to complete his campaign with a raid at the head of the Gulf in which he captured Khorramshahr, later to become familiar as a centre of British exploitation of the Persian oilfields. These forceful if peripheral demonstrations of British power were enough to induce the Shah to withdraw his forces from Herat. Outram hurried back to play his part in suppressing the Indian Mutiny, and Dost Dohammed, king of Afghanistan, showed his appreciation by refraining from taking advantage of the British difficulties at that perilous time.

The Great Game between Britain and Russia continued for so long, in Persia as elsewhere, because neither side was anxious to achieve checkmate. Except for a few zealous expansionists, both the British and the Russians wanted mainly to ensure that in the countries which separated their respective Empires—and especially in Persia, Afghanistan and Tibet—the rival power would not exercise complete control. Neither wished to repeat the costly and inconclusive experience of the Crimean War. As soon as the Germans began to probe into the Middle East, the Russians and the British in Central Asia—like the French and British in the South Pacific—quickly realized that their interests might complement rather than conflict with each other. In 1907 they signed a convention by which they agreed to respect Persian independence, but immediately negated this laudable intent by assigning each other spheres of influence, the Russians in the north-west of the country near the Caspian Sea, and the British in the south-east. The British also gained commercial influence in the south-west of Persia through the concession to the Anglo-Persian Oil Company of rights over the oilfields discovered at Abadan in 1901. The British also gained control over the main communications system in Persia through the Indo-European Telegraph Company, supervised by officers of the Indian Army, and established strong banking interests. In addition, both Britain and Russia possessed extra-territorial rights—the so-called 'Capitulations'—by which their citizens were subject only to the jurisdiction of their own consular courts.

The geographical difficulties of occupying Persia were in practice too great for either Britain or Russia to attempt it independently, and it is significant that the only occasions since the Hellenistic age when the country was occupied by European armies were the two World Wars in which the British and Russians invaded the country simultaneously from the south and north to prevent its becoming a centre for German activities in Central Asia.

The situation at the end of the First World War tempted the British to consider a unilateral domination of Persia. They and the Russians had encountered little difficulty in occupying the oilfields and the strategic areas of the north and west, and when the revolution of 1917 removed the Russians from the scene, the advocates of the 'forward' policy in the India Office decided that their time had arrived. They were encouraged by the Foreign Secretary, Lord Curzon, whose period as Viceroy of India has been marked by a policy of forestalling the Russians wherever possible. In August 1919 the Persian Government was persuaded to sign an agreement which would establish a virtual British protectorate. Independence was to be guaranteed, but only nominally, since British military and financial advisers would control Persian policy, while tariffs would be adjusted to favour British trade. But popular feeling in Persia was not so passive as had been assumed in London and Delhi; the Majlis refused to ratify the treaty.

In practice the British retained a good deal of covert influence, They still controlled the oilfields and most of the banks, and they remained the dominant power on the Gulf until the beginning of the 1970s. Furthermore, though the advisers appointed under the unratified agreement of 1919 were not allowed to take up their duties, it is instructive to compare the lists of British consular officials in Persia in 1930 with those in other Asian countries. A remarkably high proportion held ranks in the British armed forces, usually with Indian experience and often with Indian decorations; at Bushire a consul-general, a consul and three vice-consuls (a vastly inflated staff for such a post) all held military or naval rank. During the 1930s both Americans and Germans were diplomatically and commercially active in Teheran, but the British retained their influence throughout the southern coastal regions as far west as Abadan, where the British vice-consul was also Port Officer, and in the great eastern deserts that bordered on Afghanistan and Baluchistan. Thus in 1941 it would be easy for British forces to march once again into Persia, to banish the Shah Reza Khan to Mauritius, and to install the present Shah in his place. If the British never went so far as to emulate Alexander by becoming the actual imperial rulers of Persia, at least they became its king-makers, and the sphere of influence whose existence the Anglo-Russian Convention of 1907 had recognized made eastern and southern Persia an essential outwork of the Empire, to be occupied when danger demanded.

India

Afghanistan and Persia would be far out of sight of any traveller who went to India in 1930 by the safe and customary way which led him to Bombay, the first port of call after Aden for most liners sailing by Suez. By 1930 Bombay had also taken the place of Calcutta as the principal place of disembarkation, particularly for those en route to Delhi. In that city in 1912 the seat of government, the omphalos of the Raj, had been established in a new British city to be built among the ruins of the seven dead cities that commemorated the departed dynasties of Hindu and Muslim monarchs.

In 1930 in New Delhi the final touches were being put to the vast Moghul-baroque buildings of reddish stone which Sir Edwin Lutyens had designed, so that the last phase of the last alien domination of India could be enacted in the traditional capital of foreign rulers. Only the opulent Peacock Throne of the Moghuls would be missing when the inauguration ceremonies took place in February 1931. That, ironically, was kept among the treasures of the Persian royal house in Teheran; it had been taken in 1749 from the Moghul palace of the Red Fort by the Iranian invader Nadir Shah. Nadir Shah had also stolen from the Moghuls the great Koh-i-noor diamond, but this had passed out of Persian hands into those of the Durrani rulers of Afghanistan and had returned to Indian soil in the possession of the formidable Ranjit Singh, the great Sikh ruler of Punjab, from whose descendants it was seized by the British in 1849, exactly a century after Nadir Shah had taken it to Persia. Transported as legitimate booty to London, it became part of the crown jewels of England, incorporated into the crown worn by the consorts of the British Emperors of India.

The seers of the Indian bazaars are said to have prophesied, once the Mutiny was safely defeated in 1858, that whoever possessed the Koh-i-noor would rule the subcontinent, and despite the signs of unrest so evident in 1930, the average Civilian boarding the train at Bombay to return to his post in the secretariat at Delhi (or, if it were summer, to join the Viceroy's monsoon court on the heights of Simla) would have little doubt that so far as Britain was concerned the prophecy might well be correct. Whatever the strange charisma by which Gandhi appeared to bemuse his followers in that rebellious season, whatever the talk of change among intellectuals and politicians in Britain, to most of the sahibs—as to most of the British at home who gave India a second thought—it seemed as though the difficulties the Raj was enduring were minor and temporary, and that it would continue, if not for ever, at least into any reasonably foreseeable future. Few Britons in the India of 1930, and few Indians for that matter, can seriously have expected that in seventeen years the Union Jacks would be lowered for ever, and the last British soldiers would be marching through that sculptured monstrosity on the Bombay waterfront, the Gate of India, and boarding their transport ships for home.

In merely physical terms—terms of territory and military power—there was every reason for such assumptions. India projected from the underside of Asia as a vast but compact bastion defended on its continental side by the world's highest mountains, by some of its most forbidding deserts (in Sind and Baluchistan), and by some of its most impassable jungles (on the hilly borderlands of Burma). A geographical and strategic imperative even more than a historical destiny had led the British to expand their sphere of direct rule and close protection until the whole area between the seas and these natural land fortifications was under the control of an army which, with the ominous exception of the Japanese, was in 1930 the most powerful and the best-trained in Asia.

When the British first arrived as traders in the last years of the sixteenth century, India was still a relatively united country, under the rule of Akbar, the greatest Moghul. The men of the East India Company had seen that power weaken and disintegrate. The last strong Moghul emperor had been Aurangzeb, who died, pious, ascetic and cruelly intolerant, in 1707—more than thirty years after Dryden in his heroic play *Aureng-Zebe* had made him the first Indian to play an important role in English literature.

Dryden puts a meditation into Aurangzeb's mouth which might well be taken as a suitable collective epitaph for those who ruled after him in the Red Fort of Delhi, whose great hall bore in Arabic letters the inscription, 'If there is a paradise on earth, it is here, it is here, it is here.' Aurangzeb's successors would have found the greater truth in Dryden's lines:

> When I consider life, 'tis all a cheat;
> Yet, fooled by hope, men favour the deceit;
> Trust on, and think to-morrow will repay;
> To-morrow's falser than the former day;
> Lies worse, and, while it says, we shall be blest
> With some new joys, cuts off what we possessed.

Preyed on by Persians and Afghans who successively sacked Delhi, the Moghuls became the mere shadows of rulers, puppets in the hands of the Mahrattas, of the British and finally of the Mutineers, until the last Moghul, Bahadur Shah, was exiled to Burma and his heirs were slaughtered in cold blood by that God-fearing Victorian paladin, Major Hodson of Hodson's Horse.

It was partly from a need to defend nothing at first more ambitious than a trading connection, and partly by employing moderately efficient soldiers supported by the Royal Navy, that the British found their sway extending into the vacuum of power created by the decline of the Moghuls, in which contending factions and ambitious lesser rulers turned India into a land of chaos blown over by constant squalls of war. The need to save its trading enclave around Madras from French rivals led the East India Company to become a power in southern India; the need to gain security against local rulers, who were nominally agents of the Moghul but really served their own personal ends, led it to establish a territorial realm in Bengal. The Company's interests in south India brought it in conflict with the Muslim rulers of Mysore, Hyder Ali and his son Tippu Sultan, and the destruction of their power made the British not only rulers of the Dravidian-speaking south, but also inevitable rivals in the Deccan of the martial Mahrattas. It was against the Mahrattas that the most formidable British campaigns were fought; by 1818 the Mahratta Confederacy was finally destroyed, and the whole traditional heartland of India—Hindustan and Bengal, the Deccan and the south— was in British hands. The map was not entirely red; it was mottled to the end of the Raj with areas that were merely blotting-paper pink. These were the states of the native princes, Muslim and Rajput, Mahratta and Malayali, who, to the number of more than five hundred, made their peace with the British and, by accepting the Viceroy's direction of their external affairs, were allowed absolute rule in their own realms, which varied from Hyderabad's 80,000 square miles with twelve million subjects and a salute of twenty-one guns down to the tiny jungle principalities of the Gonds in Orissa with a few hundred subjects and no welcoming shots in the thunder of the durbars.

Even when Delhi fell into British hands in 1803, India was not secure until the power of the Raj extended in every direction to the most defensible natural frontier. The British accepted any challenge that might serve as an excuse to conquer the marches of Hindustan. Thus in 1849, after the death of Ranjit Singh had ended a working arrangement with the Sikhs, the Punjab was conquered and annexed. This brought the British to the natural frontier of the Hindu Kush. It also gave them control over the ancient kingdom of Kashmir, which they handed to a Dogra prince who became their puppet. With Kashmir came the tributary territories of Gilgit and Hunza, and the little lamaistic kingdom of Ladakh, formerly a dependency of Tibet, which took British power to the Karakorum and the Pamirs. To the west the British made their defences complete by annexing the Emirates of Sind, which subjected to the Raj the whole of the Indus valley, and by establishing a protectorate over the desert chiefdoms of Baluchistan, which extended British power along the southern border of Afghanistan and gave it a frontier with Persia.

To the north the line of the Himalayas had to be secured. After minor skirmishes and one serious war, a symbiotic relationship developed with Nepal, which allowed that country to retain its independence in return for acting as a reservoir of manpower, contributing to the Indian Army its formidable and reliable corps of Gurkhas, who remained unaffected by the political tensions that arose in India itself and whose first great service to the Raj was their help in defeating the Mutiny. Darjeeling was annexed to become an Indian state, while Bhutan, having been deprived of its southern Duars, became a protected state, its territory guaranteed by Britain, which managed its foreign relations.

Burma

To the east in 1930, India still included a whole alien country that had been swallowed up in the frontier rectifications of the Raj. This was Burma, which had never been part of the realm of the Moghuls or of the earlier Hindu empires.

Already, in 1825, the British had acquired from Burma the area of small principalities and tribal regions amalgamated—sometimes uneasily as in the case of Nagaland—into the province of Assam, whose northern frontier, marching with Tibet, was established on the McMahon Line, agreed at the Simla Convention between Tibet and Britain in 1914 and running—as British

defence requirements demanded—along the crest of the Himalayas.

With the acquisition of Burma the great arc of Indian land defences was complete. The country was conquered piecemeal in a
series of little wars spread over the period between 1826 and 1885.
The Burmese kings were aggressive and provocative in their
external policies, and the British were eager to accept the provocation, since they did not wish to leave this crumbling medieval
state as a prey to the French who had moved into Indo-China. By
seizing it, Britain pushed the frontiers of the Raj to the mountain
passes bordering on the Chinese province of Yunnan, and down
to Siam where the balance of British and French interests created
a buffer land. The long coastal strip of southern Burma gave
India complete command of the Bay of Bengal. Though Burma
had little in common with India, its strategic situation demanded
that it be treated as a part of the Raj, and so it remained until
1937, a situation which led to the commercial domination of the
country by a hated combination of British box-wallahs, who controlled the teak industry and wholesale business, and Indians, who
did most of the trading and by their money-lending habits
gained a financial grip on the Burmese peasantry.

India was thus a land empire, but compact and so naturally fortified that it had some of the attributes of an island continent.
Though its armies penetrated beyond its natural frontiers, to
Lhasa and Kabul and Kandahar, its rulers were always content in
the end to postpone the visions they occasionally fostered of
setting up protectorates in inner Asia. They remained satisfied
with the buffer states like Turkey and Afghanistan and Persia
where their power was in equilibrium with that of their rival in
the contest for the hegemony of Asia, the great Eurasian Empire
of the Russian tsars.

In this resolution, acquired through the follies of the Afghan
campaigns, not to exhaust themselves in the barren vastnesses of
Central Asia, and to treat the Great Game as no more than a
game, the British were wise, given the fact that both their armies
—British and Indian alike—were small professional forces in-
capable of the feats of continental occupation which the mass
conscript armies of other European powers might accomplish, but
efficient in defending the kind of accumulation of territories which

the British Empire became. And the real secret of British power in India lay in the fact that it was a country peculiarly fitted for rule by an efficient bureaucracy supported by the combination of a good professional army and boundless sea power.

The function of the navy, even in India, was important. Half of India's frontiers faced upon the sea, its greatest cities were seaports, its most fertile and industrious regions lay along the seashores or up the broad valleys, easily accessible from Calcutta, of the Ganges and the Brahmaputra. The Indian Mutiny had been doomed because it was an inland rebellion and the British controlled the ports through which, even before the Suez Canal was opened, the relieving forces arrived in a few months. After the Canal was opened, and the time of travel from England was reduced to less than six weeks, the British built from the ports the best railway system in Asia, climbing into the highlands of Darjeeling, skirting the marches of Nepal, riding to the crest of the Khyber Pass, and leaving no centre of any significance through which the mail trains did not move with slow and majestic deliberation. Thus India became a land which, so long as Britain remained the master of seas and sea routes, could be defended against all likely foes. The real reason why Gandhi's non-violent strategy appealed to the Indian nationalist movement was that its leaders were shrewd enough to read the lessons of their own recent history. The fate of all who since the battle of Plassey in 1757 had set themselves against the British in India—of the Mahrattas and the Sikhs, of the Pindaris and the Burmese, of the Mutiny itself— taught them that the violence advocated by Gandhi's great Madhratta rival, Lokamanya Tilak, could not succeed against Britain at the height of its power and the prime of its will to rule. Physically, even as late as 1947, the Raj was undefeatable by violent rebellion. The only possible way to liberation was by weakening the British will to rule, and this, in 1930, Gandhi was already attempting.

Yet in that year it was the power of Britain and not its hidden flaws that was most visible, and the Raj not only seemed to stand in its own territory impregnable against the world, but also to dominate the neighbouring seas from the shores of Malaya to the shores of Africa. East of Suez the Empire owed its extension and its survival to the effective collaboration of the Royal Navy and the Indian Army. Apart from the campaigns in Mesopotamia and Persia, in Afghanistan and Tibet, Indian troops had fought in China and Java and Malaya; they had taken part in the occupation of Cyprus in 1878 and of Egypt in 1882; and in the late decades of the nineteenth century, during the famous 'scramble' that divided Africa between the competing powers of Europe, Indian troops had assisted in the occupation of Somaliland and Zanzibar, of Sudan and Nyasaland, and of Uganda and Kenya. For, as the Portuguese realized when they sailed from the Atlantic into the Indian Ocean at the end of the fifteenth century, the control of Africa was essential to guard the routes to India.

III The African Journey

In 1956 the rulers of Britain and many of their subjects reacted with self-defeating violence to the Egyptian expropriation of the Suez Canal. They did so because they were witnessing the actualization of a nightmare that had haunted British imperialists ever since the Canal was completed in 1869, the vision of this vital waterway falling into hostile hands and, far from being a link in the defence of the Empire, becoming an avenue to its destruction. The priority given to the defence of Egypt over all other tasks than the defence of Britain itself during the Second World War indicates how acutely Churchill and his defence planners were aware that if the Germans succeeded in seizing the Canal, the Empire would be in mortal peril. Those who were stirred by Nasser's action into violent counter-action were correct within the terms of the imperial vision, for if the first seizure of the Canal—by Gladstone in 1882—marked the beginning of the most flamboyant period of British empire-building, the second seizure —by Nasser in 1956—marked that period's end and heralded the actual death of the Empire.

The strange combination of confidence and fear with which the British always regarded the Suez Canal inevitably affected their attitude towards Africa. For two and a half centuries, from the first expeditions of the East India Company down to the opening of the Canal, almost all the merchandise that travelled from Britain to India and the Far East, and in the reverse direction, went round the Cape of Good Hope, using St Helena and the Cape itself as supply and later as coaling stations.

The opening of the Canal provided the opportunity to move merchandise as well as passengers by the fast route through the Red Sea, and to send warships by the same route to the danger spots of the Indian Ocean and the Pacific. British shipping lines made such good use of the Canal that only a few years after its opening more than 80 per cent of the vessels that used it sailed under the British flag. Yet an amazing number of ships, still under sail or carrying goods whose delivery was not urgent, used the old route, and in 1878, nine years after the Canal opened, it was estimated that the volume of British trade to and round the Cape (and 85 per cent of it round rather than to) was still about 40 per cent higher than that which went through the Canal. With the steady decline of sail, the Canal attracted more and more shipping, largely because of the lower fuelling costs on the shorter voyage, but the traveller who decided to use this old route of empire would find that many ships still followed it, sometimes merely coasting down to West Africa or the Cape, but quite often sailing on to Australia or into the Indian Ocean.

This maritime presence represented the oldest British interest in West Africa, whose hinterlands were first acquired to protect the trading shores around the Gulf of Guinea, known to Europeans under such names as the Gold Coast, the Ivory Coast, the Pepper (or Grain) Coast and—representing an interest predominant among early English sailors to Africa—the Slave Coast of Nigeria. But the protection of sea routes to Asia was almost as early a concern of British merchants as local trade, for the merchandise to be found in West Africa was small in comparison with that of India and the China Coast, all of which had to pass through African waters. For this reason the East India Company seized St Helena from the Dutch in 1651, and in 1795 annexed Cape Colony.

No British Government in the decades after the opening of Suez in fact felt secure with the quick and easy way it provided through the Egyptian desert. A Parliamentary Commission on Colonial Defence which met from 1879 to 1881 was so fearful of the consequences of relying on the Canal alone that it stressed the need to provide adequately for the defence of Cape Town and the adjacent naval base of Simonstown. The members of the commission recognized that circumstances could arise in which 'the security of the route through the Suez Canal might ... become very precarious' for commercial shipping, 'in which case the long sea route would be the only one available'. They described the Cape route as 'essential to the retention by Great Britain of her possessions in India, Mauritius, Ceylon, Singapore, China, and even Australasia'. If the Suez Canal were closed, the long route was the only way reinforcements could be sent from Britain to any of the Pacific dominions or colonies. The commission concluded, in words that might define British military practice for the next three quarters of a century, 'The uninterrupted supply of men and material to meet the ordinary demands of our Eastern garrisons and squadrons is of such importance that the integrity of this route must be maintained at all hazards, and irrespective of cost.'

The subsequent seizure of Egypt did nothing to lessen anxieties about the two sea routes to India. Having temporarily occupied Egypt, the British were faced with the problem of deciding what to do with it; in the event they stayed for almost half a century, and for only a few years of that period—the protectorate from 1914 to 1922—with even a pretence of legality. Not only had they imposed upon themselves the burden of ruling a country whose people were far more wholeheartedly hostile than the Indians ever became, but they had imperilled their old relationship with the Turks, so that Constantinople no longer seemed a sure bastion to defend the routes to India, while they had given the empire-hungry Germans and French an excuse to start that dismemberment of primitive Africa which by the beginning of the First World War left Abyssinia and Liberia the only territories unabsorbed into European Empires.

Every move of their rivals at this period aroused British anxiety not merely over the protection of the Canal against rivals who might incite the Turks to recover what was at least theoretically part of their Empire, but even for the safety of the route around the Cape. The establishment of a German settlement at Angra Pequeña north of the Orange River and Bismarck's subsequent declaration of a protectorate over South-West Africa; 'the proceedings of the French in Madagascar'; the efforts of Boer republicans in Transvaal to gain a foothold on the South African coast: all these developments, which had in part been provoked by Gladstone's seizure of Egypt, implanted agonizing doubts in the minds of British ministers, civil servants and colonial administrators, and gave encouragement to the imperialists whose influence gained strength among Britons in the 1880s and rose to its peak in the decade of the Diamond Jubilee.

The old systems of consuls and agents scattered along the coasts of Africa and employed in binding native chiefs and Arab sheikhs by treaty and subsidy was no longer sufficient. What territory Britain wanted to retain—and there was none it had once claimed that it was willing to abandon—had to be occupied effectively, through the customary process of sphere of influence leading to protectorate and thence to Crown colony. But this process of deepening and securing old beach-heads, which proceeded along the whole coast of West Africa, and around the southern tip of the continent from the Orange River round to Mozambique, was not enough once the axis of British policy in the Mediterranean had shifted from Constantinople to Suez and Cairo. The Levantine orientation of the British defence system that Disraeli had completed with the acquisition of Cyprus was replaced by an orientation directed towards the valley of the Nile, which explains the strengthening of Gibraltar and Malta. But even a complete naval domination of the waters between Gibraltar and Port Said, which the British Mediterranean Fleet had sustained since the days of Nelson, was not sufficient to safeguard either Egypt or the Suez sea route from the kind of danger that arose when the Mahdi and his dervishes conquered the Sudan, and threatened both Upper Egypt and the Red Sea port of Suakin. As the Germans and the French became active in the Indian Ocean, in the East African territories under the suzerainty of the Sultan of Zanzibar, and in Somaliland, British fear of local xenophobes was deepened by distrust of European rivals, and as early as 1884 a Foreign Office official anticipated a whole movement of annexation in a minute— disregarded at the time—which remarked that 'Our alternative route to India may at any time make it important that we should have possession or at least free access to good harbours.' Not until 1918 would all the fears of Whitehall, Cape Town and Delhi regarding the long route to India be removed by the capture of the German colonies in Africa, which made Britain the leading power on the continent south and east of the Sahara and which, with the acquisition of a mandate over Tanganyika, closed the one gap in the wide corridor of land uniting Cairo and the Cape of which Cecil Rhodes and his fellow imperialists had dreamed in the last phase of Victoria's immense reign.

To the traveller who went by the long route and sailed past the desert coasts of northern Africa until the sand gave way to jungle around the Gulf of Guinea and the jungle gave way to sand again south of the Congo, the British presence presented one of its most discreet faces. There were no commanding symbols of imperial might like the rock-fortress of Gibraltar or the fleet riding at anchor in the Grand Harbour of Valletta. Four colonies were spotted around the western bulge of North Africa and in the Gulf of Guinea: Gambia, Sierra Leone, Gold Coast and Nigeria. Three island possessions—St Helena, Ascension, Tristan da Cunha— formed a loose screen in mid Atlantic. Since 1918 the German colonies of West Africa had been divided between Britain and France. A narrow strip of Togoland had been joined to the Gold Coast and a fragment of the Cameroons had been added to Nigeria. In each case the French had benefited more than the British, but there had been compensation in the complete acquisition of South-West Africa, now administered by the Union of South Africa, whose troops had captured it. Its possession meant that for a thousand miles north of Capetown the Atlantic coast of Africa was—in 1930—in safe hands.

Gambia

After the purposive activity and obvious power of strongholds like Gibraltar, Malta and Aden, Gambia seemed a singularly pointless colony. It was minute, unhealthy and unproductive (in 1930 95 per cent of its exports consisted of ground nuts). But it had been linked with Britain for more than three hundred years. Queen Elizabeth chartered a company as long ago as 1588 to trade to the Gambia River, but it was not until 1618 that a first unsuccessful attempt was made. A fort was built in the river's estuary in 1686, and British interest was sustained from that time onward. Geographically, Gambia was no more than a narrow strip on each side of the river; nevertheless, it effectively split the French colony of Senegal and served as an Alsatia for those who represented themselves as fugitives from Gallic tyranny. In 1758, after a British naval expedition captured the French forts, they were combined with Gambia into a colony called Senegambia, the only African colony of the First British Empire. Senegambia was provided by Parliament with a constitution and an administration far in excess of anything justified by its trade, which proceeded along the beaches and the river mouths, where European traders met African middlemen who brought slaves or spirit gum from the interior. At the Treaty of Paris in 1783 Senegal was given back to France, but Gambia remained in British hands, administered first by the Company of Merchants Trading to Africa, governed colonially from Sierra Leone after the abolition of the slave trade in 1807, and made a separate colony in 1843.

Gambia brought out all the irrationalities in the relationship between the British and the French. During the 1870s the French were so anxious to acquire it and complete their Senegal territory that they steadily raised their offers of compensation, until at one point Britain might have gained French Guinea, the Ivory Coast and Gabon for this tiny foothold, but such satisfaction did Victorian Governments gain from the thought of retaining a thorn in the flesh of France's imperial ambitions that they refused. Had they accepted, the offered territories would have assured the British Empire during the African scramble of the 1880s that predominance on the west coast which it never decisively attained.

In 1930 Gambia was lightly garrisoned by the West African Frontier Force—African infantry with white officers—and its most reliable defence was provided by the Royal Navy, which used the harbour at Bathurst as part of its African system of bases.

Sierra Leone

In naval terms, however, Gambia was less important than Sierra Leone on the south-easterly curve of the African bulge some three hundred miles to the south and commanding the approaches to the major colonies of the Gold Coast and Nigeria. In the early nineteenth century, when those colonies were represented merely by trading posts and high malarial death-rates, Sierra Leone was already important strategically. The colony had begun as a narrow strip of coast ceded by local chiefs to provide an asylum for liberated and destitute Africans, mostly former slaves, who began to accumulate in London after the Mansfield judgment of 1772 ended the legal validity of slavery in Britain itself. It was first administered by a philanthropic organization called the Sierra Leone Company, but in 1807, when the Company fell into difficulties, the British established a Crown colony and used the harbour of Freetown as a base from which naval vessels could operate against the West African slave trade. Slaves liberated by this means were also settled in Sierra Leone, and there arose a bitter rivalry, which continues even now that the country has attained independence, between the Anglicized descendants of former slaves in Freetown and the indigenous tribes brought under British rule when a protectorate reaching two hundred miles into the hinterland was created. Sierra Leone had little trading value, but it was important in protecting the long route to India, since Freetown had the best harbour in West Africa.

The Gold Coast

The Gold Coast, the first British African colony to attain independence under its new name of Ghana, was less important strategically than Sierra Leone; it did not possess a proper port and even at Accra ships had to be loaded offshore by lighter. Despite this disadvantage, the Gold Coast, whose territory ran inland up the Volta River and had actually much more hinterland than coast, had become by 1930 the most prosperous African colony. Gold had taken the original merchants of the Royal African Company to Cape Coast Castle in the seventeenth century, and had given the country its name. In the mid nineteenth century Britain acquired the Dutch and Danish forts on the Coast—notably the Christianborg Castle at Accra which to this day remains the seat of Ghanaian authority—and by 1901, with the annexation of Ashanti and the tribal areas of the north, the outlines of the colony were complete.

By this time, encouraged by the developmental imperialism of Joseph Chamberlain and his disciples, the cultivation of cocoa had begun. The cocoa was not grown in European plantations, like tea in Ceylon or rubber in Malaya, but on native holdings, with British traders as commercial middlemen. The result was a standard of living among Africans far higher than elsewhere on the continent. Out of this prosperity emerged an educated native middle class which by 1930 included a fair number of doctors and lawyers. The rise of this class led the British to experiment in the Gold Coast more daringly than elsewhere with the introduction of Africans into the process of government. As early as 1889 an African had been nominated to the Legislative Council, and by 1930 there were nine Africans in a Council of twenty-four members. These were chosen by a rather uneasy attempt to graft the method of indirect rule on to the British parliamentary system, for six were elected by provincial councils of chiefs and three by municipalities; there was no attempt at universal suffrage.

The system of indirect rule was highly favoured by British administrators in the first half of the present century. It was thought that if one respected customs and ruled through traditional leaders of tribal communities, the native peoples would evolve in their own time towards the kind of institutions which the West had found beneficial. Underlying the theory one detects a half-conscious calculation that Africans who kept to their villages and remained loyal to their chiefs might be easier to rule than Africans educated too quickly in Western ways.

It is instructive to compare African with Indian experiments in imperial government. In the early nineteenth century Macaulay had dismissed the ancient ways of India with contempt and had convinced his fellow administrators that the opportunity to become imitation Englishmen must be offered to the youth of India. The African method of indirect rule seems at first sight in direct contradiction to such an approach. Yet one cannot overlook the part Indian experience played in conditioning African practice. By the late Victorian period British administrators even in India had come to distrust the Western-educated men who were products of Macaulay's educational reforms; one has only to read the fiction produced by Anglo-Indian writers in the present century to realize how universally the traditional elements in Indian society—the princes, the martial peoples like Sikhs, Rajputs and Pathans, and the tribal men on the edges of Hindu society—were preferred to those whom the British had moulded mentally in their own rough image. The African administrators sought to avoid the Indian dilemma by their system of indirect rule, but on the Gold Coast the system was indifferently successful, largely because the British did not understand the intricacies of native systems of authority there.

Nigeria

The stronghold of indirect rule, where it enjoyed most dramatic success, was the colony of Nigeria, divided from the Gold Coast by the narrow French enclaves of Togo and Dahomey. The originator of indirect rule was Frederick D. Lugard, a Compleat Imperialist if one were seeking such a paragon to ornament a historical page. Lugard had seen Indian service, had fought in the Second

Afghan War, and had been active in the Sudan, Burma, Nyasaland and Uganda, before he reached West Africa in 1894 to serve
with the Royal Niger Company. Under that chartered trading corporation, and from 1900 under the Colonial Office as High Commissioner for the Protectorate of Northern Nigeria, Lugard
served for twelve years without interruption. After an interlude
as Governor of Hong Kong he returned in 1912 as Governor of
Nigeria and remained in control of the territory until 1919. He
ended his long and dedicated career as a member, from 1923 to
1936, of the Permanent Mandates Commission of the League of
Nations.

Lugard was not merely an administrator who transferred to
Africa the best traditions of the 'Guardians' of India; he was also
an articulate imperialist intellectual, and out of his experiences in
Nigeria he wrote the best of all justifications of paternalistic colonial administration, *The Dual Mandate*, which developed in terms
of practical administration the idea of trusteeship on the part of
the more advanced races that Kipling adumbrated with crude
irony in his notion of 'the white man's burden'. What Lugard envisaged was a kind of dyarchical system by which local affairs in
a colonial area would be administered in traditional ways by traditional rulers, and general matters like defence, external affairs
and the wider aspects of finance would be handled by European
administrators assisted by able Western-trained natives. The division was not quite so abrupt as this schematic presentation may
suggest, since Lugard imagined that through indirect rule the
traditional leaders of the native communities would themselves
become modernized and in their turn instruments of modernization without the need for much direct intervention by colonial
officers or for the creation of a numerous class of natives aspiring
to become imitation Englishmen.

How far Lugard's experience in various parts of the colonial
empire had led him from the glib early Victorian meliorism of
Macaulay is shown in his view of the kind of education that should
be given to those who would become the vital second stratum of
rulers in his ideal tropical African colony.

Its result should be manifest in the adaptation of the people
to the existing conditions of life and in enabling them to
effect a generation able to achieve ideals of its own, without a

slavish imitation of Europeans, capable and willing to assume its own future. The education afforded by that section of the population who intend to lead the lives that their forefathers led should enlarge their outlook, increase their efficiency and standard of comfort, and bring them into closer sympathy with the Government, instead of making them unsuited to and ill-contented with their way of life. It should produce a new generation of native chiefs of higher integrity, a truer sense of justice, and an appreciation of responsibility for the welfare of the community.

There is no doubt that Lugard, who saw empire as a trusteeship over people far back on the road of progress, had found in Nigeria the ideal place in which to develop his ideas in practice. There was the spur of necessity; as authority broadened its territorial scope in the early twentieth century, Lugard had to govern a large, populous area (almost 400,000 square miles with nearly 19 million people by 1930) with about 400 colonial officers. In the northern regions, where his experience was most extensive, Lugard found a society ready made for indirect rule; indeed, the powerful Muslim emirates would have been difficult to rule in any other way. The rest of Nigeria lent itself with varying ease to the Lugard method, though indirect rule generally was favoured by the fact that in Nigeria the British had long hesitated to establish colonial authority. British traders had operated there on their own since the seventeenth century. Early in the nineteenth century British frigates destroyed the slave trade of the Niger delta, and Palmerston terrorized its chiefs with gunboats. But when in 1849 the British Government at last decided to take official cognizance of the region, it was through the studied indirection of Foreign Office methods. A consul was appointed to look after trade in the Niger Delta, and shortly afterwards another was established in Lagos in the west. The great British drive up the Niger, which began in the 1870s, was initiated not by the Government, but by George Goldie and his United Africa Company, which later became metamorphosed into the chartered Royal Niger Company. A protectorate was not established over the southern part of the Niger basin until 1885, and even then the Company was left to rule the country while Whitehall used its presence as a bargaining counter in the competition with France and Germany for African territories. The bargaining was harder over Nigeria than over the Cold Coast, partly because the enterprise of Goldie's agents had thrust the zone of effective occupation so much farther into the hinterland, but partly also because the north-east corner of the territory that became Nigeria offered an angular thrust into French Central Africa which had strategic value. Nigeria reached the western shores of Lake Chad; from that lake's eastern shore it was only five hundred miles to the Sudan, soon to come under the Union Jack. By holding Nigeria, the British kept the power to divide the vast area of largely useless inland territory which they had deluded the French into accepting while they themselves were making sure of the most commercially desirable points in West Africa.

In 1900 the rule of the Royal Niger Company was ended and colonial government established in southern Nigeria, though in the north the protectorate continued until the two territories were united in 1914. Even then, large areas were still governed with a sophisticated and carefully distanced paternalism, almost as if the country were still a protectorate. In the south-west this practice was made easy by the fact that the Yoruba and the Beni already possessed highly developed institutions. It was only in the south-east—the country of the Ibo—that tribal institutions blurred into such obscurity that the British found it difficult always to confer the responsibility of indirect rule on those whose authority was recognized by the people of a locality. Nevertheless, because of the degree of native rulership existing in most regions at the time of annexation, Nigeria under Lugard became a model of administration in terms not only of the efficiency of a small but carefully selected colonial service, but also of the complexity of a system of indirect rule developed to accommodate a variety of native forms of social organization unrivalled elsewhere in the Empire except India.

South of Nigeria stretched hundreds of miles of coast belonging in 1930 to other powers—the French Cameroons and Gabon, the two Congos (French and Belgian) and Portuguese Angola—where the Union Jack flew only over the little British consulates that protected the considerable trade between these regions and the seaports of England and Scotland. In any roadshed or river estuary along these dune-shielded or mangrove-clogged shores a good half of the ships loading or unloading merchandise would certainly be flying the Red Ensign, for despite the havoc created by submarines in the First World War, the British merchant marine was still in 1930 the largest and the most enterprising in the world.

But on this part of the voyage it was the oceanic islands that sustained the thread of empire. First, at about the same latitude as Luanda in Angola, there was Ascension, well over fifteen hundred miles offshore in the middle of the South Atlantic. Seven hundred miles to the south-east of Ascension lay St Helena. And far south of St Helena, south even of the Cape of Good Hope, in those regions on the edge of the Roaring Forties where Bartolomeu Dias lost contact with land before he rounded the southern tip of Africa, lay the bleak but strangely appealing group known as Tristan da Cunha.

St Helena

These islands, geographically so far apart, are closely linked in history. St Helena ranks among the oldest of British possessions; it had been under the Union Jack for more than a century when the First British Empire came to an end. Named by the Portuguese in 1592 after the saint on whose day Juan de Nova Castella discovered it, the island was briefly settled by the Dutch, and seized in 1651 by the East India Company to protect the sea route to India. The Dutch took it back in 1672, but next year it was again in John Company's hands, and remained so until it became a Crown colony in 1834.

Throughout the period from 1673 until the opening of the Suez Canal almost two centuries later, St Helena was one of the regular halts for East Indiamen. It is mentioned frequently in British diaries and memoirs, for it was the only place between Madeira and Cape Town where the passengers could go ashore on a voyage from London to India that took six months.

Forty-seven square miles in area and mostly volcanic rock, St Helena was overrun by gorse, broom and pines imported from Scotland, but its stony soil and misty mid-Atlantic climate could not provide the food to support the three thousand people—mixed in breed but toughly British in their attitudes—who inhabited it. Lace-making was introduced, and also the cultivation of New Zealand flax. But any real prosperity the island owed to its importance up to 1869 as a station for ships bound not only to India, but also to China and Australia.

In the mid nineteenth century its harbour of Jamestown, neatly sheltered by the surrounding volcanic slopes, was filled with shipping, while the island had gained historic attention thanks to its celebrated residents. Edmund Halley observed his comet there in the 1670s. But St Helena reached the apogee of international fame in 1815 when—thanks to the Duke of Wellington's memories of the longueurs of voyages home from India—it was chosen as a place from which Napoleon would not easily stage another calling to the eagles. The Emperor was visited on St Helena by every traveller with the least pretension to consequence whose ship put in to St James's Bay, and his fame made the island a symbol of the exile's fate. With the opening of the Suez Canal fifty years after Napoleon's death, the island itself became something of an exile, neglected by the ships that once crowded to it, since what traffic now sailed by the Cape was mainly of the kind that hugged the African coast looking for freight. Yet the island was retained, and garrisoned, and patrolled by the navy; there was no knowing when the long route to India would again require protection and supply.

Tristan da Cunha

Both Ascension and Tristan da Cunha were originally occupied to prevent their being used to promote the rescue of Napoleon from St Helena. Until his death in 1821 they were dependent on St Helena and subject to its Governor. Then Tristan da Cunha was evacuated, but a Scottish corporal in the garrison named Glass had become enamoured of the bleak Caledonian charm of this place of teeming sea-birds, and had obtained permission to stay with some of his comrades and their wives. Rarely visited, but recruiting their numbers with shipwrecked mariners and women wooed from St Helena, the Tristanians formed into an imitation Hebridean crofting community without lairds or landlords, centred on the one settlement, Edinburgh, from which they would make occasional trips to the yet more desolate islands of Nightingale and Inaccessible. Cultivating potatoes and gnarled apple trees, rearing sheep and sturdy Scots cattle, and catching the plentiful fish of those cool southern seas, they formed perhaps the happiest community in the white Empire, uncrowded and celebrated for their longevity, sharing their goods when need demanded, and in 1930 still living this life out of Hesiod under the gentle patriarchal guidance of their oldest inhabitant, without laws or regular government and also without crime, a situation which had filled with shocked surprise a Colonial Office representative who visited the group in the 1920s. So attractive was—and is—the life of Tristan da Cunha to its own people that as recently as 1961, when the local volcano erupted and almost consumed Edinburgh, they found existence in England, to which they were evacuated, intolerable, and almost unanimously chose to return in 1963 to their distant home and its bleak and lovely solitude.

Ascension

Because of its strategic importance, Ascension's fate was greatly different from that of Tristan da Cunha. It was taken over by the Admiralty, gazetted as H.M.S. Ascension on the Navy Lists, and commanded—rather than governed—by a ship's captain, usually with such thoroughness that Darwin, visiting it on the *Beagle*, thought of it as 'a huge ship kept in first-rate order'. It passed through various stages of naval usefulness—as a supply station before the coming of steam, as a coaling station, and finally as a convalescent settlement for sailors who fell sick off the Africa coast—before, in 1922, it was finally handed over to the Colonial Office and transformed into a dependency of St Helena, as it had been in its earliest days in the Empire. It had its other rather specialized uses in the imperial pattern: the cable to South Africa emerged to dry land there, and so did the gravid turtles which were captured and taken to London to provide the rich and ritual soup at the banquets of the imperial overlords.

South Africa

Whether passing by these remote islands or risking malaria, black-water and yellow fever on the route along the Guinea coast, the voyager by the long sea route would see British soil again as he passed the shores of Damaraland in south-west Africa (blossoming in desert splendour if he came in spring but otherwise arid and colourless) and finally reached the haven of the Cape. Bartolomeu Dias, who rounded it in 1486, is said to have called it the Cape of Storms, to record his own experience, but the name it acquired among the Portuguese—the Cape of Good Hope—reflected more faithfully the sentiments of four centuries of mariners on the India or China routes, for whom the Cape, whichever direction they were sailing, meant that the rigours of their voyage were half over. In the days of sail it could also bring the first fresh meat and vegetables after months at sea, and even in the days of steam the sight of Table Bay and the neat white houses of Cape Town was still welcome, for it meant an interlude in a temperate climate, a verdurous landscape, and the amenities of a European town.

The Cape, with its multiple headlands and the great hook-shaped harbour of False Bay, was the first of many reasons for the British presence in South Africa. At Simonstown within False Bay the Dutch had maintained since 1741 a naval depot to protect their trade to the East Indies, and in 1814, when British possession of the colony was confirmed, it became the headquarters of the naval squadron in the South Atlantic. In due course the British discovered the other attractions to South Africa: land to be settled on the Cape, diamonds to be dug far inland in Griqualand, and gold on the Rand. The diamonds and especially the gold were ambiguous blessings so far as imperial interests were concerned, for both attracted the attention of potentially rapacious European powers, and gold, discovered in 1886 at Witwatersrand in Transvaal, immediately complicated the political situation and weakened the security of the British hold over the Cape because it placed the price of military strength in the hands of a rival European race.

For in South Africa, as in Canada, Britain had been faced from the beginning with the problem of dealing with a white subject people; by 1930 their memories of that relationship were distinguished by a rare mixture of shame and pride, tinged with apprehension. In South Africa, through the machinations of the diamond tycoon Cecil Rhodes and his accomplices, British imperialism had shown a face of open rapacity, concealed elsewhere since the days of the eighteenth-century nabobs of India. Both the native Africans and the Boers had suffered from the insane love of power that combined in Rhodes's brooding and humourless mind with a vast vision of an unchallengeable Pax Britannica achieved by dominating Africa from Alexandria to Cape Town and by bringing back into the imperial fold the lost American tribes of the First Empire. To create the land north of Cape Colony that was named Rhodesia after him, he had picked a quarrel with the Matabeles, destroyed their impis and driven their fat and hapless king Lobengula to a fugitive's death in the remote bush of Zambesia. With Lobengula's land in the hands of his British South Africa Company, Rhodes had pushed on into the regions north of the Zambesi, until the borders of his personal kingdom marched with the boundaries controlled by that other ruthless adventurer, King Leopold of the Belgians, who had created a personal domain on the Congo where his agents ruled without reference to the Belgian Parliament or people—the kind of independence of action which Rhodes sought to retain for himself. But Rhodes was not content with the lands he had won by force or chicanery in the centre of Africa. He realized that both his personal domain and his vision of empire were in danger while Paul Kruger, that fundamentalist flat-earther who was also an extraordinarily astute politician, ruled a virtually independent republic in the Transvaal, supported by the wealth of the Rand and drawing strength from the struggles between Britain, Germany and Portugal for the hegemony of South Africa.

Rhodes found allies among the imperialists who had steadily been gaining influence in Britain since 1882, when fears for the safety of India had led even Gladstone into the imperial act of occupying Egypt. Earlier, when he became premier of Cape Colony, Rhodes had been inclined to play down his imperial vision, largely because he hoped to unite the Boer republics of Transvaal and the Orange Free State with the largely English territories of the Cape and Natal in a federation sustained by local initiative and dedicated to eliminating competition in the exploitation of native lands and labour; furthermore, he was anxious to avoid undue interference from Whitehall in his personal plans to acquire the Bantu kingdoms of Mashonaland and Matabeleland, which he succeeded in pre-empting, and Bechuanaland, which eluded his grasp. The power and independence that gold conferred on the Transvaal upset his calculations, as did the intransigence of the Portuguese in Mozambique and the enthusiasm with which the Germans fished for advantage in the troubled waters of South African politics. It became evident to Rhodes that without diplomatic and military support from Britain his aims for Africa would never be achieved. Here he was helped not only by the appointment in 1895 to the Colonial Office of the radical imperialist Joseph Chamberlain, but also by the growing fears among even cautious British political leaders like Salisbury that if the Transvaalers were not restrained they would establish a foothold on the coast of South Africa which the Germans might use to neutralize the strategic value of Simonstown.

This conjunction of strategic apprehensions on Salisbury's part with imperial ambitions on Chamberlain's part played into the hands of Rhodes and his associates. Even now it is not wholly certain how deeply the British Government was involved in the invasion of the Transvaal in 1895 by the mercenaries of the British South Africa Company under the remote control of Cecil Rhodes and the direct command of Dr Leander Jameson. Salisbury may have avoided an intimate knowledge of the plot to unseat Kruger, but Chamberlain was obviously in agreement with as much of it as Rhodes revealed to him; this was shown in his willingness to allow the British High Commissioner in South Africa to hold himself ready to appear in Johannesburg when the *coup d'état* had been accomplished, so that when the Boer republic was toppled it would be replaced by British authority and not by a new republic ruled by the Uitlander capitalists of the Rand.

The Jameson Raid failed, at least as an attempted coup, and Rhodes had to resign as premier of the Cape (though significantly Jameson acquired that position a few years later); nevertheless, the raid succeeded in so far as it polarized the struggle between the British and the Boers. After a vain search for neutrality, the Orange Free State was forced to accept the leadership of the more intransigent Afrikaners in Transvaal. The British settlers in Cape Colony and Natal became more strident in their imperial loyalties. The native people, in so far as they developed preferences, sided with the British as their only defence against the unmitigated racialism of the Boers. Once Hercules Robinson had been replaced in 1897 as British High Commissioner by Alfred Milner, a man trained in Egypt under Cromer and ineffably contemptuous of all 'lesser breeds without the law', war was inevitable. Chamberlain, Rhodes and Milner agreed that the only way to safeguard imperial interests was to force Kruger either to accept British paramountcy, to the extent of renouncing direct relations with other countries and accepting an overriding British policy for South Africa, or to provoke him into war.

It was war that ensued. What the British had seen as an affair to be ended in a few months continued for more than two and a half years, destroying the reputations of many British generals, bringing an end to the old panoply of scarlet coat and pipeclayed helmet as Boer sharpshooters condemned their opponents to universal khaki, and demonstrating for the first time in the history of the Empire the ability of a well-disciplined, well-armed guerrilla force without outside assistance to resist a considerably larger conventional army. In the end, the British beat the Boers, as they beat the Chinese guerrillas in Malaya nearly half a century later, and as they would have beaten the American colonists except for French and Spanish intervention in the war of 1776–83; they did so by a ruthlessness with which British imperialists were willing in emergency to reinforce their administrative talents, at least as long as they thought their cause was just.

With the details of the Boer War we are less concerned than with its effects; generally speaking, it encouraged the challengers of empire at this peak of imperial power and sentiment. In Ireland the prolonged and difficult struggle which the British had to wage in order to subdue the Boers was followed by prospective rebels as if it were a war game organized for their instruction. In Europe and the United States, where British campaigns against mere blacks or browns aroused little comment, the attempt to subdue two small republics inhabited by Europeans was viewed with high and often hypocritical disapproval. (The Germans, for example, forgot their own oppression of the Poles, and almost everywhere in Europe the absence of civil rights for non-Europeans in the Transvaal was conveniently ignored, except by a few eccentrics like Ibsen, who asked his fellow Europeans to consider seriously whether they were really on the side of Kruger and his Bible.) In Britain itself, as the war continued, anti-imperialism took a new life among people who, for reasons varying from political radicalism to a mere dislike of the role of bully, found the war distasteful. But the situation was complicated by the fact that support for the war—like opposition to it—spread over a wide political spectrum. The Fabians tended towards an anti-Boer attitude based on the view that, objectively considered, British imperialism was a progressive force, while labour politicians, as well as Lloyd George, were inclined to be—in the contemporary parlance—pro-Boer.

After the end of war in May 1902, Britain was anxious to achieve both security and reconciliation. The wounds of disunity at home, and the deep resentments between European communities in South Africa, had to be healed without jeopardizing the safety of the long route to India. The result was a curious pattern of limited unification. In what was acclaimed an unprecedented act of generosity on the part of imperial conquerors, Sir Henry Campbell-Bannerman's Liberal Government granted self-government in 1907 to the two Boer states, which at the end of the war had been reduced from independence to Crown colony status. Three years later they and the two British colonies came together in the Union of South Africa, which later gained dominion status; unlike Canada and Australia, it abandoned the federal model and became a legislative union, with matters of minor importance reserved to the provinces that took the place of the former colonies.

In 1930 the uneasiness of the equilibrium by which the imperial role survived in South Africa had become evident. In terms of European population, which politically was all that counted (though there were at least four blacks to every white), the Boer colonies were roughly equal to the English colonies of Natal and the Cape, but this was no true measure of the comparative strength of the races, for there were larger minorities of Boers in the Cape and Natal than of English in Transvaal and the Orange Free State. Thus the legislative union, devised in order to frustrate future separist tendencies in Transvaal or the Free State, led to a permanent political ascendancy of the Boers. The more far-seeing Boer leaders saw that in this situation co-operation with the imperial authorities would be more productive than resistance, and Louis Botha, who had been Kruger's commandant-general during the South African War, crushed the revolt of his former comrades who imagined that the outbreak of the First World War gave them an opportunity to re-create the independent republics. Later he commanded the expedition that seized German South-West Africa, and his colleague Jan Christian Smuts served in Westminster as a member of the Imperial War Cabinet.

Smuts, who became Prime Minister on Botha's death in 1919,

represented those Afrikaners who felt the appeal of certain aspects of British imperialism: its sense of racial superiority combined at best with a high-minded responsibility embodied in the doctrine of trusteeship. His loyalty to the Empire during two World Wars was unreserved, yet after 1947 he looked on the Commonwealth with misgiving; the appearance of India as an equal partner in its councils marred his vision of an association of white philosophers benevolently guiding the world. When Smuts conscientiously wore every summer the sandals which an Indian mahatma made for him in prison, he was acknowledging an exception; Gandhi was to him the Asian whose excellence emphasized the inadequacy of his compatriots.

Even so, Smuts represented the better element among the dominant Afrikaners of South Africa. Hertzog, Prime Minister in 1930, was a convinced nationalist who found a natural ally among dominion leaders in that staunch Canadian anti-colonialist, Mackenzie King, but there were Afrikaners more extreme than Hertzog, who were destined to give new and dramatic life to old Boer ideals. Dr D. K. Malan, who would eventually lead the Afrikaner extremists to power at Pretoria, was already a man of influence; in Hertzog's Nationalist Government he was not only Minister of the Interior but also in control of the Departments of Public Health and Education.

Thus the Cape was less securely held in 1930 than the British rulers who went into the Boer War in 1899 had intended. Yet obviously a unified country with a precarious balance of British, liberal Afrikaners and conservative Afrikaners, bound to the Empire by loose and voluntary ties, was less likely to become the accomplice of hostile foreign powers than a republic of isolated antediluvian bigots like the original Transvaal. Rhodes, who had died before the Boer War ended and by 1930 had long lain in his solitary grave looking out from the wild Matopo Hills over the city that had arisen on the site of Lobengula's kraal at Bulawayo, reasoned well when he saw the solution to the imperial problem in South Africa in a union of the English colonies and the Boer republics. Despite its internal tensions, South Africa was to remain with the Empire to its end, though it became an increasingly incongruous component, and eventually, as Smuts had feared, found the Commonwealth uninhabitable.

Basutoland, Bechuanaland, Swaziland

In any case, the imperialists had taken precautions and territorial hostages. Simonstown remained in the control of the Royal Navy, which only a stronger navy could dislodge, and encysted in the territory of South Africa there were two colonial enclaves—the territory of Basutoland and the protectorate of Swaziland; the northern borders of the Union were sealed by the protectorate of Bechuanaland and the self-governing colony of Southern Rhodesia, with its predominantly British white population.

The first three were regions where tribes of mainly Bantu origin had retained their independence long enough for the humanitarians in England to become concerned with their fate and to save them from domination by white settlers. Swaziland had been ceded to the Transvaal before the South African War, but afterwards it was taken back under British protection, and in 1930 its people—a hundred thousand of them in 7,000 square miles of mountains and rich valleys—were ruled by their traditional king, who held court seated on a giant tortoise-shell, benevolently supervised by a British Resident. The half-million Basutos, remnants of the tribes who under King Moshesh had terrified the settlers of the Orange Free State, had been ruled directly by the British since 1884 in their refuge in the Drackenberg Mountains. In the same year the 300,000 square miles of Bechuanaland, a wasteland that included the Kalahari desert and was populated by a mixture of peoples from Bushmen to Zulu fugitives, were taken under protection to save them from the trekking Boers.

Since its creation in 1910 the Union of South Africa had repeatedly requested that these territories be transferred to its jurisdiction; as regularly the British had replied that this would be done as soon as the native peoples agreed, secure in the knowledge that such agreement would never be given. The territories remained under the control of the High Commissioner for South Africa, representing British interests in the region; the same man in his other role acted as Governor-General of South Africa, and in these dual offices the essential precariousness of the imperial relationship was exemplified. Britain hoped to protect its vital interest in the Cape through friendly relations with a dominion with whose most numerous European race it had fought a bitter

war at the beginning of the century, but it took hostages by retaining control of the two enclaves within Union territory and of
other colonies beyond its northern border whose occupation prevented Germany and Portugal from uniting across the waist of
Africa and threatening the Cape from the north.

Apart from Bechuanaland, this territory consisted of the old
domains of Cecil Rhodes and his British South Africa Company—
known by 1930 as Southern Rhodesia and Northern Rhodesia and
divided by the Zambesi—and the region of Nyasaland, where
Scottish missionaries, disciples of the legendary Livingstone, had
set up a theocracy which controlled the country through the
African Lakes Company.

Rhodesia and Nyasaland

Rhodes had come nowhere near success in his greater mission of
reconstituting the First Empire within the Second; it is doubtful
whether many Americans except those who took advantage of his
scholarships to study at Oxford ever knew of his ambition to make
their country a partner in his expanded Pax Britannica, and even
more doubtful if any of them responded. Even his desire to fulfil
Harry Johnston's vision of a band of British territory uniting the
Mediterranean with the southernmost point of Africa was frustrated by the pragmatic caution of Lord Salisbury, who saw the
defence of the Cape and of the long route around Africa as a
separate problem from that of defending Egypt and the short
route through the Canal. Since Portugal could not be persuaded
to give up Mozambique, it was necessary to gather under the
Union Jack enough inland territory to neutralize the Portuguese
domination of the shoreline, and this was achieved when Mashonaland became part of the territories of the British South Africa
Company, and the Shiré territory, cutting into Mozambique like a
sharp knife towards the sea, was added to Nyasaland. Nyasaland
entered the Empire as the British Central African Protectorate in
1891. The previous year, after dominating the affairs of the island
for a generation, Britain formally established its protectorate over
Zanzibar which afforded protection to shipping on the East African
coast north of Mozambique, and Salisbury now regarded the security of the Cape as assured, and with equanimity accepted the
German occupation of Tanganyika, the mainland territory to the

north of Nyasaland. His system for the protection of Suez was another matter, and to his realistic Foreign Office mind the grand conception of an African map streaked with red from end to end weighed nothing against the knowledge that if Britain allowed Germany a free hand in a well-defined part of East Africa, there would be no more German difficulties over Egypt. For the new imperialists like Rhodes and Chamberlain colonies were bricks in a great edifice; for the Victorian diplomats who still played a great part in shaping British policy they were pawns manipulated in a game of power.

By 1930 the South Africa Company had followed other Rhodesian visions into oblivion. It had not been a profitable venture, and in 1923 its rule in Southern Rhodesia lapsed; in 1924 Northern Rhodesia also reverted to the Crown. The three provinces of Central Africa at the mid-point between the World Wars exhibited three different stages in colonial development. Nyasaland remained a paternalistically ruled protectorate, whose land and people were too poor for any European to exploit except the missionaries who went there on a search for souls carried on with such Caledonian intensiveness that the people of Malawi—which Nyasaland eventually became—still speak their English with a Doric brogue.

Northern Rhodesia, a Crown colony, was too torrid to become a place of intensive European occupation, but its mineral deposits were richer than those south of the Zambesi, and by 1930 a precarious ascendancy had been attained by a small group of European settlers and mine managers who controlled the few elected seats in the Legislative Council. But the whites in Northern Rhodesia never became numerous enough to secure the position as a commanding minority which their counterparts had assumed early in the century in Southern Rhodesia.

As the end of the South Africa Company's rule approached in the early 1920s, the Union of South Africa waited expectantly for the reversion of Southern Rhodesia, which good farming had made wealthy in spite of its disappointing mineral resources. But the thirty thousand settlers, mostly British, distrusted the Afrikaners in control of the Union and voted for autonomy. It was a decision that made little difference to the position of the native people. Suffrage in Southern Rhodesia was on a restricted property franchise that allowed only a few Africans to vote; presumably this was what Rhodes had meant when he skilfully sidestepped the racial issue by declaring himself in favour of 'equal rights for civilized men south of the Zambesi'. And if there was any doubt before 1930 of the kind of society the ruling white minority sought with the tacit consent of the British Government to impose on Southern Rhodesia, it was removed that year by the Rhodesian Land Apportionment Act. Out of the country's total area of 96 million acres, 47 million—the best half of the land—were allocated to the white settlers, 31 million were left for the native inhabitants, and 18 million, much of them unusable mountain or desert, were left unassigned. In other words, of the assigned land more than three-fifths went to the whites and less than two-fifths to the natives; yet according to the most recent census in 1926 there were 40,000 whites against 930,000 natives.

Rhodesia was not a full dominion, since its Government had no control over defence or foreign affairs, but its prime minister attended the Imperial Conferences from 1932 onwards. Rhodesia's role was that of a securely held, British-dominated territory that would prevent the Afrikaners of the Transvaal from penetrating into Central Africa and would ensure, even if the British did not directly control the coastline of Mozambique, that at least they commanded it from the highlands of Mashonaland and the higher reaches of the Zambesi and the Limpopo.

Tanganyika

By 1930 the traveller on the long route whose ship touched the East African coast north of Mozambique would find that the historic Muslim ports of Dar-es-Salaam and Kilwa, where the slave trade to Arabia had once flourished, were now in British hands, conquered in the early months of the First World War. Yet so little life remained in Rhodes's dream of Cape-to-Cairo that the British accepted the mandate with reluctance, after they had suggested that the territory be ruled by Italy or the United States, both of which declined.

Tanganyika was indeed not very interesting as a colonial possession. Few settlers were attracted to it, and, since the arrival as Governor in 1925 of Sir Donald Cameron who had been trained by Lugard in Nigeria, it was administered mainly through indirect rule. Even strategically it was of minor importance, since it contributed little to the spheres of possession and influence that protected Egypt and the Cape. Any threat its ports might present to shipping in the Indian Ocean was neutralized by the protectorate over Zanzibar, which had served as a minor naval base ever since the British began hunting down slave dhows in the mid Victorian age, and by the presence of the line of island bases spaced across the Indian Ocean.

Zanzibar

Domination of Zanzibar was imperially necessary, not only for the island's strategic value and its unrivalled clove orchards whose fragrance at the proper season scented the seaways for many leagues, but also because of the Sultan's tenuous suzerainty over the coastline and the inland Arab slave routes not only in Tanganyika but northward beyond Mombasa almost to the Horn of Africa, and inland to the country of the Buganda and the lakes at the source of the Nile.

British influence in Zanzibar was linked—so intimately did the threads of empire twine together—with its interests in the Persian Gulf. At the end of the eighteenth century, when the first treaty of eternal friendship was signed with the Sultan of Muscat and Oman, that Arabian prince ruled over Zanzibar, which his slave-trading ancestors had acquired to ensure their control over the African mainland ports.

It was to further their campaign against the slave trade that the British first established their ascendancy over Zanzibar. In 1845 the Sultan of Muscat and Oman surrendered to Palmerstonian pressure and signed a treaty abolishing the slave trade within his domains. By antagonizing the slave traders who were among his most powerful subjects, this made him dependent on the support of British warships. A crucial point was reached at the death of the Sultan Said in 1856. Said divided his realm between two sons, one to rule in the Gulf and the other in Zanzibar. The arrangement suited the British, since an independent Zanzibar could be built into an effective puppet state. But the Arabs of the Gulf objected to the diminution in their own trading opportunities, and attempted to force a reunion of the two halves of Said's sultanate. while the French sought to exploit the situation by supporting a pretender unacceptable to either the British or the Arabs. In 1859 naval action assured the ascendancy of the British candidate, and two years later, presuming on a paramountcy he did not legally possess, the Viceroy of India decreed the separation in perpetuity of Muscat and Oman in the Gulf from Zanzibar and its dependencies in Africa. Strangely, this did not disturb British interests in either the Gulf or the Indian Ocean; the truncated sultanate of Muscat and Oman still preferred British protection to the chance of being dominated by Turks or Persians, while the regular presence of British ships off Zanzibar meant that, even though internationally acknowledged only in 1890, the British protectorate over the island existed *de facto* since 1861, being strengthened in 1875–6 when the Royal Navy put down the slavers' revolts against the Sultan at Kilwa and Mombasa; thereafter the Sultan increased his dependency by accepting British officers to train the army created to ensure stability.

Most of the other islands in the Indian Ocean had been acquired merely to keep them out of the hands of rival European powers. The Laccadives were a dependency of India, ruled from the Madras Presidency. The Maldives were tributary to Ceylon. With the exception of the Seychelles, all the lesser groups scattered over the Indian Ocean, like the Rodrigues Islands and the Chagos Archipelago, were dependencies of Mauritius, from which itinerant magistrates would set out on long ocean journeys and arrive once every few months to look after the welfare of the indentured Indian labourers on the ubiquitous copra plantations and to settle disputes which the islanders had not been able to compose among themselves.

Mauritius

Mauritius was quite a different matter, a large and fertile island 720 square miles in extent, and recognized as one of the most delightful refuges a colonial civil servant could find. Visited by the Portuguese in the sixteenth century, colonized by the Dutch in the seventeenth, it was seized by France in the eighteenth, and made the centre of the French Empire in the Indies until in 1789 it was replaced by Pondicherry. Its harbour at Port Louis was the best in the Indian Ocean, and during the Napoleonic Wars Mauritius became a nagging thorn in the side of the East India Company, since it harboured the French frigates and privateers that raided the Company's vessels sailing from Canton and Calcutta. In 1810 the Royal Navy seized the island, and Britain retained it. The French aristocracy stayed, and Mauritius creole society preserved an *ancien régime* elegance that vanished in the colonies that France continued to govern. Under British rule, indentured labourers were imported from India until the balance of population was permanently disturbed, with twice as many Indians as French and French-speaking mulattoes. But a voting system based on property gave the French a majority in the Legislative Council, the Code Napoléon was administered by French judges, the local defence force was commanded by a French Canadian of impeccable lineage, and only at the naval station were the British prominently in evidence; the installations there had been strengthened on the eve of the Boer War to make sure that no rival power displaced the British as the British had displaced the French.

Seychelles and Maldives

If the British interest in Mauritius was actively strategic, in the sense that the island was a base for the squadron that cruised the Indian Ocean, the interest in the Seychelles, as in the Maldives, was no more than passively strategic. Both groups had been acquired during the Napoleonic Wars, and had been retained so that hostile ships might not find shelter in their intricate waters. After the Second World War the British were to plan a military air-base in the Maldives to watch over what remained of imperial interests in the Indian Ocean, but the dismantling of the Empire had gained such momentum that the scheme soon proved abortive. The Seychelles gained celebrity because their coral island remoteness and salubrious climate rendered them pleasanter places for the exile of inconvenient political leaders than bleak St Helena. In 1930 there was no expatriate dignitary in relaxed arrest there, but not long before a Ugandan king had languished in this exotic little Siberia, and not long afterwards it gave the hospitality of its confinement to the present ruler of Cyprus, Archbishop Makarios.

The Nile

If this necklace of islands looping from the seas off Madagascar to the seas off Malabar served to protect British shipping that

struck across the Indian Ocean from the Cape, the African mainland north of Zanzibar was the southern extremity of the system
of possessions that defended Egypt and the Red Sea route. The
British could not feel secure in Egypt so long as there was a possibility that the banks of the Upper Nile might fall into the hands
of rival imperialists. Indeed, by the time the British occupied
Egypt in 1882 those higher reaches of the river were already imperilled, for the revolt in the Sudan led by the Sufi prophet
known as the Madhi had already defeated two armies sent to
suppress it. The next three years were uniformly disastrous; the
dramatic culmination came when Khartum was captured in January 1885, and General Gordon, who had been sent there to
withdraw Egyptian forces and had stayed on against orders to
fight, was killed in the palace.

The British were more responsible than they cared to recognize
for the disaster in the Sudan. The destruction of the Egyptian
army by Wolseley at Tel el Kebir left no force adequate to oppose
the Mahdi unless the British themselves intervened directly, and
this Gladstone refused to do, having realized how deeply his
own occupation of Egypt had involved Britain in the affairs of a
land whose whole governmental structure was in rapid decay.
Commanded by British officers like Hicks Pasha, hastily trained
Egyptian columns marched to their doom in the deserts bordering the Upper Nile, and in that chaos of military and political incompetence only Gordon's obstinate desire for martyrdom shone
in a perverse grandeur. His death aroused an indignation that
smouldered in Britain for half a generation until—at least in the
public eye—it was avenged when Kitchener destroyed the Mah-
dist army at Omdurman in 1898.

Vengeance was far from the intent of the British rulers, whose
capture of the Sudan in the 1890s was as much a matter of political calculation as their decision to leave it untouched in the 1880s.
In the earlier decade what concerned them most was the safety
of the ports on the coast of the Red Sea, and particularly Suakin.
Once Suakin was secured, there seemed some sense, to a country
which had interests in so many other parts of the world, in leaving
the Mahdists in control of the Sudan, since their xenophobic fana-
ticism would make it difficult for any other power to establish a
foothold.

Nevertheless, there was always an anxiety about the Nile until all its reaches were securely tucked into the Empire. In part the obsession was romantic in origin. Ever since English poets had popularized the story of Anthony and Cleopatra, the Nile had stirred the British imagination as the cradle and grave of an ancient and mysterious civilization. Napoleon's dash for Egypt in 1799, and Nelson's defeat of the French navy near one of the mouths of the great river, gave a more concrete shape to the British interest. Now the Nile appeared as something more than the river on whose banks the fate of the Roman Empire had been decided by Octavian's defeat of Mark Anthony. The fate of Britain as an imperial power might just as easily be decided by Kitchener on its banks at the end of the nineteenth century.

The cult of Gordon and its influence on popular passions and eventually on government policy have been amply discussed by writers from Lytton Strachey onwards. But other events had kept the Nile in public attention for at least a generation before Kitchener's campaign finally made the great river British from end to end. The expeditions undertaken in the 1860s to discover the Nile's source attained notoriety because of the disputes between the explorers—Burton, Speke and Baker—all of whom became Victorian folk-heroes, and the public imagination was stirred by their accounts of the strange and beautiful hinterland that bordered the vast lakes, named in honour of Victoria and her beloved Albert, through which the White Nile flowed down towards its great cataracts.

The possibility that some hostile power in control of the headwaters of the Nile might divert its flow and deprive Egypt of the life-giving annual flood haunted British imperialists, particularly when Italy gained a foothold in Ethiopia and annexed Eritrea at the end of the 1880s, while the French began to probe eastward across the continent from the Congo basin and Lake Chad. It was at this time that the Foreign Office, taking advantage of the suzerainties claimed by the Sultan of Zanzibar, made its first moves.

Uganda and Kenya

In 1886, by agreement with Germany, a British sphere of influence was established inland from Mombasa, and in 1890 a British Resident was accepted by the King of Buganda. At first the

Government hoped to save the expense of occupation by charter-
ing a trading company, and in 1887 the British East Africa Company leased the coastal region around Mombasa from the Sultan
of Zanzibar. The Company was expected to build a railway inland
to the shores of Lake Victoria, but it had neither the capital nor
the technicians necessary for such an operation, and in 1894 a protectorate was proclaimed over the cluster of tribal territories
which became known as Uganda. In the following year the Company was persuaded to abandon its charter entirely, the East
African Protectorate was proclaimed over the area that is now
Kenya, and the railway, which by now seemed of the most urgent
strategic importance, was begun; in 1901, by a series of remarkable
engineering feats, including a kind of lift which took the trains
wagon by wagon and coach by coach up the side of the Rift
Valley, it was completed as far as Lake Victoria.

The Sudan

By this time the question of the Nile had been solved by action
from the north, precipitated by the Ethiopian defeat of the Italians
at Adowa on March 1st, 1896. Italy was thus removed from the
competition for the headwaters of the Nile, but only by arms and
advice given freely to the Negus Menelik by the French, who
were now advancing from the Congo up the Ubanghi River in the
direction of the desert region known as the Bahr el Ghazal which
borders on the White Nile. It was a situation that seemed to con-
firm the imperialists' warnings of the need to control not only
Egypt but also the whole of its Nilotic hinterland if the short
route to India were to be made secure.

On March 12th, 1896, Kitchener's advance began from Don-
gola. Except for the final battle at Omdurman, it was an unspec-
tacular progress, and not until September 1898 was Khartum
captured. Meanwhile Captain J. B. Marchand, with eight French
officers and a company of Senegalese, had succeeded after almost
two years in reaching the White Nile at Fashoda, where he raised
the tricolor and waited for reinforcements from Ethiopia. Kitchener arrived instead, with an armed flotilla which had sailed
up-river from Khartum in nine days. The two men met on
September 19th and worked out a *modus vivendi* until their respective Governments decided on a course of action. There followed

the weeks of tension known as the Fashoda Crisis, during which
it seemed possible that Britain and France would go to war over
a distant tract of desert with no more than a strategic value. In
the end Salisbury outbluffed the French, and in November they
withdrew all their claims to an enclave on the Nile.

The way was now clear for the incorporation of the Sudan into
the Empire. But this had to be done in a different way from most
annexations, owing to the special relationship between Britain and
Egypt. After its conquest in 1820 the Sudan was Egyptian territory until the Mahdi freed it; since 1885 it had been ruled by the
Mahdi's successor, the Khalifa, but his government had never
been recognized and in theory the Sudan was still an Egyptian
province in rebellion. Though Kitchener was a British general,
and acted under orders from Whitehall, he conducted the re-
occupation of the country as Sirdar of the Egyptian Army, on
behalf of the Khedive, and in command of a mixed army of British
and Egyptian troops.

Nevertheless, when Khartum was taken British and Egyptian
flags were flown side by side, and this symbolized the nature of
the new order. The British intended that even if they were obliged
to leave Egypt, their occupation of the Sudan (which would give
them power *in absentia* over Egypt) would be permanent. Accordingly, they established in 1899 an Anglo-Egyptian Condominium;
in theory they shared equally with Egypt in the government of
the Upper Nile. In fact, at no time was Egypt's role more than
nominal. The administration of the Sudan was entirely controlled
from Whitehall. Like the administration of Egypt, it was under
the Foreign Office, but while in Egypt the British officials were
nominally subordinate to native superiors, in the Sudan they were
enrolled in a civil service that was openly controlled by the
British, though it was independent of the Colonial Office in
acknowledgment of the theoretical Egyptian participation in
Sudanese government.

To assess how insubstantial Egyptian participation actually was,
one need only glance through the Sudan Service List for 1930.
Among the twenty-nine leading officials in Khartum, only two
bear Muslim names (i.e., are either Sudanese or Egyptian), and
both hold offices connected exclusively with the administration of
Muslim law. Of the thirteen governors of provinces, all are
British. The Commandant of the Sudan Defence Corps rejoices

in an Arab title—El Kaid El'Amm—but he too is British, as are all his staff. It is evident that here are no Lugardian experiments in indirect rule; the Muslims are allowed to retain their Islamic law, and that is all. The Sudan is too precious in the imperial scheme for government to be anything but direct and efficient.

The British territories in north-east Africa were a perfect exemplification of the proliferation of imperial needs. Because India was the indispensable heart of the Empire, the Suez Canal had to be secured. To secure the Suez Canal, Egypt must be kept out of the hands of rival powers. To protect Egypt from outflanking movements by these same powers, the Nile Valley—the Sudan—must be secured. To protect the approaches to the Sudan, Uganda must be annexed. To provide quick access by railway to Uganda, Kenya must be incorporated. To give a shade of legality to these operations, Zanzibar with its suzerain rights over East Africa must be brought under British protection. Other interests later developed in these territories—especially white settlement in the highlands of Kenya—but even these were not sufficient, once the all-important strategic considerations were removed with the liberation of India, to sustain the habit of empire. If the traveller in 1930 had returned in 1970 to the long route round Africa, he would have found the Union Jack flying only over the rocks in mid-ocean, over St Helena of the exiles, over Ascension, over Tristan de Cunha, obstinately British in its obstinate isolation.

IV To the China Seas

Ceylon

The meeting-place of the great imperial arteries through Suez and around the Cape was Colombo, the capital and leading seaport of Ceylon. Traffic coming up from the Cape or going from the Red Sea to Calcutta almost always called there, and so did the ships bound for the China coast and for the white dominions of Australia and New Zealand and the scattered islands of the South Pacific.

Ceylon was one of the brighter jewels in the crown of empire. Those who visited this bland and populous island in 1930, and travelled up from Colombo through green jungles and pastoral villages, through rice paddies and coconut groves, through rubber plantations and gardens where fruit hung like strange lanterns on the trunks of cacao trees, to the cool mountains with their tea plantations and their intensely English club-houses, found it hard to believe that Ceylon had entered the Empire merely because of a harbour coveted by the Royal Navy. Yet there was no clearer example in the history of the Empire of a colony originally annexed for the simple reasons of strategy.

By the time the British acquired it, Ceylon had already a long history of European contacts. Greek ships came from Alexandria before the birth of Christ, and coins of Augustus Caesar and his successors have been found in large enough quantities to suggest a considerable trade with the ancient Levant. But the men of the classical world came only as traders. The Portuguese who appeared in 1505 sought to establish political domination to ensure monopoly trading and religious conversion, and at the end of the sixteenth century they formally annexed the island. Yet they never defeated the King of Kandy, who ruled in the mountainous centre. When the Dutch appeared in the seventeenth century,

King Rajasinha entered an alliance with them to drive out the Portuguese, and in 1656 Colombo was captured. But the new conquerors were no easier to dislodge than the old, and while Kandy survived as an independent highland state, the Dutch kept the seaports and the coast.

The fear that it would fall into French hands led the British to annex Ceylon. In 1783 an abortive landing was made at Trincomalee, and in 1795, when Holland was overrun by the French, the East India Company sent an ultimatum to the Dutch Governor; he refused to surrender, and the British invaded Ceylon in 1796. At first they tried to rule the island by dual control, with the Company sharing responsibility equally with the Crown. This proved unworkable, and in 1802 Ceylon became a Crown colony, difficult to govern with a turbulent, independent kingdom in its heart, until in 1815, after a series of conflicts, Kandy was invaded, the king deposed and his realm annexed.

In spite of early demonstrations of violence, British rule in Ceylon was on the whole paternalistically mild. The exactions of Portuguese and Dutch had left a depleted economy, but by 1930 the amount of cultivated land had increased more than eightfold and the livestock population more than sevenfold. The average cash income of a Ceylonese was very low by British standards, but in Asian terms his real standard of living was high; the ferry that linked India and Ceylon at Adam's Bridge always provided the traveller with a striking contrast between the rural destitution of southern Madras and the relative well-being of Ceylonese peasants.

The British had a soft feeling for Ceylon, perhaps because it became the main source of the tea to which they were so extravagantly addicted, and by 1930 they had advanced the island more rapidly in the direction of autonomy than any other colonial territory. It was not yet internally self-governing, but well on the way. Since 1923, thirty-four out of the forty-nine members of the Legislative Council had been elected representatives, and the speaker of the Council was one of them. Thanks to the Donoughmore Commission, which began its work in 1927, plans had already been laid for political changes which in 1931 would put Ceylon ahead even of India in its progress towards autonomy. Not only was suffrage to be universal (to the consternation of most native politicians), but a measure of responsible government was to be provided by giving ministers drawn from the Legislative Council control over all affairs except Finance, Justice and External Affairs, including Defence. In other words, while granting the Ceylonese a substantial measure of internal self-government to digest over the next few years, the British retained what was essential to imperial interests: control over the purse-strings, the police, and the vital naval base of Trincomalee, one of the great natural havens of the world, where the largest of battleships could shelter. Even when Ceylon became independent in 1948, one of the conditions would be that Britain retain Trincomalee; only in 1957 did the Royal Navy finally depart.

Malaya and Singapore

A ship bound for the China coast would sail almost due east from Ceylon across the base of the Bay of Bengal, passing to the south of the Andaman and Nicobar Islands, also British, and approaching the coast of south-east Asia opposite the long elbowed isthmus that links Thailand to Malaya. The Strait of Malacca, dividing Malaya from Sumatra, was the customary route between the Indian Ocean and the China Seas, shorter and less fraught with navigational perils than the route south of Sumatra and through the Indonesian archipelago. Whoever controlled the strait virtually controlled the traffic to the Far East, and the port of Malacca on the Malayan coast was for centuries the vital strategic point. Its sultans grew rich by exploiting the spice traffic from the Indonesian islands, and when the Portuguese seized the town in 1511, one of their officers remarked that 'he who holds Malacca has his hands on the throat of Venice', for the Venetians gained their spices by a long commercial chain in which this town was the crucial link.

Later Malacca was seized by the Dutch and held as the key to their own spice empire. The British meanwhile had established themselves in 1685 on the opposite shore of the strait at Bencoolen on Sumatra. Not until the later eighteenth century, when Canton was finally opened to trading, did the British pay any attention to the Malayan peninsula itself. Then, in 1786, the East India Company established a post at Penang which balanced the Dutch presence in Malacca. Malacca was captured during the Napoleonic Wars, returned to the Dutch in 1815, and finally acquired from them in 1824 in exchange for Bencoolen. But the most important British enterprise in Malaya was the settlement of Singapore in 1819 by Sir Stamford Raffles. With great foresight Raffles realized that this island at the tip of the peninsula, where the monsoon systems meet, was so placed that it could become the pivot of trade between Calcutta and Shanghai.

The date of Singapore's foundation is significant. It was the year after Java was returned to the Dutch. Java had been captured by East India Company forces, supported by the Royal Navy, in 1811, and the brief period of British rule had been utilized by Raffles to reform the administration of the island with a view to incorporating it into the British empire in Asia. When complex diplomatic considerations led to its abandonment, Raffles turned to Singapore, more suited in fact to British purposes since, apart from its commercial value, it commanded all the easily navigable channels leading into the China Seas. More than a century afterwards its strategic importance was to be recognized in 1921 when the imperial Government decided that the security of trading interests in the Far East needed a naval base nearer to Shanghai than Trincomalee; by 1930 the construction of the Singapore base was already well advanced. Towards the sea it presented virtually impregnable defences; nobody expected a foe to come by land.

During the early British presence, Malaya was regarded as subsidiary to India. There was little effort to extend control beyond the three ports of Penang, Malacca and Singapore, which in 1826 were brought under a single administration as the Straits Settlements. Even then they remained subject to the East India Company, and when the Company came to an end in 1858 they were inherited by the India Office. Only in 1867, after the trading communities in the three ports had complained emphatically about their interests being subordinated to those of India, were the Straits Settlements transferred to the care of the Colonial Office.

Yet it was the development of Malaya's own resources that stimulated British interest in the peninsula and turned it into one of the areas of the colonial empire where the thesis that colonies exist to provide prosperity for the imperial countries appeared to have most justification. Not only did it pay its way as a complex of colonies and protectorates, but, at least until the depression of the early 1930s—and again after it ended—Malayan tin and rubber brought much profit to British investors. Tin had been mined from ancient days, but it was not until the mid nineteenth century that European and Chinese miners began to exploit the deposits intensively. Indirectly, through fighting between Chinese miners and Malays, the tin mines led to British intervention in the native states—first of all in Perak in 1874. During the next decade other states accepted British residents, and an interference in their affairs rather more intrusive than that endured by most Indian native princes. In 1895 these principalities, the most prosperous in the peninsula, were united in the Federated Malay States. Three years later the first Malay rubber was tapped, and the peninsula rapidly became the leading producer of this vital commodity; by 1930 almost 95 per cent of the world's natural rubber was grown in Malayan plantations. This led not only to the absorption of the remaining native states, which in 1909 severed their allegiance to Siam and accepted British protection, but also to a symbiotic unity of interests between the states where tin was mined and rubber grown, and the Straits Settlements ports through which it was exported. But rubber and tin are no ordinary materials; in modern war they have strategic importance. And, just as Iraq and the Persian Gulf gained in importance when the Navy began to convert to oil-burning ships, so in Malaya the demand of modern war machines for tin and rubber gave the peninsula a value quite apart from its geographical setting; the transfer of the naval base from Trincomalee to Singapore was motivated partly by the calculation that in any future war it would be more important to defend one's rubber than one's tea. Thus Malaya, which the British governed so tactfully that no nationalist movement began to stir until after the liberation of India, was indeed—at the prime of empire—the Golden Chersonese which the ancients had described.

Siam

North of Malaya, at the end of the long pan-handle isthmus, Siam thrust its bulk between British territory in Burma and French territory in Indo-China. Siam was never part of the Empire, yet it fitted into the imperial pattern in the same way as Persia in the Middle East. It owed its continued independence to the fact that it was the region where French and British interests clashed; it would have been intolerable to Britain if a French-dominated Siam had existed on the borders of Burma, and equally intolerable to France if a British-dominated Siam had pressed on the frontiers of Cambodia. After much friction, Britain and France signed an accord in 1896, reinforced by a later treaty, of 1904 by which they jointly recognized Siam's sovereign independence. But British interest in Siam was never idle, and, as I have said elsewhere; 'Siam became and remained until the beginning of the Second World War something less than a protectorate but more than a sphere of influence.'* Until 1909, when they abandoned them in exchange for paramountcy over the Malay states tributary to Siam, the British enjoyed extra-territorial rights, their consular courts operating as far north as Chiengmai. Siamese princes were educated by English tutors; King Rama VI went to Oxford and served in the British army. British merchants dominated the vital teak trade and the coastal shipping lines. And in the 1890s when King Chulalongkorn began to employ European advisers, the vital adviserships on Finance and Customs were reserved for British nominees. The power of the City of London, even more than that of Whitehall, made itself felt in Bangkok and far into the Siamese hinterland.

Borneo

Ships bound from Singapore to China sailed out into the broad expanse of the South China Sea, and unless they veered northward to put in at Bangkok or Saigon they would be unlikely to sight much land before the peaks of Hong Kong's islands rose out of the sea. Yet the British had been concerned since the mid eighteenth century with strategic power in the China Seas, and in 1762 with that problem in mind they had seized Manila and held it for two years. The idea of an establishment in the Philippines was abandoned, but after the Opium Wars of 1840–2 opened the ports of China to British trade, the large island of Borneo seemed the logical place to establish a British presence that, in juxtaposition to Malaya, would ensure a virtual control over the southern end of the South China Sea.

That presence was established with such masterly indirection that until after the Second World War the only actual Crown colony was the tiny island of Labuan, less then 30 square miles in

* *The British in the Far East*, London, 1969.

extent, acquired from the Sultan of Brunei in 1846. Labuan was a fuelling station with the superb advantage that there was no need to bring its coals from Newcastle; they were dug on the spot and loaded directly into the ships that put in to Victoria harbour.

Brunei originally possessed the whole of the northern shores of Borneo, but the improvidence of successive sultans and the rapacity of adventurers drastically reduced the state's extent. By 1930, after having once ruled the Land and Sea Dyaks over almost 90,000 square miles, Brunei was confined to a residual patrimony of about a thirtieth of that area.

More than half the original dominions of Brunei were appropriated by the dynasty created by a Byronic Englishman, James Brooke, one of several originals out of whom Conrad fashioned Lord Jim. Brooke appeared in Borneo in 1840; as a reward for suppressing a revolt that threatened the Sultan of Brunei he was named Raja of Sarawak and given a small territory. He and his successors gained five further concessions until Sarawak, recognized as an independent principality in 1865, had consumed almost all the land west of the palm-leaf capital of Brunei town. To the east a shabbier series of adventurers, including an American merchant named James Torrey who gave himself the title of Maharaja and a German speculator with the apparently genuine title of Baron von Overbeck who was Austrian consul in Hong Kong, extracted almost equally extensive concessions. Eventually, after the China merchants claimed their share of the spoils, the British North Borneo Company was chartered; it brought under its rule no less than 34,000 square miles. A mere 2,500 square miles were left to the Sultan of Brunei when in 1888 the British Government stabilized the situation by declaring protectorates over the three territories of Brunei, Sarawak and British North Borneo; ironically, it was in the tiny fragment left from the ruin of the realm that rich oil wells were found which in recent years have made Brunei—still obstinately clinging in the 1970s to the status of a British protectorate—one of the most prosperous places in the Malay Archipelago.

In 1930 Sarawak was still governed autocratically by Sir Vyner Brooke, grandson of the original White Raja, and the British North Borneo Company still ruled its corner of the island, the last of the chartered companies to retain territorial government. Both the Raja and the Company had established miniature civil

services and compact private armies, and in terms of efficiency
their administrations compared well with those of the Colonial
Office. In Sarawak a traditional oriental paternalism was mixed
with Western enlightenment, and, having tamed the headhunting
proclivities of their Dyaks, the Brookes ruled over a fairly contented group of peoples with whose traditional customs they
discouraged interference.

The China Coast

Except for the presence in both places of hard-working Chinese,
it is hard to imagine a greater contrast than that between the
patriarchal rusticity of the capital the Brookes maintained at
Kuching and the modern bustle of the great city of Shanghai,
which was the nerve-centre of British commercial imperialism in
China. Except for Hong Kong, annexed unenthusiastically in
1841, and Weihaiwei, leased in 1898, no part of China was territorially contained within the British empire. In half a hundred
treaty ports British subjects enjoyed extra-territorial rights and
concessions of land for trading hongs. In more than half these
ports the British were the only Europeans, and in most of the
others they were the leading *lo fan*, or foreign devils; this was
especially so in Shanghai, the largest port of China, where the
main financial interests in the International Settlement were
British, where until 1930 the British automatically held a majority
of seats on the municipal council that ruled the settlement as if it
were a free city, and where most civic officials and most officers
in the highly trained Shanghai Volunteer Corps were British.
When Shanghai seemed in danger in 1927 from civil war in
China, and in 1932 from the Japanese, the British sent the largest
contingents of troops, as many as three brigades in 1927. And up
the Yangtse, as far as the cascades that ended navigation in the
heart of China, the gunboats of the Royal Navy patrolled unchallenged, protecting British ships and citizens.

Yet, apart from Hong Kong, headquarters of the two China
Commands, naval and military, and Weihaiwei, where the small
naval base of Port Edward was established to counterbalance the
Russian Port Arthur, the Celestial Empire lay outside the domain
of the Colonial Office. The Foreign Office writ ran here; British
affairs were overseen by consuls, with their own courts and prisons,

their own highly trained service, troops at their call, and as much power in the British concessions as a governor in a Crown colony. An even more substantial, though nominally unofficial, manifestation of the commercial imperialism of the British in China was their virtual control of the maritime customs. Even before the Opium Wars, foreign merchants had objected to the capricious exactions of Chinese mandarins in charge of customs operations, and in 1854 they had established in Shanghai an international board of customs inspectors. As the most formidable maritime power in the China seas, the British quickly gained control, and in 1863 the Imperial Maritime Customs was established, staffed by European officers, of whom more than half were always British, and under the autocratic control of an Inspector-General who was a virtual nominee of Whitehall.

Ruling—in fact if not in name—the key ports of China, sailing its greatest river, influencing its fiscal policy through the maritime customs, and maintaining a miniature British garrison at the embassy in the heart of Peking (in 1930 it was commanded by a Major Colchester Wemyss), Britain at the beginning of the 1930s still wielded in China the power of a solidly based commercial imperialism. There had been times indeed when it seemed on the verge of transformation into a territorial imperialism like that which had supplanted the Moghul Empire. Britain, as the veteran imperialist L. S. Amery remarked in 1953, had taken the leading role 'in opening up an empire hitherto sealed off from the outside world'; at the time of the Diamond Jubilee, Amery added with a loose kind of justice: 'No one was clamouring to see Queen Victoria Empress of China as well as Empress of India. But no one at the time of her Diamond Jubilee would have dismissed the idea as inconceivable.'

Yet now, at a safe distance from the heyday of empire, it is not difficult to see why, with the special exception of Hong Kong, the British urge to paint the world map red flowed no farther than the mangrove swamps of Borneo. The mere logistics of distance provides one answer. By 1900, even if one counts the Opium Wars as a single incident, the British had made three major military interventions in China; on two occasions their troops had marched into Peking. Yet the total result of these experiences was to convince even ardent imperialists in the 1880s and 1890s that to maintain control of a country as large as China at a distance from

London almost twice that of India was virtually impossible. Another factor, emphasized in 1900 during the Boxer Rebellion, was the sense of racial superiority and solidarity which had made the Chinese not only less receptive to Western influences than the Indians, but also less willing to accept foreign rulers. It would have been impossible to recruit among the Chinese an army like that which the British raised in India. But without such an army control over the country would have been very difficult to sustain.

If China had been less distant and less intractable, the British might well have occupied it in the period around the middle of the nineteenth century when they were almost unchallenged as the leading European power in the Far East. But after 1860 China was the focus of many rival ambitions, some of them nurtured by powers whose home bases were far closer than Britain or even India; the time for even attempting a British hegemony had passed. France was becoming active in southern China, while Russia was occupying Siberia to its Pacific limits and, on the lower reaches of the Amur, trespassing on land the Chinese regarded as theirs, with the intent of establishing a sphere of influence in Manchuria.

Japan

In 1902, seeking for a combination that would not involve embarrassing commitments in Europe or concessions in Egypt, Britain entered into an alliance with Japan directed mainly against Russia. It represented a tacit abandonment of all pretention to extend the British Empire into China. Indeed, as early as 1898 it was clear that if the commercial advantages and political influence Britain had gained in China was even to be preserved, there would have to be an arrangement with most of the rival powers gathering around the dying Chinese Empire. Accommodations with France in 1896 and 1904 recognized a French sphere of influence in Yunnan; a similar German sphere was recognized in Shantung; both France and Germany accepted British pretensions in Shanghai and on the Yangtse. But neither of these powers, however menacing it may have appeared in Africa, showed itself as serious a rival of the British in the Far East as Russia.

The rapid modernization of Japan brought a great change in the regional balance of power. For a few decades after Japan was opened to foreign contacts in 1853, it had seemed almost as if the country would succumb to the same kind of commercial exploitation as China. Treaty ports were created, foreign concessions established; British troops did garrison duty at Yokohama in the 1850s. But Japan became receptive rather than resistant to Western ideas and techniques. In 1899 the treaty privileges of foreigners were withdrawn by agreement, and Japan began to emerge as a modern military power so efficient that in 1905 her forces defeated the Russians on land and destroyed their fleet at sea. From this point the British alliance with Japan began to take on a new complexion. It had begun as a protection against Russia: now it seemed more like a flimsy assurance of Japanese non-belligerence, and it was not long after the defeat of Russia that the three British dominions on the Pacific—Canada, Australia and New Zealand—began to regard Japan as a menace, so that the alliance became a source of dissension even within the Empire.

Nor was Japan the only rival power that at the turn of the century was assuming importance in the Far East. American trading interests dated from the early days of the nineteenth century, and American political interests began to assume importance after Perry's expedition to Japan in 1853 first opened that country to Western contacts. At the end of the century the American presence in the Pacific assumed the shape of open imperialism, through the annexation of Hawaii, the capture of the Philippines from Spain, and the acquisition of such strategic points as Guam, Wake Island and the eastern part of the Samoan archipelago.

The First World War marked an end to the possibility of extending British territorial possessions or commercial power east of Singapore. Germany was eliminated from the region, but Japan's power increased through its participation in the war on the Allied side. Economic difficulties in Britain, and the sheer costliness of new and sophisticated naval equipment, made impossible a return to the old principle on which British sea power had been based: to have a navy as strong as those of any two other powers combined. To keep its navy as strong as that of any one power was now as much as Britain could hope, and the Washington Treaty of 1922, which established a ratio between the British, American and Japanese navies of 5:5:3, gave overt recognition to this changed situation. The Washington Treaty was devised with the Far Eastern situation especially in mind. Britain had decided that her forces must be used primarily to defend the territorial empire, and the treaty was an attempt to establish a tacit arrangement by which British naval forces could be reduced east of Malaya. But America could not be relied on to protect Whitehall's interests in the China Seas, and Japan would remain an ally only so long as it remained convenient not to be an enemy. In the British decision to build the Singapore base there was more than a thought of having a fixed position from which quick relief could be sent to lightly garrisoned concessions in China; there was also an intent to guard more closely the way from the China Seas to the Indian Ocean, the central lake of the territorial empire.

Thus it was in the Far East that by 1930 the British Empire had most evidently reached and passed its point of greatest power, and here too the signs of strain were evident. Even the most incurious traveller could not fail to become aware of them as he listened to the talk of the *taipans* at the long bar in the Shanghai Club, the talk about what had happened in Weihaiwei and Hankow.

V Britain in the Antipodes

Australia and New Zealand

Whether one travelled by the ships that sailed from Colombo to Fremantle in Western Australia and thence to Adelaide, or more slowly via Singapore and through the Malay Archipelago to Brisbane and Sidney, the route that led to Australasia would take the traveller in 1930, as it takes him today, into a realm that even in imperial terms was completely different from anything experienced on the long or the short route to India, or on the Far Eastern journey from Colombo to Shanghai.

He would sail far enough to reach the temperate regions, which up to now he had experienced only at the tip of South Africa and in certain Indian hill stations where altitude performed the role normally associated with latitude. And in these Antipodean distances he would find the communities which were most clearly linked in race, customs and loyalties with their British past.

Though in New Zealand the Maoris had been accorded an equality of status so far denied to the scanty remnants of aborigines in Australia, they formed less than five per cent of the population and no longer retained the power to influence the fate of the country as they had done in the Maori Wars of the 1860s. In Australia the non-European population, including aborigines, half-castes and Asians, was less than two per cent of the total, and the vast majority was of English, Scots or Irish descent. In New Zealand there were proportionately more members of the Church of England than in England itself, and the English traveller found himself in landscapes and among life-styles often poignantly reminiscent of those he had left behind.

When the traveller had time to look more deeply into the Australasian pattern of existence, there were indeed aspects of it — and particularly its rough egalitarianism and the consequent simplicity of its class system—that suggested the slow emergence of a distinctive culture and independent political attitudes. But if Australia and New Zealand moved forward, and in moving forward moved inevitably slowly away from Britain, they did so as homogenous communities. They had to accommodate within their views of a national future no large minorities of alien language and tradition like the French in Canada and the Boers in South Africa. Indeed, if one uses the word in its pure, original sense, Australia and New Zealand, with Newfoundland and a scattering of small and remote places like the Falklands and Tristan da Cunha, were the only true *colonies* in the Second Empire, for they were the only places where parts of the British swarm hived off and became new and self-contained communities.

Distance, which had made Australia and New Zealand reserves of archaic zoology, conspired perpetually to keep the two countries as true colonies in the antique sense. Because they were so far from the routes of trade and empire established by the Spanish and the Portuguese in the fifteenth and sixteenth centuries, it was long before they were even discovered; the first sightings of these southern lands by Dutch mariners in the seventeenth century produced an impression of such commercial unprofitability that they were left almost unnoticed until the later eighteenth century when, in 1768, James Cook set out on the first of his great voyages, circumnavigated the islands of New Zealand and discovered the east coast of Australia, which he named New South Wales and claimed for England in 1770.

The settlement of Australasia began as an almost direct result of the collapse of the First British Empire, for the loss of the American colonies faced Britain with an urgent domestic problem: there was nowhere to send convicts who had been sentenced to transportation overseas. It was decided to make use of the distant shores, far beyond the recognized sea routes, which Cook had discovered, a land so remote that escape of any kind would be difficult and unsanctioned return to Britain would require superhuman ingenuity. In 1788 the ancestors of some modern Australians arrived in the contingent of 786 convicts—188 of them women—and 210 marines and officers who landed at Botany Bay, but settled finally at Port Jackson on the great harbour where Sydney later rose.

Once the convicts had been established, it was natural that adventurous free men should follow them, and as early as 1813 the great pastures beyond the Blue Mountains were discovered and Australian sheep farming began. From that time the settlement of the rest of the country, or at least of the fertile rim to the vast barren Outback, became inevitable, and, although Britain was then unenthusiastic about acquiring new colonies, it feared that the French, who had shown interest in the Pacific ever since Bougainville's voyage there in 1767, would lay claims to Australia if they were not anticipated.

In New Zealand, where the success of settlement in Australia inspired private colonizations by individuals and by organizations like Edward Gibbon Wakefield's New Zealand Company, the be-lated intervention of the Colonial Office was provoked by the same anxiety, and the British representative who went to negotiate terms with the Maori chiefs arrived only a short time before the warship sent to lay claim to the islands in the name of Louis Philippe, King of the French. At the Treaty of Waitangi in 1840 the Maoris ceded sovereignty to Britain, and New Zealand entered the Empire, to develop a bond with Britain that was as much economic as sentimental. No colony became more bound by trade to industrial England, which absorbed the greater part of the meat, wool and dairy products grown on the lush pastures of North Island and the vast dry ranges of South Island. By 1930 more than 70 per cent of New Zealand's exports went to Britain. But the bond of tradition was as strong as that of commerce, and the fact of New Zealand's being the most remote of all the dominions, the farthest from any competing influences, helped to strengthen it. No colonial towns were more variedly British in character than English Christchurch and Scots Dunedin, with their respective Anglican and Presbyterian traditions; no schools in the Empire more faithfully inculcated muscular English Chris-tianity than those of New Zealand; and to the First World War went a higher proportion of New Zealanders than of any other territory in the Empire.

Yet the British loyalties which appeared so strong in New Zealand and Australia were accompanied by an inclination to-wards political and social radicalism more advanced than existed in Britain until after the Second World War or existed at any time in the other dominions of Canada, South Africa and Newfound-land. It is true that this development was mainly peaceful. While

Canada's progress towards nationhood was accompanied by no less than four armed rebellions, the first in 1837 and the last in 1885, not to mention invasions by disaffected Canadians and by American supporters of the Fenians, Australasians could boast no more than the minor incident of the Eureka Stockade. This was a gold-miners' uprising in 1854 which was mainly a product of the hypertense atmosphere common to nineteenth-century boom settlements and which had no effect on the general political progress of the country—though the historiographers of Australian radicalism have not neglected to exploit the romantic possibilities of this single example of insurrectionary violence and to make martyrs of the twenty-five diggers who died after their demands (derived from those of the English Chartists) had been rejected. It adds spice to the legend that Eureka was not a place but a public house, that the incident began with the death of a miner in the same pub, and that the principal leader of the insurgent diggers, Peter Lalor, having lost an arm fighting at the Stockade, went into hiding and eventually emerged to be elected to the legislative assembly of Victoria, not, as one might have expected, as a socialist or a radical or even a liberal, but as a conservative.

But, Eureka notwithstanding, the Australasian dominions proceeded in general by the same path of non-violent political evolution as Britain, though more quickly. New Zealand, in 1893, was the second country in the world to grant the vote to women (the Isle of Man was the first). New Zealand also pioneered in old age pensions and State life insurance, factory laws and industrial arbitration. In Australia the trade unions became and remained more militant and more powerful than their British counterparts, at least until the First World War, and after taking a leading part in a series of coalitions from 1904 onwards, the Labour Party won an absolute majority in both Houses of Parliament in 1910. This did not mean a wholly enlightened form of government, for until comparatively recent years the Labour movement in Australia has been unrelievedly xenophobic, and has supported legislation intended to keep non-Europeans from immigrating.

Roughly a decade beforehand, Australia displayed a polarization of politics into social-democratic and conservative groupings, with the centre virtually eliminated, of the kind that would come into being in Britain with the collapse of the Liberal Party during the 1920s. In 1930 Labour was in power again in Australia, elected in

1929 (the year of Britain's second minority Labour Government) after being out of power during most of the 1920s.

When Labour first came into office in 1910, Australia as a united dominion—or Commonwealth as its people chose to call it—was less than a decade old. In New Zealand a tendency towards centralization had developed early; the original division into ten provinces, each self-governing in its own affairs, had proved cumbersome in a country little larger than Great Britain, and in 1876 the provinces were abolished in favour of a legislative union, a solution short of ideal, since it left a lasting sense of grievance among the people of South Island, who rightly believed their interests were subordinated to those of the more urbanized North Island which by 1930 already contained two-thirds of the dominion's population. Australia, by contrast, scattered as its population was in the coastal pockets where rainfall was sufficient—with the desert heart a vast no man's land except for its mining settlements—fell naturally into the pattern etched out by boundaries of its six states, each of which centred on a knot of communication, industry and urban settlement around its leading city.

To the end of the nineteenth century these fragments continued as politically separate entities, and when at the Diamond Jubilee in 1897 eleven premiers of the self-governing colonies drove behind Queen Victoria, each in his separate coach, there was a touch of braggadocio about the matter, for six came from Australia and only five from the rest of the Empire. It took forty years of negotiation to bring the six colonies together in 1901 in a federation similar to that which Canada had established in 1867. The Labour movement was suspicious that it might increase the power of capitalist interests, and it took two sets of referenda to acquire a people's mandate for the Commonwealth. Less than 30 per cent of those entitled to vote supported the idea in 1898, and though it was carried in the following year, only 43 per cent of the electorate registered their approval. Fear of domination by the populous eastern colonies remained so strong in Western Australia that its people did not agree to join until a year later than the rest.

Yet there were many reasons—apart from a dawning nationalism—that made some form of unification inevitable. The imperial authority was inclined to regard self-government among its colonies as a sign of their ability to defend themselves and an excuse to withdraw its own troops to guard India, Egypt, Shanghai, and the dependent territories which guaranteed the routes of empire. And even before the 1880s both the Australians and the New Zealanders had become uneasily aware that distance was no real protection. In fact, when the 1880s dawned, the scramble for Africa was to be reproduced on a smaller scale among the multitudinous scattered islands of the South Pacific, and in the end the British Empire was to incorporate a goodly share of them.

The Pacific Islands

But the pattern here was different from that in other parts of the world, since there were no interests in the South Pacific that directly concerned Whitehall. None of the islands lay on the route to India or China, and none directly threatened communications with Australia or New Zealand. It is true that there were certain pressures in Britain to assume protective responsibility for the islands of the Pacific, including Hawaii, which for a brief period in 1843 fell under the control of the Royal Navy, but this came mainly from the humanitarians, who were appalled by the reported brutalities of the blackbirders recruiting labour for the Queensland plantations, and from the missionaries, who played political power-games on such a scale among the islands that for periods they became virtual rulers in places like Tonga and Hawaii. Traders on the whole preferred the islands as they were, since local chiefs, suitably bribed with guns and alcohol and offers of support against their neighbours, might condone practices that European administrators would almost certainly not permit.

Yet not until the 1870s did Britain appear as anything more than a powerful naval presence among the South Pacific Islands, and then only after European—largely Australian—settlement in the Fijian islands had created a politically tense situation. Cakobau, the paramount chief of Fiji, had found the group virtually ungovernable by the 1860s, owing to the intervention of Tongan invaders, yet at this time the imperial powers were so little interested that he offered his kingdom in turn to Britain, the United States and Germany, and in each case was refused. In 1874, urged on by Australian politicians, the British finally decided to accept the group.

Britain followed the annexation of Fiji by establishing in 1877 a Western Pacific High Commission, at first concerned merely with regulating the behaviour and protecting the interests of British subjects. Whitehall would have been content with such a shadowy presence if it had not been for the tension created in the 1880s by the actions of Germany and the consequent anxieties of Australia and New Zealand. It would indeed be no exaggeration to claim that almost all the island colonies which the traveller might visit in 1930 (provided he could endure the primitive and irregular boat services that traversed the vast and hurricane-swept ocean distances from group to group) had been acquired to safeguard the white dominions of the southern hemisphere in the same way as Aden and Malta were acquired to protect the Indian Raj.

The German penetration into the Pacific had been a matter of the flag following trade, for as early as 1868, before the German Empire came into existence, the Hamburg firm of Godeffroy began trading in Samoa and spread its activities far into the scattered atolls of Micronesia. Godeffroy went bankrupt in 1880, but German interest in the Pacific did not vanish, and it was evident that sooner or later the expansionist Reich would move into the vacuum created by the failure of the traders. The Queenslanders became especially anxious, for the unclaimed eastern half of New Guinea, which lay across the narrow Torres Strait from the north-eastern tip of Australia, was already attracting active German interest. In 1883, acting on its responsibility, the Queensland Government sent a magistrate to Port Moresby to raise the Union Jack and claim the region. The act was repudiated by Whitehall, but in November 1884, after Germany had laid claim to north-eastern New Guinea and the Bismarck Archipelago, a naval vessel officially took possession of south-eastern New Guinea, which became known as Papua. In Samoa, where the German interests were long-established, the British were not so successful, for though a British-American-German protectorate was established in 1889, the Germans and Americans in 1899 divided the group between them.

Elsewhere, in the Gilberts and the Ellices, in the Solomons, in the Cook Islands, in Tonga, on Pitcairn Island, British protectorates which often developed into Crown colonies were declared during the late 1880s and 1890s. The authority of the High Commissioner for the Western Pacific became one of territorial government, exercised over hundreds of islands inhabited by Polynesians,

Melanesians and Micronesians, and scattered over eight million square miles of ocean. They included the one regular monarchy other than Britain in the whole Empire, that of Tonga, where in 1930 Queen Salote had already been ruling for twelve years from her little palace of white painted wood decorated with ginger-bread fretwork.

They also included—or at least half included—that strange governmental hybrid, the Condominium of the New Hebrides. In 1886 the British and French had set up a Joint Naval Commission for this group of islands; the Commission's overt aim was to safeguard order and its ulterior motivation was to keep out the Germans. The Germans still tried to gain a foothold, and it was for this reason that the French and British, by now united in the Entente Cordiale, set up in 1906 a system of joint rule so complex that it provided not for a single administration but for three, the result being a situation whose bizarreness must have impressed the visitor in 1930 as it does those who journey to the New Hebrides today.

For the islands are ruled by two equal Resident Commissioners, one British and one French. Together they preside over a Con-dominium Government, which deals with limited fields of com-mon interest; in other fields they maintain separate and equal administrations, with their own civil services and armed forces. The peculiarities of the situation can be illustrated briefly by the fact that the modern visitor, landing at Vila, is faced by two immi-gration desks, one for French subjects and one for British; sub-jects of other nations can choose which power shall admit them. But while immigration is a matter of separate and equal concern, customs is a joint responsibility, and the visitors' bags are exam-ined by Condominium officials at a single desk. Roads and ports are under Condominium jurisdiction, as are land titles and labour conditions; education, health and police are separate but equal areas, so that in an age of intense welfarism rival French and British schools and hospitals proliferate, and rival police forces arrest natives to be lodged in rival prisons and tried by rival magistrates. Only British police can arrest British subjects and French police French subjects, but Americans are fair game for both.

In 1930 government in the South Pacific was extremely simple. The medical and educational needs of the natives were met mainly by missionaries. Order was maintained by widely scattered district commissioners and by roving gunboats, and little interference took place in the lives of most island natives. Except in the New Hebrides, where the land thefts were spectacularly scandalous, a limit had been put on the activities of speculators, and in most parts of the South Pacific the land remained in the possession of the indigenous peoples. In Fiji—and only in Fiji—the British presence had resulted in startling demographic changes through the introduction of indentured Indian labourers to toil on the sugar plantations where the Fijians refused to work. Already in 1930 there were 73,000 Indians to 92,000 Fijians, and the Indians were breeding so much more quickly that the time was already in sight when, even though the Fijians retained most of the land, the Indians would exceed them in numbers.

Despite the beauty of the atolls and the high volcanic islands, despite the charm of many of their peoples, despite the abundance of useful products such as copra and sugar and phosphates, despite the anthropological secrets and the treasures of primitive art which they still concealed, these small and scattered islands were governed by Britain without enthusiasm, and even before the end of the nineteenth century Whitehall had begun to shed some of its burdens by transforming the Australasian dominions into colonial powers in miniature. After 1890 the Cook Islands were administered from New Zealand; in 1906 Australia assumed control over Papua. New Zealand later acquired Niue and the Tokelau Islands. When the First World War broke out in 1914 it was left to the two dominions to seize the German possessions in their localities. Australia took German New Guinea, the Bismarck Archipelago and the rich phosphate island of Nauru; New Zealand appropriated Western Samoa. When the time came to assign mandates, Britain allowed the dominions to retain their acquisitions, so that in 1930 the British Empire in this region was represented by three different Governments, not counting the Condominium of the New Hebrides. The Australian colonies, in fact, considerably excelled, both in area and in population, the British-administered colonies in the South Pacific. They also formed the world's largest reservoir of surviving neolithic cultures.

VI Remnants of an Old Empire

West and south from Britain, and then east through the Mediterranean or round the Cape, lay the countries of the Second Empire,
the lands by which Britain retained the status of world power that
was threatened by the defection of the thirteen colonies of North
America. West across the Atlantic lay the lands that remained
after those colonies departed. Only two British possessions in the
Americas were acquired after 1783, and one of them, British
Columbia, had been absorbed into Canada in 1871. The Falkland
Islands, which guarded the Strait of Magellan, had been occupied
temporarily by British forces between 1765 and 1774, but were
not permanently annexed until 1833, when the British expelled a
small Argentinian garrison and settled the islands with sheep-
farmers from Merioneth and the Scottish Isles, men accustomed
to austere remotenesses and glad to graze land of their own.

It was not that the setback of 1783 had deprived the rulers of
the Second Empire of expansionist designs in the Americas.
Where territorial expansion seemed likely to pass unopposed, as
in the great northern plains over which King Charles's charter to
his uncle Rupert had given the Hudson's Bay Company a tenuous
suzerainty, it had been effected and a vast new nation sketched
out—'From Sea Even Unto Sea', as the Canadian motto has it—
with the creation in 1867 of the first self-governing dominion in
the Empire. But elsewhere the efforts had remained, at least in
terms of territorial empire, tentative. The abortive occupation of
Buenos Aires in 1806–7 had taught the British a notable lesson,
for after the Spanish authorities had fled, the Argentinians themselves rallied to harass and expel the invader. It was evident that
the former Spanish colonies would involve far more trouble to
occupy than they might be worth strategically or territorially.

One of the reasons for British reluctance to become further embroiled in the Americas at this period was the War of 1812, which opened an unwelcome additional front during the Napoleonic Wars when the young United States reacted decisively to British efforts to inspect neutral vessels during the blockade of continental Europe. The war is now almost forgotten in Britain and the United States and remembered with pride only in Canada, where it is believed to have shown the emergence for the first time of an intimation of national consciousness; Canadians may not by 1812 have shown much consciousness of what it might mean to be Canadians, but at least they displayed a determined unwillingness to become Americans. The British burned Washington, the Americans burned Toronto (then known as York), there were some spirited miniature naval battles on the Great Lakes, Tecumseh led his Indian levies into an alliance with the British against the hated American 'Long Knives', and the Canadians believed they had won the war; but it had all been an expensive and rather alarming diversion for a Government already heavily involved in Europe, and Britain was happy to have got out of the affair without losing any territory.

Yet it would be wrong to assume that fear of the United States or rivalry towards it—though both existed—entirely or even mainly dominated British actions in the Americas after 1783. It has often been suggested that the Monroe Doctrine was obliquely aimed at Britain as the principal European imperial power. In fact, it was promulgated when both Britain and the United States were anxious to prevent continental European powers from intervening in Latin America to restore Spanish rule. Canning had approached the American Government with a proposal of joint action, and Washington decided on a unilateral declaration. The enunciation of the Monroe Doctrine seemed offensive to the British only because it implied that the Americans were seeking to rival them in gaining the goodwill of the newly independent South American States.

Once only—during the disputes between Britain and Venezuela in the 1890s over the boundary between that country and British Guiana—was the Monroe Doctrine invoked as a result of British action, and even then the evidence suggests that American intervention merely ensured what the British had always wanted: serious negotiation and arbitration. Otherwise, throughout the nineteenth century and well into the twentieth, British interests

were helped rather than hindered by the warning stance the
Monroe Doctrine appeared to offer. No rival European power was
likely to attempt an imperial adventure in which it might face the
combined powers of Britain and the United States, and this fact
effectively halted the Russian attempt to spread southward from
Alaska during the early nineteenth century, and discouraged the
Spaniards, after their attempt to establish themselves at Nootka
Sound at the end of the eighteenth century, from attempting any
further adventures north of California.

Britain, in fact, had no need after Waterloo to increase its
territorial empire in the Americas. The liberation of the former
Spanish colonies had opened their ports to commerce, and British
merchants were foremost in taking advantage of the new freedom
of trade. Surplus capital from the City of London moved into the
newly independent nations, and in several South American
countries the whole infrastructure of the emergent modern
society—railways, power installations, the banks, insurance companies, even many of the great cattle-rearing haciendas—was controlled by British interests. This situation continued in Argentina
and Uruguay until the later 1940s, and though the region of La
Plata contained the largest concentration of British capital, the
interests of the City were strong in Brazil and Bolivia as well.
Thus, except in Canada, the advances made by the Second British
Empire in the Americas were wholly in the direction of commercial imperialism; in financial terms the stake which Britain held in
Latin America was greater than its stake in any part of the territorial empire outside India and the white dominions, and far into
the twentieth century this financial power was translated into
political influence. It was no accident that the embassy in Buenos
Aires was, apart from that in Washington, the most important
British mission in the Americas, and considerably more important
than—for example—the embassy in Lisbon, the capital of Britain's
oldest ally but also one of its poorest friends.

The actual British possessions in the Americas were scattered
in a vast arc from Ellesmere Land in the High Arctic to Graham's
Land, a dependency of the Falklands, on the continent of Antarc-
tica. A more curving global arc, of surprising regularity, was that
which would take the voyager from Britain to the two North
American dominions of Newfoundland and Canada and then to
the thickly scattered colonies of the Caribbean. This second arc

would not touch the Falklands, but they can fairly be left in their Antipodean remoteness; once the difficult sea route around Cape Horn had been superseded by the Panama Canal, their strategic role fell into abeyance, to be revived only in wartime when the islands provided Britain with a useful naval base.

Wales

The traveller setting out to visit the American remnants of the First Empire would pass, before he left British waters, the relics of the even earlier European empire that the Plantagenet kings had attempted to create in the Middle Ages. Just out of Liverpool his ship sailed north of a colonized land whose very identity had for centuries been almost submerged. The last native prince of Wales had died in 1282 defending his stronghold in Snowdonia, and though the Principality continued to exist in name and Welshmen still sang of it as 'the land of the free', it had been absorbed for all but a few minor administrative functions into the kingdom of England. In 1930, though there was a minister for Scotland, which had joined England by legislative union and not by conquest, there was none for Wales, and the Welsh had fought their last rebellion long ago at the beginning of the fifteenth century, when Owen Glendower held the land for a few years against the English barons. Even the Welsh language was declining fast by 1930, and though a Welsh Nationalist Party had been founded in 1925, it would have to wait forty-one years for enough support among the Welsh themselves to elect a single member to Westminster. There was nothing in Wales like the spirit of rebellion that long before the end of the nineteenth century had made every Irish M.P. a nationalist, varying from his fellows only in the degree of his militancy.

The Isle of Man

Perhaps through the accident of history, perhaps because it had an area and a population both about a fortieth those of Wales and because it was strategically of minor importance, the Isle of Man, lying to the north of the shipping routes from Liverpool towards North America, was a fragment of Celtic world that had retained autonomy, even though since about A.D. 800 it had remained under foreign overlords, with Norsemen, Scots, and English

alternating according to the fortunes of war until, in the reign
of Edward III, it fell permanently under English suzerainty.

During all these changes of lordship, Manxmen retained the
power over their own affairs which all other Celts had lost, no
matter whether they were Irish, Scots, Welsh or Cornish in the
British Isles, or Bretons in France. Yet they retained it through
an institution of alien origin, the Tynwald, introduced by the
Norsemen in the ninth century. It consisted of a Council and an
elected House of Keys whose laws were proclaimed in public
from the Tynwald Hill on Old Midsummer Day, July 5th. From
the laws of the British Parliament, unless they expressly mentioned
the island (which they rarely did), Manxmen were exempt, and
except for a customs union with Britain they taxed themselves,
and did so leniently, for there were no death duties in 1930 and
the rates of income tax were much lower than on the mainland.

Ireland

The good sense with which the Manxman's desire for independence had been accommodated within the British scheme of empire, even in the Middle Ages, made all the more surprising the
agony for both sides which the British relationship with Ireland
had involved since those fateful days in the twelfth century when
the Fitzgeralds and the Fitz-Stephens first landed as Norman
knights on Irish soil, followed in 1170 by the formidable Richard
de Clare, called Strongbow. The tortuosity of the relationship, the
sense of a bitter feud between kinsmen, emerges when one reflects
on the fact that both the Fitzgeralds and the Fitz-Stephens were to
become absorbed by the Irish, and that while an extraordinary
proportion of the great writers in English were Irish by birth (so
that English literature would seem vastly impoverished if one
subtracted Congreve and Sheridan and Swift, Shaw and Wilde
and Yeats, Joyce and Synge and MacNeice), the race of English
descent known as Anglo-Irish was in compensation to provide
some of the greatest fighters for the freedom of Ireland, from
Wolfe Tone, a good Protestant born within the Pale, down to the
Ulsterman Roger Casement, and to Yeats's beloved Maud Gonne,
the red-haired daughter of an English army officer.

Ireland had been for centuries a wound on the conscience of the
English, and yet, in an age when supremacy at sea was vital for

the greatness and indeed for the survival of England as anything more than an imperilled island, the Irish seaports could not be left for enemies to use. Through the long centuries of conflict with France, from Crécy down to Waterloo, the possession of Ireland had seemed necessary to prevent the outflanking of England, and the waning of France as the great threat to British sea power after Waterloo had not removed strategic anxieties about Ireland. Even in the sixteenth century there had been a danger that Spain would use it in the attempt to destroy England, and in the nineteenth century Ireland was regarded as a potential political vacuum which, if it were not filled by Britain, would attract one of her enemies. The rise of Germany as a naval power gave weight to such anxieties, and even Home Rule as conceived by Gladstone and advocated by his successor Asquith on the eve of the First World War stopped short of the full dominion status that would have made Ireland responsible for its own defence. There remained always the fear that by some quirk of the national character the Irish would be willing to sacrifice their territorial integrity to a foreign power just for the sake of a slap at England.

All the horrors of the relationship between England and Ireland can be traced to this long-sustained feeling that Ireland was indispensable for English greatness. Economically, Ireland was no great asset to Britain, for the money that absentee landlords could wring from the impoverished countryside hardly counterbalanced the cost of holding the country. The settlements in Ireland were intended less to get rid of surplus population in England and Scotland than to create loyal Protestant enclaves in this land of disloyal Catholics and so to make it a more reliable outer bastion. Repressions in Ireland were fiercest when the danger of the country being used by enemies in actual war was strongest, e.g. during the Napoleonic Wars, when the United Irishmen rose in rebellion, and during the First World War, when the discovery of the link between the Irish Republican Army and Germany, through Sir Roger Casement, led to the savage treatment of participants in the Easter Day rising of 1916 and gave the Irish cause the martyrs it needed. It was also largely for the sake of security during the period of the Napoleonic Wars that the Parliament of Ireland, which—though elected only by Protestants—gave a semblance of independence, was abolished and the Irish in compensation given a disproportionately large representation in the imperial

Parliament, with the unforeseen result that the Nationalists, by holding the balance of power between the Conservatives and Liberals, created much disturbance in British political life.

Britain paid in more than noisy sessions at Westminster for the Irish connection. Even during the long calm following the Indian Mutiny, when for fifty years the British army overseas was engaged in extending borders rather than in crushing insurrections, Ireland, even when there was no open violence, existed in a state of chronic tension. And because this situation persisted from the eighteenth century to the twentieth, Ireland became a perpetual example which other subject peoples of the Empire could consider when they became conscious of their subjection. Throughout the nineteenth century, and up to the First World War, the pattern of Irish resistance alternated between times of legal agitation for Home Rule and times of open rebellion in which anything less than republican independence seemed beneath consideration. It was the rebel Ireland that struck the imagination of the world and echoed in insurrectionary movements elsewhere in the Empire. Ireland had erupted into its eighteenth-century cycle of insurrection at the same time as the Thirteen Colonies, and the American and Irish uprisings gave moral and physical support to each other. There were links between the Fenians and the Canadian rebels of 1837–8, and a Fenian was a member of Louis Riel's provisional government on the Red River in 1869. Irishmen fought at Eureka Stockade in Australia, and there were close sympathetic links between the Irish and the Boers. Even the Indian nationalists, particularly those who sought freedom through violent means, followed the progress of the Irish movement and studied the methods of its activists, though there was scanty reciprocation of interest, for the Irish were little concerned for the freedom of the colonial subject peoples.

Just as crucial for the eventual fate of the Empire were the sentiments which the Irish cause aroused in the United States. Irish Americans contributed most of the funds used by activist movements in Ireland from the early nineteenth century onwards, and attacks on Canada by Fenian volunteers recruited in the United States were a recurrent threat, particularly immediately after the American Civil War. But the most important effect of the Irish question on relations between Britain and the United States came from the power of the millions of voters descended from those who had sailed the Atlantic in the noisome emigrant ships during the years of the great Irish famine and had carried their resentments with them. It was, of course, an American revolutionary tradition to sustain a principled disapproval of Britain as an imperial power, but that disapproval was kept green and growing by the friends of Ireland, and Irish sentiment played its part in shaping the diplomacy through which, during and after the Second World War American leaders sought to hasten the end of the Empire.

In 1930 Ireland rested in an interregnum of dominion status. Violent insurrection after the First World War had led the British to a degree of coercion—involving the use of the notorious counter-revolutionary Black-and-Tans—that had shocked public opinion at home and abroad, and some arrangement became inevitable. Events had pushed the area of choice beyond Home Rule —or local self-government—which the Irish would have accepted had they been given it in Gladstone's time, and now it lay between dominion status and republican independence. Most of the Irish leaders accepted an offer of the same 'constitutional status in the community of nations known as the British Empire' as Canada and Australia, and it was on this basis that the treaty establishing the Irish Free State (but retaining the six counties of Northern Ireland as a locally self-governing part of the United Kingdom) was signed. The Irish Republican Army repudiated the treaty, and a bitter civil war among patriotic Irishmen continued until 1923. By the treaty, Ireland remained within the Empire, and British strategic fears were appeased by the Royal Navy's retention of its bases at Cork and Lough Swilly, so that the great grey ships still steamed into Irish havens with white ensigns floating from their sterns. But republicanism in Ireland, though disarmed, was still powerful. In two years from 1930 the old leader of the Irish Republican Army, Eamon de Valera, would come to power; events would move again.

Newfoundland

After losing sight of Ireland, the first landfall across the Atlantic was Newfoundland, a jagged-edged triangle of bleak British territory, somewhat larger than Ireland and thrust like a great irregular plug into the Gulf of St Lawrence, so that ships bound for the

Canadian river ports of Montreal and Quebec had to make their way through narrow and difficult channels to the north or south of the island.

Newfoundland is now a part of Canada, but it took depression and bankruptcy to drive it—in 1949—into a land which its people still defy in song, as they have done for a century past.

> Men, hurrah, for our own native isle, Newfoundland;
> Not a stranger shall hold one inch of her strand;
> Her face turns to Britain, her back to the Gulf.
> Come near at your peril, Canadian Wolf!

In 1930 anti-Canadian feeling was running high and triumphant in the island owing to the dispute with the larger dominion over Labrador, an inhospitable but mineral-rich area of 110,000 square miles which actually lay on the Canadian mainland but which in 1927 the Privy Council had finally awarded to Newfoundland. This was regarded on the island as an eminently just decision, since Newfoundland was Britain's oldest colony, claimed by Humphrey Gilbert in 1583, the year he disappeared at sea. By the twentieth century it had become in many ways a living fossil, preserving ways of speech and folk songs that had come from the West of England with the first fishermen-settlers and had survived in stark Newfoundland outposts with names like Come by Chance and Hearts Content. Despite a large element of Irish descent, Newfoundland had remained fervently loyal to the British connection, and in 1930 a great deal of its trade was still with English ports. Yet for all its loyalty, it maintained a sense of independence not entirely in keeping with its economic situation.

Having chosen a solitary path by refusing to join the Canadian confederation in 1867, Newfoundland was accorded by courtesy the title of dominion; it made no effort to control its external affairs independently and it did not rank a Governor-General. It was in fact the last survivor of the self-governing North American colonies which had existed before the creation of Canada. But its condition was perilous, for the refusal of its people to join Canada meant that Newfoundland tried to enter the modern world with a meagre economy based mainly on cod and newspaper pulp. Its budgets had not balanced since 1920, and railways, highways and schools—inadequate though they were by contemporary standards —had eaten up vast loans, so that in 1930 Newfoundland was on

the verge of becoming the most sensational imperial victim of the
world depression; it would shortly go literally bankrupt. Having
escaped the Canadian wolf, Newfoundland in 1930 was about to
enter the cage of the lion known as the City of London.

Canada

Canada's very vastness rendered it immune from such perils; it
had so much of so many things that its bankruptcy seemed and
doubtless was impossible. It was the largest country in the Empire
and the second largest country—exceeded only by Russia—in the
world. On the Mercator's Projections with which one customarily
illustrated the vastness of the Empire it dwarfed the United States
with a vast surge of red, exploding northward to the Arctic
islands, which were so swollen that Ellesmere Land—in reality
smaller than Britain—looked as large as Europe without Russia.
Even if one disregarded such cartographical distortions, Canada
was still an unconscionably vast country which then took five
days and nights to cross by train: a land of vast forests, vast
mountains, vast rivers, vast wheat-growing plains, vast northern
emptinesses, and as large an area of fresh water as the rest of the
world combined; a land united by the great railways which had
turned it from a wilderness of primitive hunters and pioneer farmers into a modern nation. Though Canadians were still mainly
country people living by primary industry, they dwelt usually near
the railways in a narrow corridor of populated land that in few
places reached farther than two hundred and fifty miles north of
the American border.

It was that border, running four thousand miles from the Bay
of Fundy to the Gulf of Georgia, which made Canada unique
among the lands of the Empire. No other dominion or colony
stood in so close a physical relationship with a major world power
other than Britain; indeed, one of the strengths of the Empire,
except in North America, had been that it did not have to defend
the kind of land frontiers with powerful military and industrial
neighbours that were customary in Europe. In theory the border
between Canada and the United States was 'the world's largest
unguarded border'; in practice one had only to try and filter
through the woods from Canada to realize that if not fortified, the
frontier was manned.

To Canadians the United States was both a threat and an invitation. American expansionism ran high for at least a hundred years after independence. The doctrine of Manifest Destiny proclaimed that the whole sweep of North America from the Pole to the Rio Grande must be embraced in a single commonwealth. During the Oregon Boundary Dispute of the 1840s, and later at the time of the Red River rising in 1869, there were many influential Americans who called for the expansion of the Union as far as the Arctic Seas. And menace contained temptation, for the United States throughout the nineteenth century and into the twentieth presented the image of a dynamic and expanding culture in which the material standard of living kept consistently above that in Canada. Yet from 1812 onward, Loyalists in Upper Canada and French Canadians in Lower Canada, and the immigrants who joined them, were virtually united in opposition to the American political style. Annexationist movements failed for lack of mass support, and nothing contributed more to the failure of the movement led by William Lyon Mackenzie in 1837 than his proclaimed desire to reproduce north of the border the presidential form of government, with all its in-built tendencies towards dictatorship. When the colonies of British North America became self-governing in the 1840s and 1850s, the pattern they chose was responsible government on the Westminster model, and the pattern was repeated in the dominion created in 1867.

That Canada became the first dominion—and thus set on foot a transformation of the Empire that is the central theme of the latter part of this book—was a fact dependent on the proximity of the American republic. In the mid nineteenth century, faced by expanding responsibilities in India, where the Punjab had just been acquired, and in China, where the treaty ports had been opened, concerned over the annexation of New Zealand, and involved in the thankless task of sustaining Turkey against Russia, the imperial Government could not accept the responsibility of ensuring that the northern half of North America should remain British. Later, when the Civil War ended with a residue of Anglophobe belligerence, it reached the politic decision that the creation of an autonomous North American nation might deter the Americans far more effectively than the British troops whose very presence reminded the citizens of the republic, and especially the Irish among them, that George III's descendants still reigned north of

the 49th parallel. When the regiments sailed from Canada in 1871
—leaving garrisons only at the naval bases of Halifax in the east
and Esquimalt in the west—the possibility that the United States
would attempt the political absorption of Canada retreated for
ever. At the same time the first self-governing dominion had been
created and the process of transformation from Empire to Commonwealth had begun.

Canada's role as a differentiating factor in the Empire began
with the presence of the French Canadians, who, by their retention of a vigorous sense of separateness, prevented the dominion
as a whole from developing into even as relatively faithful a copy
of the Old Country as New Zealand became. But it was also ac-
centuated by the ambivalence of Canada's relationship with the
United States. For while the Canadians refused to accept anything
other than a British political pattern, they were affected by the
culture which developed in the United States. American books
and periodicals always competed with those from Britain for
Canadian readers; American educational patterns were imitated in
Canada; American films and radio had by 1930 a vast Canadian
audience. Even the almost universal imperial game of cricket,
adopted enthusiastically by Indians and West Indians and Malays,
gave place in Canada to the American game of baseball.

And, given a border that ignored natural frontiers, so that the
prairies and the Rockies were quite arbitrarily divided by the
great line cutting from east to west, there was the inevitable
pressure towards economic assimilation. Geographically Canada
was the natural leading customer of the United States and *vice
versa*; the weaker of the two was the obvious first choice as a
destination for the surplus capital of the stronger, and the investment of surplus capital is the forerunner of commercial imperialism. In the early decades of the dominion, British trade and
British investment were dominant, but this was a declining survival from the colonial period. Even before the end of the nineteenth century the trend had changed to such an extent that an
astute observer like Goldwin Smith could regard assimilation as
inevitable, and when the First World War depleted Britain's
financial power, the trend towards American domination through
Canadian overseas trade developed so rapidly that in the year ending on March 31st, 1930, the ratio of Canadian imports from the
United States to those from the British Empire was approximately

10:3, and that of exports to the United States in comparison with those to the Empire was approximately 7:5. More than two-thirds of Canadian imports came from the United States; about 45 per cent of Canadian exports found a market south of the border.

But during Canada's crucial years of national growth, the shift into the American economic orbit encouraged a growing political independence of Britain. Thus the position of Canada between Britain and the United States in what John Bartlet Brebner called 'the North Atlantic Triangle' gave it the leadership of the movement towards a multi-national pattern within the Empire which in 1930 and 1931 came to a point of sharp definition with the events leading up to the Statute of Westminster.

The West Indies

Looking at the map with a historical eye, one sees superimposed on the North Atlantic Triangle an older and more polygonal figure, with lines that run down towards the West Indies. Even in 1930 the region of the Empire with which Canada maintained the greatest volume of trade, apart from Britain itself, was the Caribbean area, comprising the British West Indies and the mainland colonies of British Honduras and British Guiana. During the eighteenth century, when cane sugar and rum had been materials of high commerce, the island possessions seemed so valuable that at the time of the Treaty of Utrecht it was seriously debated in Britain whether to keep the sugar-growing island of Guadaloupe or to retain Canada. Under the so-called mercantilist system of the First Empire, Britain, the Thirteen Colonies and the West Indies had formed a closed triangle of trade operated mainly by British ships, which, having unloaded manufactured goods at one of the ports of the mainland of North America, would proceed to the islands and load up with sugar, molasses or rum for transport back to Bristol. After the loss of the Thirteen Colonies, a link remained, for the clippers from Nova Scotia and New Brunswick played an important part in the trade of the islands far into the nineteenth century, and Canadian economic interest continued in a variety of ways. On more than one occasion the proposal was raised that the West Indies should be admitted into the Canadian confederation. It was always abandoned.

In fact, the Caribbean islands sustained a sense of local independence that had frustrated all attempts at union, and this fissiparous inclination was foreshadowed even in colonial days by the lack of any effectively centralized administration. The mainland possessions, and the Bermudas which lay in mid Atlantic in the same latitudes as South Carolina, were too far away from the actual West Indies to be effectively included within a regional grouping, but even in the Caribbean itself the attempts at administrative consolidation had been no more than nominal. In 1930 the only token of common interest in the British West Indies was the fact that the Governor of Jamaica, who held locally the ancient Cromwellian title of Captain-General, was regarded as the senior official in the region and by virtue of this fact held the additional title of Governor-in-Chief. But it was no more than a title, except for the small groups of the Caymans and the Turks and Caicos Islands which were dependencies of Jamaica. The Bahamas, the Windward Islands and the Leeward Islands, Barbados and Trinidad, all had their own complete colonial Governments. Barbados and the Bahamas, like Bermuda, retained the Houses of Assembly which had been customary in the First Empire; they were not strictly speaking Crown colonies. And within the Windward and Leeward groups, the separate islands—Antigua and Dominica, St Kitts and Montserrat, Grenada and St Lucia and St Vincent—possessed their miniature local Governments, presided over by Administrators or Commissioners, or in the case of Antigua by a President, and issuing local postage stamps for the delight of philatelists.

The administrative chaos of the West Indies had its origin in the varied mode of their acquisition. The English had been interested in the region ever since 1527 when George Rut, sailing south from Labrador, entered the Caribbean, which up to this time had been virtually a Spanish lake. During Elizabeth's reign, English mariners sailed there for piracy or trade, and the trade was often hardly more respectable than the piracy, since it was often in slaves, for which there was so much demand in the Spanish West Indies that evasions of the strict laws governing commerce were often connived at by the local authorities. British settlements on unclaimed islands began in the early seventeenth century, when English gentlemen adventurers were given grants by the Stuart kings. The Bermudas, discovered through shipwreck, were claimed in 1609, and provided the inspiration for one of the few great poems of the Empire, Andrew Marvell's 'Where the remote Bermudas ride . . .' Barbados, the Bahamas and St Kitts were settled shortly afterwards under grants to various court favourites. Jamaica, on the other hand, was conquered from the Spaniards in 1655, and remained in the Empire as the sole monument to that frustrated Western Design which made Cromwell the first self-conscious imperialist in the British tradition. There were few Spanish settlers in Jamaica, and little sign survived of their presence, but the Spanish influence in Trinidad, captured in 1797, remained strong, as did the French quality of Grenada and St Lucia, which were among the few fragments Britain gained in the settlement of 1783 to compensate for the loss of the United States and of Minorca.

British Guiana

Of the mainland colonies, British Guiana pointed back to the old obsession with the basin of the Orinoco and the fabled city of El Dorado which had led Raleigh on an unsuccessful voyage that spelt his doom. A Captain Leigh made an unsuccessful landing in Guiana in 1605, in 1619 the Amazons Company attempted a settlement but withdrew when the Spanish protested, and in 1627 the Company for the Plantation of Guiana under the powerful patronage of the Duke of Buckingham repeated the experiment, but those settlers who had not died of ague were driven out by the Portuguese. In 1651 the first successful British settlement was established at Surinam, and lasted long enough for Mrs Aphra Behn to live there and gather the material for her novel *Oroonoko*; it was captured by the Dutch in 1667. What became known as British Guiana, west of Surinam, was captured from Holland in 1796, and in 1930 the old Dutch Court of Policy had been replaced only two years ago by an ordinary Crown colony form of government.

British Honduras

British Honduras, in an angle of coast between Guatemala and the Mexican territory of Quintana Roo, was the one lasting result of a series of British efforts to establish settlements or at least spheres of influence in Central America. Unsuccessful expeditions had been

made from Jamaica to the Bay of Campeche in Mexico during the
1670s, and in 1749 the British appointed a Superintendent of the
Mosquito Coast and established a protectorate over the Mosquito
Indians which lasted until Nicaragua took over the territory with
tacit British agreement in 1855. Farther south, in what is now
Panama, one of the few attempts by the Scots before the Union
with England to establish an empire of their own came to disaster
in the seventeenth-century colony of Darien.

British Honduras, an intermittent source of international friction because Guatemala claimed but dared not take it, had been a
minor focus of British interest since the 1640s; ships' crews, and
buccaneers when their normal employment became too risky, took
to cutting mahogany and cedar in the forests along its shores.
Those who remained there became known as the Baymen, and
in 1765 Admiral Burnaby placed them under naval protection and
framed a rough constitution based on local usages, but it was not
until 1862, when the Victorian fashion for heavy mahogany
furniture gave the region a certain commercial importance, that
the British decided to regularize the situation by declaring it a
Crown colony.

By 1930 the whole Caribbean region had become the backwater
of the Empire, so neglected that it was difficult to remember the
prosperous times when a small West Indian island had seemed
worth all the possibilities of Canada. The sugar market, the mahogany market, the sponge market of the Bahamas: all had declined
catastrophically, though the Bahamas, being near the coast of
Florida, had gained a special blessing when prohibition became
law in the United States and smuggling flourished. Successive
British Governments, their interest directed towards Asia and
Africa, tacitly accepted the rise of American power in the Caribbean. The Clayton–Bulmer treaty of 1850 had provided for a
rough equality there between Britain and the United States, and
Britain had been granted the right to share in any canal driven
through the isthmus of Panama. But one Suez was enough, and
in the Hay–Pauncefote treaty of 1901 Britain abandoned all rights
over the Panama Canal. In 1905 British garrisons began to withdraw from the West Indies and Bermuda. The maintenance of the
vestige of British power was left to the Navy.

Their usefulness to the Empire ended, the islands fell into

almost complete neglect. Between the turn of the century and the early 1940s virtually nothing was done to mitigate their economic difficulties. The contrast between the model administrations of the African colonies, like the Gold Coast and Nigeria, Sudan and Uganda, and their antiquated and inadequate counterparts in the West Indies was so extreme that it was hard to believe they came under the control of the same Colonial Office. Yet the traveller who went to the West Indies in 1930 after he had visited the rest of the Empire would hardly be inclined to see in them the signs of any general decay; they would seem to him merely a half-forgotten niche in a structure of government so vast that every corner could not possibly be ruled with equal efficiency and care. It might be a depressing destination to reach on the last great route of empire, a kind of Sargasso Sea of hopelessness, but if that image had occurred to a traveller in 1930, when men still believed in progress—even the progress of empires—he would doubtless have said that in the age of steam there is no need for ships to stay becalmed and that the tales about the Sargasso Sea were in any case exaggerated. Few saw the omens of that year of 1930 as we see them now.

Part II
And they shall have Dominion

VII The Settlement Colonies

As the pioneer dominion, Canada dominates the narrative of the evolution of white settlement colonies into virtually independent nations by 1931, just as India, the first non-white possession to gain independence, will dominate the narrative of the subsequent liquidation of the colonial empire. There is an essential link between the two developments, for if Canada had not created the precedent of self-government attained by mutual agreement, assisted by small insurrections which acquired mythical stature in popular memory, the struggle for the liberation of India, when it came, would undoubtedly have been far more prolonged, violent and difficult.

There are other important links, parallel and analogical, between Canada and India as the key imperial possessions. The decisive battles which preluded British domination in the two countries were fought within two years of each other, and both stemmed from the ancient feud between Britain and France. Clive survived his triumph at Plassey in 1757; Wolfe won and died on the plains of Abraham in 1759. These two victories not only laid the foundations for the Second British Empire. They also doomed France's hopes of creating an empire that would rival the British.

The loss of the American colonies in 1783 elevated the importance of both Canada and India in the imperial scheme, which was consolidated during the Napoleonic Wars. The last war to ensure the presence of Canada within the Empire was fought and won between 1812 and 1814 by an alliance of British soldiers, Canadian militia and Tecumseh's American Indians; hardly was it over than in India the armies of the Company began the final campaign against the Mahrattas that by 1817 secured British domination over the subcontinent.

From this point the pattern changes, and parallels turn into contrasts. As Canada was released stage by stage from the old mercantilist subjection of colony to metropolis, and proceeded towards self-government, India fell under the steadily tightening control of the alien oligarchy of the Indian Civil Service. Between 1848 and 1849 the colonies of Canada (embracing what is now Ontario and Quebec) and Nova Scotia were granted responsible government; in 1849 the last independent realm of any significance on the Indian subcontinent, the Sikh kingdom of Punjab, fell under East India Company control. 1858, the post-Mutiny year when India was finally brought under direct British rule, was the year when the idea of Canadian federation was first seriously mooted. And in 1876, nine years after the dominion of Canada was created and three years after it was made complete with the accession of Prince Edward Island, the Queen of England assumed the titles of the Moghul rulers of India and became Empress.

So, within a decade, Britain showed a democratic example to the world by creating in North America the first self-governing State that had existed within any empire, and at the same time in India acknowledged the autocratic implications of its rule by openly accepting the imperial style for the first time in British history. Thus the double faces of the Victorian outlook, its unprecedented combination of the liberal and the authoritarian, found more or less simultaneous expression. And, as the self-government established in Canada became a model for the white settlement colonies in moving towards dominion status, so the incorruptible but coldly impersonal regime of the Indian Civil Service became the model for the administration of the new colonies that were acquired after 1870; it was even applied to some of the older colonies, for a number of West Indian islands retrogressed during the nineteenth century from the First Empire pattern of local government by an elected assembly to the Crown colony pattern of rule by a Governor with a mainly nominated legislative council.

When the colonial empire finally began to move in the same direction in which Canada had led the dominions a century before, it was India and the adjacent colonial territories of Ceylon and Burma that led the way. The whole history of the Empire's decline and death—or of its transfiguration into the Commonwealth, which is much the same thing—could in fact be written in terms of the constitutional history of Canada and India. Without them it could hardly be written at all, for even Ireland and South Africa had, in comparison, a peripheral importance.

From the later 1820s, a good decade before those winter days of 1837 when Louis-Joseph Papineau raised his insurrection in the country districts of Quebec and William Lyon Mackenzie led the rebels of Upper Canada in their abortive march on Toronto, to precipitate the critical decisions in Britain that led towards self-government for the settlement colonies, it was the Canadian leaders who pressed constantly on the opening door of autonomy. It was they who established precedent after precedent of independent decision, until the day in 1931 when William Lyon Mackenzie King, the enigmatic grandson of William Lyon Mackenzie the hunted rebel, saw the actions of his grandfather, and of many other Canadians between them, brought to fruition in the Statute of Westminster which established the dominions as separate international entities.

The South Africans, like the Irish, played their part in the final stages of the evolution that led to the Statute of Westminster, but the initiative rested with Canada to the end. Australia and New Zealand, homogenous and almost entirely British in population, with no rival European culture as in Canada and no centuries-old bitterness as in Ireland, followed—sometimes reluctantly—in the rear of the march towards independence.

The obvious and most often quoted reasons for Canada's leadership—the presence of the French Canadians and the proximity of the United States—are not the only or even the most important factors. Canadian attitudes to the United States, as we have seen, were always ambivalent (as for that matter was the kind of freedom produced by American political institutions), but if there is one constant in Canadian history, from 1776 onwards, that balances the example of American democratic liberties, it is the distrust harboured by Canadians in general for American gigantism. During the American Revolution, the French in Quebec and the descendants of the New Englanders in Nova Scotia adopted a more or less neutral stance, but the War of 1812 showed a surprising unity of anti-American sentiment in a group of colonies— from Upper Canada to Nova Scotia—which had no political unity and little intercommunication. The failure of Canadians to respond to the American myth of Manifest Destiny was to be clearly demonstrated throughout the nineteenth century in the failure of annexationist movements to attract anyone but cranks and American citizens. This is not to minimize the strong American influence on events in Canada, but in so far as the United States has been an example to Canadians, it has to be regarded as negative more often than positive.

Similarly, while the presence of the French Canadians was as important as that of the Americans, their actual role can be misinterpreted. The obvious comparison is with the Boers in South Africa, but the comparison immediately tells us that, while the Boers trekked into the wilderness in search of a place to be free and themselves, and only ceased that search when the British had successfully closed the frontiers north of the Transvaal through the activities of Rhodes and his South Africa Company, the French Canadians chose obstinately to stay. Except for a few officials and seigneurs, they did not return to France at the time of conquest, and except for a few *voyageurs* who eventually mingled with the Indians and were lost to Quebec, they did not move on into the vastnesses of Canadian *terra incognita*. They left the prairies for other men to break and cultivate, and concentrated on building up, in the lands along the St Lawrence River, which their ancestors under the *ancien régime* had broken, a social world governed by a Christianity which the harshness of the environment shadowed with a Jansenist gloom not unlike the presbyterian darkness into which the indifference of the Nova Scotia wilderness drove many pioneers of the Atlantic colonies.

In social terms the main effects of the British conquest of Quebec were to weaken the power of the traditional seigneurial class and the hold of the modified feudal system of Quebec on the *habitants*, to transfer the vital fur trade of Montreal to dynamic Highland Scots who established themselves shortly after the conquest, and to allow much unappropriated power to fall into the hands of the Church. In terms of actual power the Church became stronger after the conquest, for with the decline of authority the village priest became the local focus of social and political influence, and the Catholic hierarchs, on the tacit understanding that their position would not be imperilled by the new rulers, offered positive support or benevolent neutrality whenever the established Government was challenged either by invasion from the south or by internal rebellion. In 1776, in 1812, in 1837, and during the Métis risings of 1870 and 1885, the Church never wavered in its refusal to give countenance to any movement that threatened British authority or, later, the authority of the federal Canadian Government.

If the Church accepted the unwritten contract by which its bishops shared authority with an alien Government, the ordinary people of Quebec—who so long accepted *La Survivance* as an ironic motto to express their hopes—were concerned to maintain their way of life (and their language as its essential expression) in the land to which their ancestors had come in the days of La Nouvelle France. The revolution of 1789 had detached them from a fatherland whose secularism they rejected; it would be many years before the links between Quebec and metropolitan France were even loosely retied. They had nothing in common with the New England Protestant republicans who in their eyes represented the United States. And though from the early years of the nineteenth century there were separatists of one kind or another in Quebec, at no time have the majority of French Canadians decisively shown a desire to secede from the grouping of political entities which after 1783 was known as British North America and after 1867 as Canada.

There has indeed been a kind of pendulum swing in the relationship between French Canada and English Canada, but whenever Anglophobia has run high in Quebec a point has always come when anger has been moderated by the sense that independence would present French Canadians with an even less congenial road than continued association. Yet a strong desire to be —as the *Québecois* themselves put it—*maître chez nous* has always contended in their minds with the shrewd unwillingness to shed the advantages that may accrue from being part of a larger political and economic entity. This inclination of the *Québecois* towards local independence has considerably influenced Canadian history, keeping alive after confederation what one might call a centrifugal federalism, the urge towards maximum provincial autonomy, and at the same time forming a permanent nucleus of isolationist feeling towards the world beyond North America that has helped sustain the Canadian shyness of imperial and even international entanglements.

It would therefore be a mistake to follow the ideologues of contemporary Quebec separatism, and to create a false image of unified feeling among French Canadians at any period after 1760.

Even today no analysis of the situation in Quebec is complete unless it recognizes the extreme stratification of French Canadian society, which leads to a continuing struggle of elites often masked as a struggle for liberation from those perpetual demons of French-Canadian political propaganda, *les Anglais*.

One of the paradoxical features of events in 1837, the fateful year in imperial history when Canadian discontents first took violent expression, was the contrast between the Lower and the Upper Canadian movements, which on the surface appeared to represent identical urges towards independence from imperial authority. The extreme reformers of Upper Canada who rose under William Lyon Mackenzie were for the most part egalitarians, dazzled by the rhetoric of Jacksonian democracy in the United States, and genuinely intent on destroying the power wielded by the rich landowners, office-holders and Anglican clergy who formed the so-called Family Compact and who favoured the continuation of Canada's political subordination to the imperial Government. It was a relatively simple situation in which social and political conservatism were on one side and social and political radicalism on the other.

In French Canada, however, the rebel leaders were socially conservative members of the seigneurial and professional classes, seeking to use politically radical means to regain the authority their class had lost at the conquest. What the French Canadian leaders sought was the political authority to consolidate a hierarchical social system with themselves at the head. Yet despite its reactionary overtones the movement of 1837 in Lower Canada played its part in the eventual disintegration of the Empire, and thus reminds us—as the example of the Boers in South Africa does sixty years later—that the forces which eventually produced the Empire's end were not entirely those of social justice or political enlightenment.

Though the presence of the United States and that of the French-speaking population of the St Lawrence Valley created circumstances which gave the Canadian urge towards independence from central imperial control a peculiar impetus and persistence, the main factors that made Canada a pioneer among the dominions were temporal and quantitative.

Quantitatively, in area and in the volume of external trade, Canada by 1930 exceeded the other dominions of Australia, New

Zealand and South Africa in combination; its total white population also exceeded the sum of theirs. Next to Britain and India it was physically, as well as historically, the most important constituent unit of the Empire.

In temporal terms Canada's membership of the First Empire had given it almost a century's start over the other dominions in attaining the beginnings of practical democracy. Within what eventually became Canada, the maritime colony of Nova Scotia with its mixed population of Scots, Germans and emigrant New Englanders, led the way, gaining in 1758 a constitution with an elected assembly. Though other Canadians have been inclined to obscure the fact, it was also Nova Scotia that in 1848 was the first imperial territory outside the British Isles to be accorded what colonials called responsible government and what the British usually called cabinet government: the rule of a ministry directly responsible to the elected representatives of the people and removable at the will of parliament.

Halifax, therefore, rather than Ottawa or Canberra, or even Delhi, stands as the geographic metaphor that exemplifies the difference between the new country of the United States that emerged from the eighteenth-century disintegration of the First British Empire and the new countries that have emerged from the twentieth-century disintegration of the Second Empire. With no recent historical precedents to guide them, and a strong resentment of the corrupt eighteenth-century British Parliament, the framers of the American constitution relied on pseudo-historical myths and literary conceits, in which a vague knowledge of the Roman Republic and of the early Swiss confederations mingled with the theorizings of Rousseau and of Locke, to create what seemed then—but no longer seems today—a foolproof pattern in which executive, legislative and judicial factors would balance each other by their mutual independence. In practice the pattern became a system in which a strong executive wielded a quasi-dictatorship, as in the administrations of Andrew Jackson, Abraham Lincoln or F. D. Roosevelt, or a weak executive became locked in chaotic strife with an antagonistic legislature. On the other hand, except in countries—like Pakistan, Burma and many former African colonies—where democracy failed to take root at all, the successor States of the Second Empire, created without the bitterness of actual wars of independence, rejected the American experiment and based their political constitutions on the practical experience of Westminster, which established a balance of forces governed by the fact that the prime minister, unlike the American president, depends for the continuance of his power on those who at least approximately represent the will of the people.

It was when Nova Scotia was thus formally granted cabinet government, and Canada (into which the early colonies of Lower and Upper Canada had been temporarily welded after the Durham Report of 1840) gained responsibility in 1849, as Lord Elgin created precedent by accepting a law repugnant to the executive but voted by the majority in the assembly, that the constitutional evolution from imperial dependence to the post-imperial ambiguities of the Commonwealth was first adumbrated.

In comparison with the ninety years that separated the grant of an elected assembly from actual responsible government in Nova Scotia, and the fifty-eight years that intervened in the Canadas, where an elected assembly was first granted under the Constitutional Act of 1799, the political evolution of New Zealand and the Australian colonies was sharply telescoped. Because New South Wales and Van Diemen's Land (which became Tasmania) were convict colonies before they became settlement colonies, autocratic forms of government to ensure internal order were maintained much longer than in the North American colonies. It was not until the 1830s that agitation for representative government began seriously to emerge, and not until 1842 that a two-thirds majority of the legislative council in New South Wales was elected on a very narrow property franchise; even then Van Diemen's Land and South Australia had only been granted councils to which members were nominated by the Governor. An attempt in 1850 by Lord Grey, the Colonial Secretary, to persuade the Australian colonies to accept a federal legislative council was wrecked on the reefs of local jealousy, and it was only in 1856 that these territories and New Zealand (which was not widely settled until the 1840s) gained assemblies elected by full manhood suffrage and at the same time were granted responsible government similar to that accorded to the Canadian colonies.

In South Africa the presence of Boers in Cape Colony and Natal, and the existence of intermittently independent Afrikaner republics in the hinterland, created a more complicated pattern.

Only in 1872 did Cape Colony, and in 1892 Natal, attain responsible government. Transvaal and the Orange Free State passed from precarious liberty to dependence in 1877, when the British formally annexed them with a promise of internal self-government which had not been redeemed by the time the Boers rose in 1881 and humiliatingly defeated the British regulars at Majuba hill. From that time until their eventual defeat in the South African War, the Boer republics maintained a virtual independence of a peculiarly xenophobic kind; only in 1907 did they accept responsible government on the Canadian model.

After local self-government, the next stage towards that state of quasi-independence known as dominion status was the unification of the colonies into larger entities that could assume national responsibilities. The colonies of British North America, federating in 1867 into what we know as Canada, were again the pioneers. Though New Zealand abandoned its provincial Governments only nine years later, it was a whole generation before the Australian colonies became united in their local Commonwealth.

Canada also provided the title by which these new self-governing protonations would be collectively identified when, the title of *kingdom* having been discreetly put aside as likely to cause offence south of the 49th parallel, its founders accepted the style of Dominion. At the final Colonial Conference in 1907 all of the participants except Britain accepted that title as defining their special status within the Empire. The change in title from Colonial Conference to Imperial Conference, made at the same time, removed the suggestion of subordinate status. The dominions were now, in theory at least, imperial partners rather than subject realms, and from this point the question before them would be one of defining the terms of the partnership, of deciding how and how far the self-governing parts of the Empire were still bound to Britain. The original group of dominions, apart from Canada, were Australia, New Zealand and Newfoundland, with South Africa and the Irish Free State added by the time the defining of the partnership culminated in the Statute of Westminster.

It would make for neatness in a historical account to present the progress towards independence within the Empire as in every case a regular evolution through the various stages of popular representation to responsible government and then to the quasi-national status of a dominion. But this did not always happen;

there were cases of regression. Jamaica, for example, lost in 1866 the elected assembly which it had shared with the other American colonies of the First Empire and reverted to the status of a Crown colony, and so did some of the lesser islands of the West Indies. Malta, with its sensitive combination of extreme strategic importance and a volatile European population, fluctuated for decades between autocratic government and some measure of popular representation.

The most striking setback in the process of political development was that of Newfoundland. Less than sixty years from its original rejection of union with Canada, the ambitions which local pride aroused had driven Newfoundland hopelessly into debt. Its creditors demanded some kind of receivership, but, since the crisis came to a head in 1933–4 after the Statute of Westminster, the British Government could not actually impose a solution. The dominion of Newfoundland had to be persuaded to commit suicide, which it did when the assembly accepted the *force majeur* of economic circumstances and abandoned responsible government for a form of autocracy unique in the history of the Empire; an appointed commission, half British and half Newfoundlanders, ruled the island by a policy of strict economy until after the Second World War.

Newfoundland never regained its status as a separate dominion; in 1948 the prospects of a pauperly independence daunted enough of its inhabitants to carry by a small minority a plebiscite which committed Newfoundland to final union with detested Canada. Only in this limited sense—as part of a larger dominion—did Newfoundland regain its former status.

But Newfoundland and the other possessions subjected to constitutional retrogression were at best marginally viable in an economic sense; with the sole exception of the Boer republics, which for two brief periods of a few years fell into subjection to British autocracy, there is no case where a possession that was capable of paying for its own administration and defence slipped backward from a condition of self-government. So the example of Canada can be considered a model of the characteristic evolution of the white settlement colony, from an autocratically governed territory, usually under initial military rule, through the stages of representative assembly and responsible government on the local level to the quasi-nation which gains international standing, externally as well as internally determining its own destiny.

The process in Canada can be divided into four phases. These are roughly consecutive, though the last two overlap. The first phase, from 1760 to 1849, covers the evolution from the autocratic rule of a military governor, through the transitional stage in which an executive appointed from Britain is balanced by an elected assembly, to the point of responsible or cabinet government, which means virtual political autonomy within the local territory of the colony.

The second phase, from 1849 to 1867, is that in which the self-governing colony develops into a satellite nation. Today we have become accustomed to small fragments of land which the convenience of imperialists gave a separate administration, claiming sovereignty and an international status at least formally equivalent to that of the United States and the Soviet Union. But the age when the Canadian colonies gained local autonomy, an age which saw the submersion of the small principalities and republics of Germany and Italy in large nation-states, tended—unless a country was fortunate enough to be as geographically remote as New Zealand—to equate size with security and with the ability to sustain sovereignty. Certainly, at a time when American aggressiveness was at its height, fed by the annexation of parts of Mexico and the successful assertion of Lincolnian centralism against Confederate fission, the unification of British North America into a geographically cohesive State seemed the only precarious guarantee of survival for the Atlantic colonies and for the two Canadas, which as a unified State could inherit the rights that Britain had accumulated over the rest of the northern part of the subcontinent, and build westward to prevent American intrusion on the Prairies and the Pacific.

In the third phase, beginning in 1867 and not yet formally ended, Canada has reached, by a series of constitutional changes that have reduced the areas of imperial power to a symbolic vestige, the condition of independence within the Commonwealth, recognized in formal terms at the accession of Queen Elizabeth II when she became specifically Queen of Canada. The jurisdiction of the British Parliament over the Canadian constitution (embodied in the British North America Act) now depends entirely upon Canadian wishes; disagreement among Canadians rather than any desire of Britain to retain the shreds of imperial power has so far kept the British North America Act alive as a statute of the Westminster Government. In this phase Canada has shed the powers of veto and disallowance on the part of the imperial Government that lingered until 1931 in British law and in the ambiguous role of the Governor-General, who for sixty years after confederation combined a surrogate headship of state with an incompatible role as representative of the Government in Westminster.

But political equality and independence within the Commonwealth may, in the shifting power-relations of the modern world, mean subordination elsewhere. The fourth phase of Canada's moving towards independence contains an element of ambivalence not present to the same extent in the history of other white settlement colonies. It is the phase of attaining international standing and recognition, free of formal suzerainty on the part of any other country. In the case of Canada, this process was made inevitable from the beginning by its special relationship of neighbourhood with the United States. Once confederation created Canada as a nation with a border coterminous with the American states it was inevitable that, sooner rather than later, she should enter into direct diplomatic relations with Washington. Only in 1923, after many disillusioning experiences of relying on British diplomatic intermediaries, did Canada finally begin to negotiate and sign its own treaties.

For almost as long, though British troops were withdrawn from all of Canada except the naval depots of Halifax and Esquimalt, Canada remained under the military tutelage of Whitehall by accepting a British general as commander of the Canadian armed forces; only in 1909 was this arrangement brought to an end. Yet in the field of actual warfare Canada progressed more quickly in asserting her independence than in the field of diplomacy; for Canadians could directly control the degree of their participation in Britain's conflicts, while diplomatic status depended on a willingness on the part of countries outside the Empire to recognize Canada's coming of age, which did not occur until after the First World War, and then, at first, only in the case of countries like the United States and France whose interest in Canada was, for differing reasons, exceptionally close.

The issue of Canada's participation in Britain's wars emerged in 1885, less than twenty years after confederation, when the British Government was planning Wolseley's expedition to relieve Gordon on the Nile; it recurred during the Boer War. Repeatedly between the end of that war and 1914 the question of the creation of a co-ordinated imperial armed force was raised at Imperial Conferences and as repeatedly opposed by Canada, whose insistence on playing an independent role in the First World War contributed greatly to the achievement of diplomatic status during the 1920s. At the same time, though political independence within the international community was substantially won under the Statute of Westminster, it was not finally validated until after the Second World War. Even in 1939 the Canadian legal officers had to rule that when Britain was at war Canada was also automatically at war, since the headships of state vested in the monarch were not formally separated until Elizabeth's accession.

By the time of the Suez crisis, however, it was clear that no vestige of diplomatic dependence remained, and that the Commonwealth was no longer the binding and unquestioning alliance which the Empire had been. For it was Canada and India, members of the Commonwealth, dissociating themselves from Britain (while Australia and New Zealand still supported her), who played the actively neutral role of peace-brokers and brought the crisis to an end. Thus, at this crucial point when the hollowness of Britain's power was finally revealed (a revelation from which the final decline of the Empire in the 1960s seemed to follow naturally), the fates of Canada and India, which had paralleled each other at the very beginning of the Second Empire, drew together again. There emerged what a Canadian editor had foreseen more than fifty years before, at a time when few people in the white dominions were conscious of a relationship between their subordination to Britain and the predicament of the autocratically ruled possessions. In 1898 the *Toronto Globe* remarked: 'Our conception of the growth of the Empire is not that Canada should become more like India, but that India should become more like Canada; the ideal being not a group of dependencies governed from one central point but a league of self-governing communities.'

The Suez crisis showed dramatically how independent of British leadership the former imperial possessions had become; the extraordinary paradox was that though the events of that time spelt the end of what remained of the Empire, they guaranteed the survival of the Commonwealth by forcing it to exist as a completely flexible association of States.

In the following chapters I shall examine more closely these phases of Canada's detachment from imperial ties, and the clues they offer for the final breakdown of the Empire. In doing so I shall necessarily touch at times on a theme whose complete exploration would require another book: the shifting of Canada from the British orbit of formal political dependence to the American orbit of informal economic and cultural dependence. At every stage America was an element in determining Canada's relationship with Britain, establishing the need for unity and internal independence before these became urgent issues for the other dominions, but at the same time fostering—in reaction against American influences—an adherence to British political forms. Paradoxically, if Canadians today are embarking on a second struggle for liberation, this time from a colonialism far more insidious than the British, they are aided by a flexibility of political attitudes inherited from Britain and by the fact that, with much that was patrician in the transatlantic heritage, they inherited also the traditions of English and Scottish working-class radicalism which gave toughness and tenacity to Canadian labour movements and have made them a more enduring part of Canadian political life than they ever became in that of the United States. But, interesting and timely as the subject is in all its ramifications, it is only as far as it has influenced Canada's role in encompassing the death of the British Empire shall I consider the special relationship with the United States.

I shall go on to show how the example of Canada was adapted to their special circumstances by Australia and New Zealand, whose particular problem was isolation from a friendly power rather than the proximity of an overbearing neighbour, and how South Africa and Ireland proceeded on divergent courses to the same end, so that in 1930, when the dominions formulated the demands that Britain willingly embodied in the Statute of Westminster, they had all reached the same stage of political evolution, an evolution whose consequences the temper of the times gave something of the transvaluing quality of a revolution.

VIII The Fight for
Self-Government

By the end of the 1820s it became an assumption among colonial administrators in Whitehall that the French-speaking inhabitants of Quebec had accepted leaders determined to bring an end to the system by which their province was administered by a Governor responsible, not to the people of the colony, but to the Parliament in Westminster; they wished, in other words, to control locally the political destinies of Lower Canada, and this Britain would not accept.

Looking at the situation a century and a third afterwards, we are inclined to condemn the British view because we assume in imperial rulers at that time an understanding of democratic procedures, and therefore a level of anti-democratic perfidy, neither of which in fact existed. To understand the situation on the eve of the Victorian era we must relate events in Canada to those in Britain, where the Reform Bill was passed only in 1832. Even the Reform Bill, with its severely restricted franchise, was hardly democratic by twentieth-century standards. It was framed, with a British talent for compromise, to give political recognition to the changes in the power structure that had been brought about by the rise of the rich manufacturing class; it was not designed to produce political equality, but to diminish class antagonism by a minimal absorption of new elites.

Since the rise of the Levellers during the Commonwealth there had indeed been Englishmen who advocated political democracy manifested through universal suffrage, and as early as 1797 the great Whig leader, Charles James Fox, established a powerful faction within the existing elite that demanded radical parliamentary reform on such lines. Detaching themselves from the Whigs, Fox's followers assumed the name of Radicals; it was they in the 1830s who endeavoured, by whatever political advantages the Reform Bill offered, to extend popular participation in the process of government. Not until the latter part of the decade did a substantial working-class movement, represented by the Chartists, bring mass support to the Radicals and much perturbation to those who felt that the Reform Bill had gone quite far enough.

England was in fact passing with difficulty from an age of corrupt oligarchy into one of cautious democratization; its executive as well as its legislative institutions were in transition. The idea of a cabinet responsible only to the people through Parliament was still a novelty, and only after the death of William IV and the accession of the young queen Victoria did it finally become established that a Government need not enjoy 'the confidence of the Crown'; as late as 1834 William IV had dismissed a Government headed by Lord Melbourne that enjoyed the confidence of Parliament but not his own.

With Britain itself in the process of evolving a satisfactory system of responsible government, the politicians and officials who controlled colonial affairs did not readily conceive such an institution taking roots in the colonies, which, by definition, were dependent territories, less advanced in political experience than the mother country, territories in which the imperial Parliament considered it had a duty to ensure the rights of interests and minorities. The concern for minorities was to complicate imperial relationships—and sometimes to serve as a cover for the dubious exercise of power—to the end of the Empire, when Whitehall still felt itself obliged to protect Muslims from Hindus in India and Turks from Greeks in Cyprus. In the case of Canada it seemed a matter of peculiar urgency, since the minority happened to be Englishmen who were loudly demanding protection from their historic enemies, the French.

One can imagine the frustrated righteousness with which the men of Whitehall in the last years of King William's reign must have regarded Lower Canada. By the Quebec Act of 1774 they had recognized the rights of French Canadians to live by their own customs, language and religion; by delaying the immediate calling of the Assembly for which it provided they had saved the French Canadians from rule by the tiny minority of British merchants who would have dominated that gathering, since Catholics even in Canada were not yet enfranchised. Finally, in 1791, they had made an exception unique in the Protestant Hanoverian Empire by allowing French Canadians who had sufficient property to vote for the Assembly regardless of religion. Few conquered minorities in history had been treated so generously. Now, when they heard the complaints of the English in Montreal that the French were using their control of the Assembly to maintain antique and discriminatory civil laws and systems of land tenure which hampered the growth of commerce, it seemed to the men of Whitehall that their generosity had been ill-repaid. The French Canadians, as they saw it, were displaying democracy's worst features by seeking to deny the rights of others by the weight of numbers; in such circumstances they were inclined to believe that the only way to ensure equitable justice was to insist on the independence of the Governor and his executive from the control of the Assembly. Perhaps the surprising fact is that not all British officials or politicians accepted this attitude of pessimistic authoritarianism.

In considering the attitudes of those who became rebel leaders, one must equally guard against the assumptions of a hindsight vision. To us, who are painfully conscious of the defects of the American system of government, it can seem strange that Canadian radicals did not realize in 1830 that it embodied the very feature of British colonial government to which they most objected: a supreme executive officer (the President) who was not obliged to accept the will of the people's elected representatives. But the flaws inherent in the fixed American system, as compared with the more flexible parliamentary democracy that was evolving in Britain, were not yet evident because America in the 1830s was still a developing country with a relatively simple political life. Only between 1835 and 1840 did Alexis do Tocqueville publish his classic *Democracy in America*, in which he pointed out the dangers of tyranny which such a system embodied. To Papineau and Mackenzie, who struggled for years with no apparent success to shed the autocratic administration imposed on them by Whitehall, the United States became attractive as the sole existing example of escape from English tutelage.

Even so, their desperate conclusion was unrepresentative of feeling in British North America, as the failure of their rebellions to attract more than a few hundred supporters was to demonstrate. The people of the North American colonies were divided in their views of what the link between Britain and Canada should eventually become, but very few among them wished that link to be broken. The dissociation from Britain which Canadians now take for granted was not what most of their predecessors in the early nineteenth century expected or even desired. A century ago there were reasons which no longer exist for a continued and relatively close association with Britain.

Some of these reasons were political. Memories of 1812 were strong. The war had brought a virtual end to American immigration into Canada; it would not recur on an appreciable scale until the opening of the prairies in the 1880s. The loyalists in Upper Canada and in the Maritimes had been reinforced after Waterloo by large-scale migrations from Britain, including many officers of Wellington's armies and many zealous Orangemen. At the same time the Catholic hierarchy of Lower Canada, and traditionalist *Québecois* in general, nurtured no illusions about the chances of their antique French culture surviving meaningfully in the expansionist and assimilationist atmosphere of the United States. Whatever struggles may have gone on between the French Canadian elites, and between the Assembly and the Governor, there is no sign that any large proportion of French Canadians would have welcomed union with the Americans and especially with those nearest and most detested of traditional enemies, the New Englanders.

Canadian separatism, indeed, was an idea more talked about among Manchester Liberals in Britain, concerned about the expense of an empire, than it was among Canadians, who realized in the heyday of American bellicosity, when the Oregon boundary agitation and the anti-Mexican agitation were rising to a territorially profitable climax, that immediate independence would be certain to invite aggression and annexation. Autonomy under the aegis of Britain was as much as most Canadians desired; even in later years, after confederation had turned Canada into an internally self-governing nation, the sense of identity with Britain remained extraordinary strong, and Canadians like R. B. Bennett, Bonar Law and Lord Beaverbrook were among the fervent advocates of imperial federation.

Bennett, Law and Beaverbrook were all Maritimers; and this reminds one how complex loyalties were in Canada during the century that preceded the Statute of Westminster. Not only did ethnic and cultural differences divide English and French; there were also strong regional differences, dominated as much by economic as by political considerations. The Maritime Provinces came into Canada only hesitantly, and the reasons for their hesitation were not merely those of parochial sentiment; they were due to the fact that the trade of all these territories was directed principally towards Britain. Indeed, for all the Canadian provinces, Britain was the best customer until well into the nineteenth century, and Canadians would have preferred closer trading links than the Free Traders, who were extending their influence in Britain itself during the years after the Reform Bill, wished to sustain. There was little rejoicing in Canada when the Corn Laws were repealed in 1846 and the Navigation Acts in 1849. Such loosenings of economic links meant harder times for the farmers of Upper Canada and for the shipbuilders and shipowners of the Maritimes.

Yet, if most Canadians were unsure about their power to defend themselves, unwilling to lose their economically privileged relationship with Britain, and unenthusiastic about abandoning their local rivalries, they became increasingly anxious, after the difficult years of the Napoleonic Wars, to gain internal self-government. This applied—for all their social conservatism—to many of the Loyalists as well as to the French Canadians and to the English and Irish radicals who found their way to Canada after Waterloo; Joseph Howe, the great fighter for responsible government in Nova Scotia, was a Loyalist's son, and it was Loyalists who in both Upper Canada and New Brunswick dominated the early Assemblies and began the task of extending their duties and rights. If their experiences between 1776 and 1783 had left them no desire to follow the republican destiny of the America they had abandoned, they still hoped to find within the monarchical system a means to regulate their lives according to their local needs, which were incomprehensible to men in Whitehall.

The divisions of view between British rulers regarding the destiny of the colonies may indeed have been deeper than those among Canadians. The active British ruling class was still, in the early nineteenth century, relatively small: the ministers and the more vocal members of the two Houses of Parliament; the politically powerful landed magnates and the handful of financiers and industrialists who challenged their influence; the narrow circles of higher government professionals—leading civil servants and a few generals and admirals who had political interests and influence. Even among this restricted group, comparatively few were interested in colonial questions. To the end of the Empire's life the House of Commons would fill for a debate on India and empty when any other dependency but Ireland was being discussed.

And even among those who did become concerned with questions of colonial government, which in the earlier days meant specifically Canadian government, few understood from close experience the issues they discussed. Some, like Edward Ellice, an influential conservative adviser on Canadian affairs, had links with the Montreal merchants or the Hudson's Bay Company; others, like radicals J. A. Roebuck and Joseph Hume, were in close touch with Canadian reformers; a handful of M.P.s had served in Canada as officers; a handful of peers had been Governors of various North American colonies. But for most British politicians and civil servants in the early days of the nineteenth century, Canada was little more than a snowy screen on which to project their own views of Britain's role in a world where the defeat of Napoleon had conferred on her an unaccustomed lack of continental rivals, a naval power that was great because it was unchallenged, and a reputation for luck in warfare that until the advent of Bismarck made challengers hesitant.

What made the future at once exhilarating and bewildering was the fact that to this combination of strength and prestige was added a completely new factor—that of the industrial revolution, which for a generation placed Britain in a position of trading eminence as little challenged as its sea power. It was natural to hope—particularly in a country that had experienced the financial drain of repeated wars with France since the accession of William of Orange at the end of the seventeenth century—that the combination of far-flung markets with an apparently invincible navy would reduce the need for both overseas possessions and military expenditures. With the powers of Europe at least temporarily bled to exhaustion, with Germany and Italy still politically fragmented, with no present need for large armies to fight on the continent or funds to pay continental mercenaries, it seemed possible, at least for the few halcyon decades before the rise of new Emperors in Paris and Berlin, that Britain could enjoy all the benefits of her

favourable situation merely by ensuring the widest possible application of the doctrine of Free Trade, formulated by Adam
Smith and David Ricardo in the late eighteenth century and
eagerly adopted by British manufacturers and merchants.

Britain had in fact established the first industrial imperialism,
as distinct from the trading imperialisms of the Portuguese and
the Dutch and of their own First Empire, and the fact was so impressive that it created illusions on many sides. If the capitalists at
first believed that industrial-plus-commercial power was sufficient
without actual political power over dependent territories, the
anti-capitalists—because Engels and Marx witnessed the Free
Trade stage of British imperialism at close quarters—fell into the
complementary fallacy that the tyranny of man over man was
economically motivated; and thus ignored the deep psychological
bases of the urge to power. In practice, the urge to power remained undiminished, and continued to be expressed in territorial
acquisitiveness. Logically, Free Traders should have been opposed
to all types of imperial possession. In fact, very few of them proceeded to such extremities of consistency. Even Gladstone, even
John Bright, accepted—with some pious Exeter Hall phrases to
justify them—the naked fact that the success of Free Trade was
bound up with the maintenance of British power and prestige, and
that without India neither would exist, so that whenever that
bastion was threatened—or whenever in later years the territorial
greed of another power threatened to constrict the scope of
British commerce—even the purest of Manchester Liberals could
turn aggressive. Quite apart from Rosebery and the Liberal
Imperialists, quite apart from the colonialist Radicals represented
by Joseph Chamberlain, even Liberals whose temperamental and
theoretical inclination was anti-imperialist, like Gladstone, would
resort in practice to measures that defended the Empire as it
existed or even initiated whole series of territorial extensions.
There was the case of Egypt. There was also the more curious case
of North Borneo in 1882, when Gladstone's Government chartered the British North Borneo Company under the specious
argument that this was merely a matter of regi stering a commercial
enterprise and that the Government had only to safeguard Britain
against diplomatic complications with other powers; in fact this
pretence at commercial penetration was an act of territorial annexation, and the imposition of a protectorate six years later by

a Conservative Government was the inevitable consequence of Liberal support for the traders who formed the Company.

Free Trade was abandoned only in 1931, when the startling realization of Britain's economic weakness at the onset of the great depression forced an uneasy recognition of the general weakening of its imperial power and of the need to build up economic defences. The paradox of Free Trade surviving throughout the high imperial period from 1880 to 1918 finds its parallel in an ambivalence of attitude that characterized those politicians generally regarded as imperialist as much as the so-called anti-imperialists; even Disraeli could refer to the colonies as 'mill-stones' around Britain's neck and yet at other times rejoice in the imperial glory that the possession of India conferred.

The attitude of Victorians to their colonies was in fact rather like their attitude towards the monarchy. There were times when Queen Victoria was unpopular and a great deal of loose criticism of the Crown went on, but true republicans were very rare, even among radicals and socialists. In the same way, the loose talk that went on against colonies did not mean that the British wished to get rid of what they had, though at few times except during the jingoistic heyday between the Diamond Jubilee and the outbreak of the Boer War were they really avid for more. Personal and class interests determined the degree of imperial enthusiasm, but one cannot assume that there was no interest in the colonies outside the middle classes who administered them, traded with them or invested in them. Victorian working men petitioned the Queen to facilitate emigration to British possessions; the nonconformist missionary societies, supported and staffed by working-class adherents, were anxious to extend British colonial protection to non-European peoples threatened by rapacious traders; the sense of divinely ordained superiority which almost every Englishman and Scot sustained during the nineteenth century made it seem natural and fitting to most British Islanders that the totemic figure known as the Great White Queen (whom the Fijians had declared their paramount chieftainess and whom even the distant Tibetans regarded as the incarnation of one of their most formidable deities) should rule—on their behalf—over palm and pine and all who dwelt in their shadows.

Yet imperial possessions were expensive and politically trouble-some, particularly where their inhabitants were European. The liberties enjoyed by Britons at home could hardly be denied to Britons living in imperial territories beyond the seas, and what was extended to Britons must—if one believed in public-school doctrines of Fair Play—be extended to people of French and Dutch descent who lived under British rule, and ultimately (though few said this outside the most enlightened circle of Indian civil servants) to men of other breeds. As long ago as the seventeenth century the pioneer republican James Harrington had foreseen in his *Oceana* a day when colonies would 'ween themselves' of the mother country, and Edmund Burke had declared, during the debates on the Quebec Act in 1774, that 'No free country can keep another in slavery. The price they pay for it will be their own servitude.'

In arguing thus Burke did not go so far as Adam Smith, who in the same year remarked that 'Great Britain derives nothing but loss from the dominion she exercises over her colonies', adding, in words that formed a virtual text for a century of Manchester liberals, 'The inconveniences resulting from the possession of its colonies every country has engrossed to itself completely. The advantages resulting from their trade, it has been obliged to share with many other countries.' Smith was the theoretician, seeing everything in cold economist's vision; the very fact that the Empire did not wither away under the blast of his doctrines was proof that in terms of political realities in the eighteenth century he was as unrealistic as he seemed logical. For if in 1774 the Quebec Act—reasserting the rights of the imperial Government to determine North American political patterns—marked the point of no return so far as the republican activists of the Thirteen Colonies were concerned, there were still those in North America who wished to continue in a political form their relationship with Britain. Burke spoke to them in 1775.

> My hold on the colonies is in the close affection which grows from common names, from kindred blood, from similar privileges, and equal protection. These are ties which, though light as air, are as strong as links of iron. Let the colonies always keep the idea of their civil rights associated with your government;—they will cling and grapple to you; and no force under heaven will be of power to tear them from their allegiance. But let it once be understood, that your

government may be one thing, and their privileges another; that these two things may exist without any mutual relation; the cement is gone; the cohesion is loosened; and everything hastens to decay and dissolution. As long as you have the wisdom to keep the sovereign authority of this country as the sanctuary of liberty, the sacred temple consecrated to our common faith, wherever the chosen race and sons of England worship freedom, they will turn their faces towards you.

It is obvious that Burke does not here anticipate the later complexities of imperial development. He still sees Britain as possessing sovereign authority over the colonies, and the freedoms he means are internal ones: those of self-governing extensions of Britain rather than separate and equal entities such as the dominions later became. He failed to realize that when Britons lived abroad they formed new communities, with their own collective characters and needs; one of the few eighteenth-century Englishmen who did was the early radical John Cartwright, who in 1771 talked of the transformation of the Empire into a 'brotherly League' of nations which he proposed to call the Grand British League and Confederacy.

It was among the Radicals who may be regarded as Cartwright's heirs that the most realistic and prophetic thinking on imperial matters emerged in the early nineteenth century. Jeremy Bentham, the most prestigious of all philosophical radicals, moved from a wholehearted condemnation of colonies and colonialism at the time of the French Revolution to a view of imperial relationships based on mutuality (a view that eventually permitted him to encourage and assist Edward Gibbon Wakefield in his Australasian settlement schemes). In his words, 'If wisdom alone were listened to, the ordinary subject of contention would be reversed—the mother-country would desire to see her children powerful, that they might become free, and the colonies would fear the loss of that tutelary authority which gave them internal tranquillity and security against external foes.'

J. A. Roebuck, the Radical M.P. who defended the cause of the Canadian reformers throughout the 1830s, saw the issues with a clarity and foresight that suggest a remarkably early recognition of the dynamism implicit in imperial relationships. Roebuck not only issued a warning of the perils of American imperialism that today rings with a deadly truth; he also saw that the only way to save the Canadas was to nurture their political strength, which was dependent on their progress towards independence. Even in practical matters, Roebuck was well ahead of his time; thirty years before the confederation of Canada, he submitted a plan for reforms in Canadian government which included a federal assembly of all the North American colonies. It was rejected by the British Cabinet in April 1837; it is just possible that its acceptance might have prevented the rebellions which came with that year's winter.

The difference between Roebuck and the *laissez faire* Manchester Liberals was that while the latter would theoretically have let the colonies go as needlessly expensive luxuries, Radicals like Roebuck wished to see an orderly and friendly progression towards separation, should that prove to be inevitable; this led eventually to the kind of colonial reformism that found one extreme of expression in Joseph Chamberlain's radical imperialism and another in the socialist imperialism of the Fabians. Undoubtedly it was the Radicals—particularly if one includes Lord Durham ('Radical Jack') among them—who prepared the way for a more or less ordered dissolution of the Second Empire, in dramatic contrast to the violent end of the First. And the basis for the whole process was laid by the events in Canada and the debates in Britain which centred around the rebellions of 1837.

But before turning to those episodes, it is useful to view at least briefly the more conservative English attitude towards the colonies. In general terms, those who held this view had accepted up to the time of the American Revolution that the colonies existed for the benefit of the mother country. While for the Greeks a colony had been an instantly independent entity, for them it was—and the idea still held much of the word's feudal flavour—a dependency, and dependency implied vassalage, the tendering of tribute. A colony provided raw materials; it was a captive market; it was a place to send one's convicts and to settle one's surplus population; it was, perhaps most important of all, a counter in the game of power, for history had not known a powerful nation that was not also, in some degree, an imperial nation.

Modified by the concepts of trusteeship which Victorian evangelicism had encouraged, these attitudes survived until the

end of the Empire. They were complicated by the slow evolution—even in Britain—of democratic forms of government, and
by the inability among traditionalists from the Royal Family
downwards to conceive of sovereignty as other than indivisible.
The Prince Consort expressed it succinctly on behalf of the Queen
when he wrote to Stanley in 1843, 'I don't think the Crown of
England could allow the establishment of a responsible Government in Canada, as that would be tantamount to a declaration of
separation from the mother country.' Even an enlightened Whig
like Lord John Russell, the great advocate of the Reform Bill, was
aware of the dilemma in terms of current constitutional theory,
when he remarked in 1840, while he was Colonial Secretary,

> It may happen ... that the Governor received at one and the
> same time instructions from the Queen and advice from his
> Executive Council, totally at variance with each other. If he
> is to obey his instructions from England, the parallel of con-
> stitutional responsibility entirely fails; if, on the other hand,
> he is to follow the advice of his Council, he is no longer a
> subordinate officer, but an independent sovereign.

Not until ninety years afterwards, at the Imperial Conference
preceding the Statute of Westminster, did the rulers of Britain
entirely abandon the view that, if sovereignty is to be regarded
as indivisible, then the King's Government is the Government in
Westminster alone, and the Governor is ultimately responsible to
it, so that in the event of any conflict of interests he must accept
the instructions of the British Cabinet.

It was, strangely enough, the presence of India within the
Empire that provided a precedent for the idea of a divided
sovereignty. Until the deposition of the last puppet Moghul in
1858, the British Crown had no formal rights in India. The East
India Company functioned as vassal of the Moghul, and the
Company's actions were merely supervised by the British Parliament. The defeat of the Mutiny was to turn the last Moghul, who
had allowed himself to be used as a puppet by the mutineers in
Delhi, into a conquered sovereign whose realm was forfeit.

But it remained a separate realm. The Governor-General was
also the Viceroy, surrogate for an absentee sovereign, and the
method behind Disraeli's act of apparently romantic flattery in
conferring the Imperial Crown of India on Queen Victoria lay in

the recognition that sovereignty over India was separate from sovereignty over England; even in this sense the two great poles of the Empire balanced each other. In practice the British Parliament decided questions of policy relating to India, but even here there were the special features—the India Office, the Council of India, the direct responsibility of the Secretary for India to Parliament—that distinguished it from the other dependencies. India was a separate nation within the Empire, and the fact that it was ruled autocratically by an alien sovereign (as it had been since Akbar) while Britain was ruled democratically by the same alien monarch (still of the House of Hanover) did not alter the fact that here was a clear case of divided sovereignty.

But India was a country with a long and in some ways glorious independent history. It was more difficult for British traditionalists to accept the idea of separate sovereignties existing in countries which had developed as offshoots of Britain, and here perhaps there was an essential difference between the conservative and the radical imperialist. The first believed that the Empire could survive only as a pyramidical structure of authority, in which the other parts were subordinate in all but local considerations to Britain; the second acknowledged the possibility of separate nations existing within the Empire, united by common interests and traditions. It is against this spectrum of imperial attitudes in Britain, ranging from conservative autocrats and Free Trade crypto-imperialists to radical imperial federalists, liberal imperialists like Rosebery with his pioneer advocacy of a Commonwealth of Nations, and socialist imperialists like the Fabians, that we must view the vital developments in nineteenth-century Canada, since the final result was produced by reciprocal action between Britain and the dominion rather than by unaided Canadian initiative.

Canada entered the nineteenth century with a pattern of colonial Governments, all in theory subordinate to Westminster, which showed an extraordinary variety in form. The whole of the west, from Sault Ste Marie to the Pacific and from the American border to the Arctic sea, was the domain of the Hudson's Bay Company, held under Charles II's charter of 1671, with later extensions to cover the land beyond the Rockies, and here there was no real government except locally in the Red River settlement and in the fur-trading posts scattered through the wilderness; it was arbitrary government where it existed, with the traders and factors acting as petty despots. Newfoundland was still ruled autocratically by the naval governors, who would arrive at the start of each fishing season. Not until 1832 was it granted an Assembly like the other maritime colonies—Nova Scotia, Prince Edward Island and New Brunswick—all of which had constitutions like that of the original colony of Virginia, with a Governor appointed by the Crown, an appointed Council to advise him, and an Assembly which passed on money votes and could make local laws not repugnant to the laws of England or to imperial policy. Unacceptable laws could be vetoed by the Governor or by the British Cabinet. The only appeal was a petition to the British Parliament, so that the strings of imperial power were all held in Westminster, and the Cabinet with a majority in the Commons need not fear a petition against it.

The Governments of Lower and Upper Canada created under the Constitutional Act were more complicated, since they provided for a four-tiered division of authority mirroring that evolved in Britain during the eighteenth century. The Governor represented the king, but, as head of the executive which paralleled the cabinet, he was also his own prime minister, so that locally he wielded more power than the king retained in London. The Legislative Council, entirely appointed, corresponded to the House of Lords and the Assembly to the Commons. The idea was that the excesses of a popular assembly, as yet unaccustomed to parliamentary procedures, would be tempered by a council of independent-minded men expected to be impervious alike to popular passions and to private interests.

In practice there were difficulties almost from the beginning between the Governors and at least some of the people they ruled. The grievances differed in detail between Upper and Lower Canada, but in both cases they revolved ultimately around the distribution of power. Should local affairs be governed by the representatives of the people gathered in the Assembly, or by an executive taking its instructions from London?

In Upper Canada the first difficulties were as much religious as political. Non-Anglicans—Scottish and Ulster Presbyterians, Irish Catholics, American Methodists, German Lutherans and Mennonites—formed the majority of the population, and yet tracts of choice land known as the clergy reserves were kept for the benefit of the Anglican Church. There were other difficulties over land, for the members of the executive and legislative councils, chosen for their pro-British attitudes, were rewarded with considerable grants, while large areas were given to speculative land companies with influential sponsors. The Family Compact, as the reformers called it, seemed to many farmers in Upper Canada and many artisans in the small towns along the shores of the Great Lakes to be an oligarchy which identified its own interests with those of Britain and neglected the welfare of the colonies. But the tensions of the War of 1812 prevented discontent from taking a political form until the middle of the next decade, when the reformers, led by William and Robert Baldwin, became a substantial party in the Assembly, and William Lyon Mackenzie founded in 1824 *The Colonial Advocate*, devoted to attacking oligarchical rule and the abuses of the land system, thereby gaining a considerable following not only among the urban poor but also among the less prosperous settlers.

Mackenzie was a tempestuous Scot with a violent pen and tongue, a kind of Canadian Cobbett. When a gang of young Conservatives broke up his presses in 1826 he not only gained heavy damages in the courts, but also became a popular hero and assumed the leadership of the reformers. From the beginning Mackenzie was attracted to the American republican system and—in so far as one can find a clear direction in his rather chaotic outpourings—seemed to favour a form of government in which the Governor would be elective and would acquire something resembling the powers and reponsibilities attached to the American presidency. Robert Baldwin, the leader of the more moderate reformers, was concerned rather with adapting the British parliamentary system to the Canadian setting, and it was he who first, in 1836, worked out and presented to the Colonial Office a detailed proposal for a system of responsible government in the Canadas.

In spite of growing opposition, a succession of Governors in Upper Canada gained friendly majorities in the Assembly, supported by the Loyalists and the British middle-class settlers, so that they ruled, not without criticism—for Mackenzie was always there to head the chorus of denunciation—but with little difficulty in gaining the funds to carry on government. Indeed, the majority of the Assembly was docile enough to discipline even its own recalcitrant members, and Mackenzie, elected in 1828, was expelled in 1831 for a statement regarded as a breach of privilege; though he won five consecutive by-elections for his seat, he was re-expelled as many times, and did not return to the Assembly until a Reform majority was elected in 1834.

Mackenzie had filled his time while under expulsion from the Assembly in preparing an indictment of the establishment in Upper Canada, and in 1832, when the Reform Bill raised expectations among radicals in Canada, he hurried to London with a list of grievances which alerted the British authorities for the first time to the serious extent of discontent in Upper Canada, of which the incumbent Governor had kept them in ignorance. Faced already with trouble in Lower Canada, and nervous about any situation that might lead to a repetition of the previous century's disputes with the Thirteen Colonies, the Colonial Office was anxious to conciliate the reformers, and took what might have seemed the reasonable step of dismissing the law officers of Upper Canada, who had been mainly responsible for the votes expelling Mackenzie from the Assembly. The result was a curious sign of the volatility of Canadian politics, for the Conservatives now protested angrily against Whitehall's interference with the rights of the Assembly, and most unexpectedly talked of finding a political system that would not subject them to the vagaries of English politics.

In 1834 the reformers gained a majority in the Assembly, and a group of the more radical members, headed by Mackenzie, compiled the Seventh Report of the Committee of Grievances, which they forwarded to Westminster. Glenelg, the incumbent Colonial Secretary, was not the most intelligent or decisive of men, but he and his staff, who included James Stephen, the formidable grandfather of Virginia Woolf, were impressed by the authenticity of the tone of grievance, quite apart from the merits of the accusations, and they not only censured the Governor, Sir John Colborne, who had neglected to report the true state of affairs, but dismissed him and sent out in his stead, with instructions to achieve political reconciliation, Francis Bond Head.

Head had served as a soldier and fought at Waterloo, had managed a silver-mining enterprise in South America which failed, had written some racy travel books, and at the time of his appointment was serving as an assistant poor law commissioner in Kent; the variety rather than the particular appropriateness of his experiences seemed the only reason for choosing him, and the appointment appeared so inappropriate that it was widely rumoured he had been picked by mistake and that the man the Colonial Office really had in mind was his cousin Edmund Walker Head, who was subsequently a successful Governor of New Brunswick and later Governor-in-Chief of the Canadas.

There is no doubt that Francis Bond Head must rank as one of the minor conspirators involved in the death of the Empire. Head's principles were impeccably liberal, but he was a head-strong and a volatile man, and his personality rather than his ideas acted as the detonator that precipitated the rebellion in Upper Canada. He began reasonably well, with the intention of choosing an executive that would be generally acceptable. At best, his task was delicate, since both Reformers and Conservatives in the Assembly were impatient of interference from England, and were more or less agreed that it was better to fight out their feuds on local terrain than to subject themselves to the interference of arbiters from the imperial centre. With some difficulty, nevertheless, Head persuaded two Reform leaders, Robert Baldwin and John Rolph, to join a number of representative Conservatives on the Executive Council. It seemed a genuine advance; for the first time the Council appeared to represent, however inadequately, the actual political forces at work in Upper Canada.

In less than a month the Executive Council resigned unanimously because Head had failed to consult it on important matters of government. Head then assembled a completely Conservative Council. The Reform majority in the Assembly denounced it as unrepresentative. Head thereupon dissolved the Assembly, and in the ensuing elections of 1836 secured a Conservative majority. His success prevented the Colonial Office from recalling him, but it intensified the frustrated indignation of William Lyon Mackenzie, who was among the defeated candidates. But the particular incident that led Mackenzie from radical agitation to open rebellion was undoubtedly the rejection of the idea of colonial autonomy in the Russell resolutions, which were passed by the British Parliament in 1837. Yet these resolutions, while they affected the upper province, had their real roots in Lower Canada.

Relations between Britain and Lower Canada were constantly

troubled by an element which has often been loosely described as
racism, but which a recent writer* had described more felicitously
as cultural chauvinism. The British did not think the French
belonged to an inferior breed of men; they did think they had an
inferior civilization. English officials sent out during the Napoleonic Wars were also inclined to distrust the French in Quebec
and to favour the English from a sense of insecurity towards a
people related to their enemies, but the *Québecois* were inclined to
regard this attitude as part of a deliberate intent to undermine the
liberties and equalities that had been granted to them in 1774 and
widened in 1791.

There have been many crises in the relationships between the
so-called founding races in Canada, but if any can be regarded as
uniquely crucial, it was probably the arrival of Sir James Craig as
Governor in 1807. Craig was an imperial veteran of multiple
experience; he had been wounded at Bunker Hill and captured
with Burgoyne at Saratoga, had governed the Cape of Good Hope
during the first British occupation in 1797 and commanded a
division in India. He accepted without question the views of the
Anglophil oligarchy in Lower Canada, and instituted what French
Canadian historians like to call a 'reign of terror'; Craig was no
Hitler, but he did dissolve the Assembly and arrest the editors of
Le Canadien, which criticized his regime. Craig was in fact a sick
and dying man, who realized his own errors before he left Canada
in 1810. He was replaced by Sir George Prevost, a French-
speaking general of Swiss descent who played his part of con-
ciliator so capably that the French Canadians not only refused to
assist the Americans in 1812, but even inflicted a notable defeat on
them at the battle of Chateaugay.

But Craig and his policies were not entirely forgotten; French
Canadians were inclined to believe from this point that the British-
dominated executive was intent on a policy of anglicization
and assimilation. The only way to ensure that this would not
happen was to gain and maintain control over the Assembly, and
to press continually for the extension of its powers. But this
intent was what precluded an acceptable agreement during the
1820s and 1830s, since successive Governors—and successive
Colonial Secretaries in London—were unwilling to accept a

* Peter Burroughs in *The Canadian Crisis and British Colonial Policy 1828-41*,
Edward Arnold, 1972.

situation in which the British merchants in Montreal and the British settlers in the Eastern Townships would be subject to a Government responsible to a permanent French Canadian majority.

Just as William Lyon Mackenzie acted as catalyst in Upper Canada, so did Louis-Joseph Papineau in the lower province. Papineau was a lawyer and a seigneur; he retained throughout his life a rather patrician social attitude, and one is tempted to compare him with Thomas Jefferson, a comparison Papineau invited, since he named his Quebec estate Montebello. In the beginning, Papineau was not an Anglophobe; he fought under Sir Isaac Brock during the War of 1812 and was present when the Canadians captured Detroit. He was elected to the Lower Canadian Assembly in 1814, became Speaker in 1815, and remained so for the next twenty years, using his post without scruple to gain political advantage for the Radical Party. In 1822 Wilmot Horton, the parliamentary under-secretary to the Colonial Office, introduced into the Commons a bill for the unification of the two Canadas, and Papineau went to London to organize opposition to it. The bill was defeated, but what he had heard in London convinced Papineau that Horton represented a considerable group who hoped that French culture would be submerged in Canada by the building up of an English-speaking majority; in the meantime, the political union of Upper and Lower Canada would neutralize any advantage the French Canadians enjoyed through their majority in the Lower Canadian Assembly.

When Papineau returned, Lord Dalhousie was Governor, and for the next five years a conflict of wills ensued between that stiffnecked Presbyterian autocrat and the equally proud and headstrong Speaker. On one occasion Dalhousie tried to expel Papineau from his office. He also imprisoned critics of the Government, dismissed magistrates he regarded as disloyal, and, according to his critics, appropriated provincial funds illegally when the Assembly refused him supply bills. When complaints reached London, the Government was sufficiently embarrassed to send Dalhousie to India as Commander-in-Chief, and when a deputation arrived from Lower Canada in 1828 with a statement of grievances, a Committee of the House of Commons was appointed to consider them.

The hearings of the Canada Committee were important not

because of any positive results in terms of legislation, for none
ensued, but because the opportunity was given for a first statement of British radical views on the Canada question which laid
the foundation for many later developments. Important was the
evidence of James Stephen; while most of his colleagues at the
Colonial Office opposed concessions to the Lower Canadian
leaders, Stephen spoke sympathetically on the Assembly's constitutional claims. He argued that a local body was much better
fitted to administer affairs than an authority far away in London,
and he expressed his belief that the progress of the colonies towards autonomy could not in the long run be prevented, and that
resistance might lead to another war of independence on the
North American continent. Yet even he feared giving too much
power to the French and argued for uniting the two Canadas to
avoid it.

The parliamentary radicals, led by Henry Labouchère and Sir
James Mackintosh, criticized the idea of imperial interference, and
argued for local control and for equal rights for all colonists,
which meant avoiding political manœuvres aimed at diminishing
the rights of the French Canadians. The report of the Committee
followed very closely the lines of radical argument. It blamed the
troubles in French Canada on maladministration. It recommended
that the constitution should be amended only at the specific request of the colonial assemblies, and that minor adjustments to
suit local conditions should be left to the representatives of the
colonial peoples. It declared specifically, 'Canadians of French
extraction should in no degree be disturbed in the peaceful en-
joyment of their religion, laws and privileges, as secured to them
by the British Acts of Parliament.'

Clearly the framers of this report already foresaw the steady
evolution of colonial autonomy, and there was a perceptible step
in this direction in 1831 when the Lower Canadian Assembly
gained final control over all sources of revenue. But the executive
still remained responsible to the alien Government in Whitehall,
and as the radical majority in the Assembly increased after 1832
they became considerably more militant and, under the embittered
leadership of Papineau, more openly Anglophobe. For the first
time in Quebec the ideas of French revolutionary thinkers were
seriously discussed, and the formulation of republican proposals
by the *Patriotes*, as the radicals now began to call themselves, went

side by side with a progressive estrangement from the Church. Year after year supply bills were rejected. In 1833 the Assembly called for a constitutional convention, and in the following year Papineau drafted his Ninety Two Resolutions, which Aylmer, the incumbent Governor, described as a Declaration of Independence; in fact, they were much less, and their proposals for a new form of government were not nearly so precise as their criticisms of what existed. But the Resolutions were passed by 56 votes to 23, and aroused fresh discussions in Britain, where the demands for an elective executive council and other radical reforms were hardly suited to gain the support of Peel's Tory Government.

Lord Aberdeen, the Colonial Secretary whose name is cele-brated in the great floating slum of Hong Kong, agreed to some minor concessions regarding revenue and land tenure, but re-jected the idea of an elective executive and found the suggestion of a constitutional convention distinctly un-British. He decided to send Lord Amherst on a special mission with a set of non-negotiable offers, but before Amherst could set off the Tory Government had fallen, and it was for the Whigs to take up the problem of Canada, which they decided to do by sending Lord Gosford on a mission of investigation.

Gosford's mission sent back a series of reports which cannot have differed greatly from those the Tory commissioner Amherst might have sent, for they rejected the idea of an elective executive on the grounds that it would imperil British interests in Lower Canada. Though Gosford was specifically deputed to consider the situation in Lower Canada, his recommendations were by impli-cation applicable to Upper Canada, and this meant that the moderate proposals of Robert Baldwin and the wilder demands of William Lyon Mackenzie were rejected, as were the Twelve Resolutions passed in the Nova Scotia Assembly early in 1837 calling for responsible government and the surrender of Crown revenues.

Any hope that the British Government would prove more liberal than Gosford was dashed when Lord John Russell intro-duced his resolutions on the Canadian question in March 1837. They denied both the principle of responsibility as applied to colonial Governments, and the possibility of making either execu-tive or legislative councils elective. The resolutions were passed by heavy majorities, and Roebuck's compromise proposals were rejected out of hand by the Cabinet. Nevertheless, there was one innovation embodied in the resolutions whose importance none of their opponents fully realized. It was that in which Russell proposed that henceforward an appointed executive council should contain only two or three officials and the rest should be chosen from among the members of the legislature. It was through this loophole that responsible government was eventually to enter Canada.

But at the time the resolutions, framed to give prominence to their rejections and to conceal their one important concession, created only disappointment among the reformers in the colonies and anger among the more militant of them. The resultant deadlock paralysed efforts at conciliation on both sides, and in the summer of 1837 an economic depression swept the Canadas, intensifying bitterness and desperation. The only people who acted decisively were the bishops in Lower Canada; offended by Papineau's anti-clericalism, they issued a statement denouncing any attempt to overthrow the Government.

How serious or extensive were the revolutionary intentions of Papineau and Mackenzie in 1837 is still a matter of debate. Certainly their followers played with fire, organizing, arming and drilling, but the actual outbreak of fighting may well have been accidental. Papineau did not even take part in the actual revolt; when the *Patriotes* held a meeting in Montreal in November 1837 and apparently spontaneous rioting broke out, he slipped away, evidently not wishing to be involved; he was certainly not active in the fighting when Government forces took the initiative against the rural rebel strongholds, and when his followers were being killed and imprisoned he was over the border. The Upper Canadian revolt was sparked off by the news of that in Quebec, though there is little evidence of direct links between the two groups of rebels. This was a much more deliberate act of rebellion. As soon as Mackenzie heard the news of fighting in Quebec, he issued a spirited insurrectional proclamation, calling not for reform but for independence and promising free land to every man who rallied to his standard. It was rather like a clan rising in his native Scotland as the farmers in homespun trooped with their wretched arms to the rendezvous outside Toronto. But far more volunteers rallied behind Sir Francis Bond Head, who enjoyed a last and rather ludicrous hour of public glory as he marched his motley troops up Yonge Street to the burlesque battle of Mont-gomery's Tavern.

Both Mackenzie and Papineau were among those rare men whose greatest hours were times of failure. Neither of them, after he returned to Canada under the amnesty laws of the 1840s, recovered the prominence or the influence he had attained in the active years of the 1830s; they had been passed by by the events they had set in motion and made to feel outmoded in a world they had dramatically helped to create. Yet they are now rightly re-garded as among the architects of Canada as it has become, and there is no doubt that the consistently provocative attitudes they took to political questions between 1822 and 1837, and the catalytic effect of the rebellions associated with their names, precipitated the vital first stages of Canada's progress towards independence and decisively affected the development of the Empire.

John George Lambton, first Earl of Durham, is one of the more enigmatic figures of imperial history. There is the arrogant, ir-ritable aristocrat who rides into Quebec City like a conqueror on his white horse; there is the determined advocate of parlia-mentary reform whom devoted British working men christened 'Radical Jack'. There is the political hero whose celebrated *Report on the Affairs of British North America* was hailed by English-speaking Canadian reformers as a masterpiece of radical enlighten-ment; there is the political villain whose same report has gone down in French Canadian memory as English cultural chauvinism at its worst. Outside Canada, where more equable views have pre-vailed, it is considered that the Report was a milestone in the development of governments within the Empire, and Durham has taken his place in political history as one of the precursors of the devolution of the Empire into the Commonwealth.

Certainly Durham can be regarded as the dominant personality in the period of imperial history immediately after the Canadian rebellions, but it is still not easy to assess his true role. He ac-cepted reluctantly—and it is said only after the personal interven-tion of Queen Victoria—the appointment as Governor-in-Chief of British North America and as Lord High Commissioner deputed to investigate in depth the problems that had brought violence into the two Canadas. His health was not good, and he was conscious that Melbourne, the Whig Prime Minister, had chosen him mainly because his radical reputation would make him acceptable to reformers in Canada and to critics of the Government in England.

As a governor-general, Durham's achievements were as slight as his tenure was brief. He arrived in Canada on May 28th, 1838; he resigned his office on September 28th, not because he had been unable to win the good will of the Canadians, but because Melbourne had failed to support him in a political crisis. By the time Durham arrived some of the Lower Canadian rebels had already been executed; faced with the problem of dealing with those in captivity, he decided on the clement course of banishing them to the rather delectable solitude of Bermuda. Since Durham had no jurisdiction over that colony, the banishment was technically an illegal act, and Lord Brougham used it in the House of Lords as an excuse for attacking the Government. Melbourne declined to defend Durham; instead he disallowed the banishment and Durham resigned, thereby gaining considerable popularity among Canadians, and leaving to his successor the task of dealing with a further abortive revolt by the *Patriotes* at the end of 1838.

Having resigned his post as Governor-in-Chief, Durham insisted on fulfilling the obligations he had accepted as investigating commissioner; he spent his last months of life and his remaining strength compiling the report on what he had found and framing the recommendations on what might be done to alleviate Canadian discontents. The Durham Report is written with a natural authority and elegance rare among such documents; it is strong in opinion and sometimes weak in information, giving the appearance of independence and yet on examination revealing the presence of a multitude of influences. Durham travelled with two advisers whom he had chosen over Melbourne's objections to their unsavoury social reputations. Charles Buller had been involved in a well-publicized divorce and Edward Gibbon Wakefield, later to play an important role in the settlement of New Zealand, had spent three years in Newgate for abducting a young heiress. But both had thought seriously on colonial questions and Wakefield's views on subsidized immigration and the need for strict control of land distribution had their effect on Durham's thinking.

As for the Canadians, Durham's attitude towards them was sharply divided. In Upper Canada he sympathized with the views of the moderate reformers, and the influence of Robert Baldwin on his arguments is especially evident. On the other hand, it is evident that in Lower Canada he was impressed by the English-speaking merchants of Montreal, many of whom were Highland Scots strong in personality and a good deal more knowledgeable about Canada and its potentialities than the somewhat parochial lawyers and physicians who were the spokesmen of the *Patriotes*.

A tone of almost emotional revulsion from French Canadian attitudes characterizes his report, which immediately shocked and antagonized the *Québecois* by its systematic belittlement of their culture and of their hopes of creating a French community in the heart of North America. For Durham, as for many of his contemporaries, the traditional French society of Canada represented an obscurantist past from which generations of British radicals and dissenters had sought to free themselves, and in comparison the merchants of Montreal and the gentlemen settlers of Upper Canada seemed to stand for the march of liberal progress.

The extent to which this conflict weighed on Durham's mind is demonstrated in the ringing sentence which, so often quoted out of context, has given a distorted view of his report as a whole. 'I expected to find a contest between a government and a people; I found two nations warring in the bosom of a single state; I found a struggle, not of principles, but of races.' When Durham stated his cultural views, it was evident that he had abandoned the sympathy for the French Canadian cause which he had once shared with the London radicals like Roebuck and Hume, and had taken his stand with the Tory politicians and the Colonial Office bureaucrats who aimed at assimilation. 'I entertain no doubts', he insisted, 'as to the national character which must be given to Lower Canada; it must be that of the British Empire.' And to realize this aim he made one of his main recommendations: the legislative union of the two Canadas, the very measure which had aroused Papineau's opposition in 1822 and which the French Canadians in the Assembly had opposed ever since.

At the same time, he called for the extension to all the colonies of British North America of the 'British constitutional practice of cabinet government'. Durham regarded greater responsibility as a safeguard rather than a diminution of essential imperial rights; he wished to retain for Britain the overriding powers of providing for defence, of regulating imperial trade and of disposing of lands in newly opened territories, but he insisted that, where it operated,

British government should be good government. As one of the results of his proposed reforms Durham envisaged the emergence of nations out of colonies. Discussing ways of countering the influence of the United States, he revealed his consciousness of the evolution of separate identities within the Empire.

> If we wish to prevent the extension of this influence [of the United States], it can only be done by raising up for the North American colonist some nationality of his own; by elevating those small and unimportant communities into a society having some objects of a national importance; and by thus giving their inhabitants a country which they will be unwilling to see absorbed into one more powerful.

It was this ultimate acknowledgment of the principle of local independence emerging from the sense of local identity that made the better features of Durham's proposals in the long run negate their less worthy aspects. As the modern Canadian historian, Kenneth McNaught, has said of the report, 'Its basic constitutional liberalism, which was to pave the way for the long-term survival of a French-Canadian nation and for the development of a multi-racial and freely associated Commonwealth of Nations, thus stands in ironic relationship to its Anglo-Saxon racism.'

Durham's report was issued late in 1839. By the following summer its brilliant author was already dead, at the age of forty-eight. Before he died, the Act of Union which gave one of his proposals the force of law had been passed in the British Parliament, and Upper and Lower Canada were united.

Edward Ellice had urged a federal union of all the North American colonies, but this was rejected because the ministers in London feared that such a body might usurp powers reserved for the imperial Government, and the union became a legislative one. The two sections into which Canada was divided for electoral purposes, Canada East and Canada West, corresponded to the superseded colonies. They were given equal representation in the Assembly, though at the time of union the population of Canada West was considerably less than that of Canada East. The aim was to prevent the French Canadians, with their larger population, from dominating the Assembly, and this was at first a source of great grievance in Quebec. Before long the grievance shifted to the inhabitants of Canada West, whose population grew more rapidly, and the French Canadians began to regard the equality of representation as an essential protection against cultural submergence. The use of French as an official language was abandoned, and when it was proposed in 1843 to reinstate it, the Tory Colonial Secretary, Lord Stanley, refused permission and in doing so admitted the assimilationist intent of the British Government. 'The avowed purpose of the Enactment', he told the Governor-General, Sir Charles Metcalfe, 'was to promote the amalgamation of the French and English Races.'

In fact, the French and English races did not amalgamate, but they did co-operate in a way the British authorities had not expected. With Mackenzie and Papineau exiled south of the border, the reform movements fell into the hands of moderates, and a working arrangement was established between Robert Baldwin and Louis Hippolyte Lafontaine, the leaders in Canada West and Canada East respectively.

In spite of the overtly reactionary nature of the Act of Union, circumstances were in fact much more in favour of the colonists than at first seemed evident. People in Britain, including their representatives in Parliament, were becoming impatient of recurrent colonial crises, to such an extent that in 1849 the Colonial Secretary, Lord Grey, told Lord Elgin, then Governor-General, 'There begins to prevail in the House of Commons and I am sorry to say in the highest quarters, an opinion (which I believe to be utterly erroneous) that we have no interest in preserving our colonies and ought to make no sacrifices for that purpose.' And even the most conservative ministers during the 1840s were so sensitive to the possibility of a repetition of the risings of 1837 that they were inclined to send out Governors who—though not all of them succeeded—would try to work smoothly with the Assembly. This led to an inevitable series of arrangements and compromises, each bringing nearer the final governmental surrender on the question of responsible government.

From the beginning of the union the principle was accepted that the Governor-General should pick his Executive Council from the legislature. Lord Sydenham in 1841 selected a non-partisan group of advisers from the Assembly and presided as his own prime minister, hoping to give an illusion of cabinet government while retaining the substance of authority. Since the active role remained with the Governor, responsible government was avoided, and the reformers found no satisfying place for themselves in what Sydenham in his more cynical moods described as 'a council to be consulted, and no more'. Though Sydenham showed considerable skill in creating a Cabinet that would accept his methods and that also commanded a majority in the Assembly, it was the kind of juggling that could not long succeed.

Sydenham evaded a confrontation by falling off his horse and dying. His successor, Sir Charles Bagot, was an experienced politician and diplomat; more than thirty years before, he had been under-secretary for foreign affairs; he had held the post of ambassador to Washington during the difficult years after the War of 1812 and had negotiated the Rush–Bagot agreement which eliminated warships of the Great Lakes; more recently, he had represented Britain at the Hague and in St Petersburg and Paris. Bagot came with explicit instructions from Lord Stanley to follow the methods laid down by Sydenham and to give no more ground to the reformers.

But Bagot was too experienced an observer of politics to imagine that Sydenham's game could continue for very long, and when the ministry which his predecessor had created was defeated in the Assembly, he acted as if he were a constitutional monarch and accepted the reformist spokesmen, Baldwin and Lafontaine, as leaders of a new ministry. Stanley was not pleased and Queen Victoria was vocally unamused, but Bagot carefully explained the realities of the Canadian situation as he saw them. 'Whether the doctrine of responsible government is openly acknowledged, or is only tacitly acquiesced in, virtually it exists.' It was not yet party government, for Bagot insisted on representatives of the Conservative minority being included in the new administration, yet he did his best, by absenting himself frequently from meetings of the Council, to allow the reformist leaders to prove that a cabinet system would work in Canada.

Bagot, however, was defeated by the same kind of misfortune as had destroyed so many of his predecessors. Like Craig and Durham, he was attacked by fatal sickness while in Canada, but at least, unlike Sydenham, he was able to go home to die; he resigned in 1843, as he was about to transfer to his ministers the all-important patronage of official appointments. The Government in Westminster was as pleased with Bagot's resignation as it had been

enraged by his concessions, and sent to replace him Sir Charles
Metcalfe, trained in the autocratic school of Indian administration.
Metcalfe's refusal to follow Bagot's policy of granting responsible
government by default was enthusiastically supported by the
British Court and Cabinet. Patronage was the obvious point of
confrontation. Metcalfe insisted on making an appointment that
was repugnant to Baldwin, Lafontaine and their followers. They
resigned, and, instead of choosing another ministry, Metcalfe
ruled alone and in defiance of the Assembly for nine months until,
in 1844, he called an election and won a slight majority which
enabled him to install a Conservative executive, willing to sustain
Lord Stanley's view that anything less than the independence of
the Governor-General from the Assembly would 'convert
Canada into a republic, independent of the Crown of this country'.

But the fate that seemed to hang like the curse of an Egyptian
tomb over the Governors of Canada attacked Metcalfe too; like
Bagot he fell fatally sick and went home to die. He was an example
of the just and uncorrupt kind of administrator which India
produced in the early nineteenth century, but his experience there
had made him insensitive to the political realities of a colony
inhabited by two European peoples of different cultures, and his
attempt to turn back the clock on Bagot's progress in the direction
of responsible government was doomed to failure, not only because it found a steadily dwindling support among Canadians, but
also because it was out of tune with the prevailing drift of British
opinion.

In 1846 the Whigs returned to power under Lord John Russell.
Grey, the new Colonial Secretary, who had been sympathetic to
Durham's proposals, selected Lord Elgin as Governor-General
of Canada. Elgin was not merely a reformer, but had just married
Lady Mary Louisa Lambton, Durham's daughter; he went to
Canada with a conscious intent of completing his father-in-law's
work. Without any formal statement of intent to establish responsible government, he made it known that he was willing to work
in harmony with any advisers who enjoyed the confidence of the
Assembly. The Conservative ministry formed by Metcalfe was
still in office when he arrived, and he ruled for a year with its
advice. When the Conservatives were defeated in the elections of
1848, he entrusted office once again to Baldwin and Lafontaine.

Yet it was not in the united province of Canada that responsible government was first explicitly acknowledged, but in Nova Scotia, where the ground had been prepared by Joseph Howe, who used both his position as a leader of the Reform Party and his literary eloquence (expressed in a series of open letters to the British Prime Minister) to put the case for responsible government in a particularly clear and attractive way. When Sir John Harvey was sent to Nova Scotia as Governor, Grey instructed him to ensure that the Executive Council would always be constructed as to accord with the views of the electorate as represented by the majority in the Assembly. This was the first time the principle of majority government—which soon led to party government—had been conceded.

Grey instructed Harvey that the areas of reserved imperial jurisdiction were foreign policy and trade, defence and the form of the constitution. Everything else was to be the province of an administration chosen not any longer by the Governor, but by the leader of the majority party, for it must be recognized, as Grey put it to Harvey, that 'it is neither possible nor desirable to carry on the Government of any of the British provinces in North America in opposition to the opinion of the inhabitants'. In January 1848 the Reform Party won the Nova Scotian elections, and James Boyne Uniacke was invited by Harvey to form a Government, the first responsible administration in the British Empire; Nova Scotia thus became the pioneer colony in the attainment of full internal self-government.

Because the situation in Canada was more volatile, Grey allowed Elgin to proceed according to his own judgment, and the Governor-General interpreted this to mean quietly and undemonstratively giving his constitutional support to whichever ministry might be in office. But he waited for a suitably dramatic opportunity before making an explicit and practical application of the principle of responsible government. It came in 1849 when the Baldwin–Lafontaine ministry submitted a Rebellion Losses Bill to compensate those who had suffered losses during the rebellion in Lower Canada. A similar bill relating to losses in Upper Canada had been passed already and sanctioned by Metcalfe, but the list of people to be compensated in Lower Canada included a number who were reasonably suspected of having themselves been rebels, and when the bill was passed, the Conservatives of Montreal demanded that Elgin should refuse his assent. Elgin personally shared their repugnance for a law that seemed to reward rebellion, but he realized that this was a testing point for the sincerity of the British Government's acceptance of responsible government in the colonies. He signed the bill, whereupon the Tory mob burnt down the parliament building in Montreal, a gesture which could not negate the fact that responsible government had been given its first effective expression in Canada.

Within five years it had been granted to all but one of the colonies of British North America; it came to Prince Edward Island in 1851, to New Brunswick and Newfoundland in 1854. The only remaining Crown colony was a newcomer, Vancouver Island, on the far Pacific coast, founded in 1849; the remainder of the west, and the great basin of Rupert's Land, still remained under the seventeenth-century chartered rule of the Adventurers of England Trading into Hudson's Bay. But the settled regions of British North America had proceeded by 1854 to a stage in constitutional progress which no British possession, in North America or elsewhere, had previously achieved, and with the acquisition of self-government their peoples had been given a lever that would shift and eventually shatter the structure of the Empire.

IX Self-Government to
Independence

When responsible government was achieved in the Canadian colonies—and a few years later in those of Australasia—it seemed already that this qualified autonomy might lead in several possible directions. As the imperialists later argued, it could produce a federal union of the English-speaking realms to which in the fullness of time the lost territories of the United States might return. Sharing in trade and defence, speaking a common language and perpetuating a common culture, the members of such a federation would be invincible. To be sure, the imperialists were never exalted enough to think of a thousand years of Pax Britannica, but until the South African War revealed the military inadequacies of Britain (which historically had won most of its wars by naval superiority and by the use of largely mercenary forces) they were unshaken in their belief that if only the colonies could be persuaded to play their proper part in strengthening the imperial forces, Britain would still be able to repel the threat of Russia in the wild borderlands of Asia, and the threat of Germany at sea and in international commerce, and in the end convert the cousinship of the United States into a renewed brotherhood.

Today—but here again we must beware of the temptations of hindsight—it is hard to understand how British imperialists, and among them men as tough and shrewd in their own fields as Cecil Rhodes, should have failed to perceive that among the great nineteenth-century powers the most consistent and logical enemy of the British Empire was the United States. Germany, Russia, even France, were countries with the same kind of imperial approach as Britain, and no one, before 1914, realized that the internal hatreds of Europe had built up to the point where the rivals for leadership would be willing to destroy even themselves rather than accept a modest compromise. Only the United States stood out as a country whose very existence dated from the breakdown of an empire, and there was no reason even then to suppose that it could rejoin that empire in its renewed form or even adopt an attitude towards it any less than covertly hostile and destructive. When eventually Britain and the United States did recognize certain common perils and fought beside each other in two World Wars, the Americans never really wavered from the view that, though Britain itself must be preserved as a bastion of capitalist democracy, the preservation of the Empire as a pattern of sovereignty and dependence was not to be attempted.

But all this could be safely ignored by the imperialists until as late as the 1940s, for once the tensions of the 1860s had passed it was not until Britain had been isolated by her enemies in Europe and Asia, and the Empire seemed likely to disintegrate because of the threatened destruction of its centre, that the Americans during the Second World War set about the task they had long intended: to promote the salvation of Britain and at the same time hasten the final destruction of its Empire.

It was not only the imperialists in Britain who conceived of the Empire as a single organism, with Britain its head, the dominions its members and India its vast body; there were Canadians and Australasians and South Africans—there were even a few Indians—to whom such a concept seemed attractive, and even though the Americans did not return to a transformed Empire, the imperialists still believed that there would be enough Britons (not to count on the unmentioned Boers and *Canadiens*) to defy the world, provided they could be induced to organize themselves properly and to accept the views of Lords Roberts and Kitchener and the much admired Admiral Fisher on how—through conscription and dreadnoughts—to set their defences in proper order.

The imperialist attitude had much in common with that of nineteenth-century evangelical missionaries, who were convinced that the day would come when the whole world would be converted not only to Christianity, but specifically to their own sect of Christianity. The imperialists believed that, like the missionaries, they were bringing light into darkness; the very superiority of the way of life they carried into the less advanced parts of the world was a guarantee of its eventual acceptance. Among the generation of Chamberlain and Milner and Rhodes there was a genuine altruism that irradiated even if it did not excuse their imperial recklessness. And it was understandable that those particular Canadians and Australians who found their commercial interests tied to Britain should be attracted to the dream of playing a high role in the evolution of what Sir Charles Dilke called 'a greater Britain'. There were even times in Canada when nationalism and imperialism appeared to go hand in hand; some of the leaders of the 'Canada First' movement, which in the 1870s and 1880s sought to create a recognizable Canadian national character *vis-à-vis* Britain as well as the United States, were convinced that once Canada had established itself as a nation it should play its part in the mighty super-nation that would emerge from a willing partnership between Britain and her dominions.

Yet from the beginning there were the forces which would militate against such an eventuality, and they were at work in all the settlement colonies that during the 1840s and 1850s attained the status of internal self-government. There were always local circumstances which the colonies did not share with the mother country: the presence of the United States on the borders of Canada, the growing fear in the Australasian colonies of the Asia that lay between them and Europe. There were the elements in each colony that were traditionally suspicious or resentful of Britain or British rulers; the French in Canada, the Irish and the descendants of the convicts in Australia, and, later in South Africa, the Boers; only New Zealand lacked these suspicious minorities, and New Zealand was consistently the most loyal and the most 'English' of all the dominions. There were the divergent interests: Britain was dedicated to Free Trade, while the colonies, needing markets for their raw materials and protection for their nascent industries, were interested in creating a trading system that would ensure reciprocity within the Empire. Britain pressed in a series of Colonial and Imperial Conferences for a system of imperial defence, but to the colonies it seemed like a return to taxation without representation, when they were expected to contribute financially to an army and a navy controlled by Whitehall and used to defend parts of the Empire in which they were not interested, or, even worse, to fight the wars in which Britain might become involved owing to her position as a European power. Perhaps there is no better example of the kind of dilemma faced by a colonial leader than that experienced by Sir John A. Macdonald, the Conservative Prime Minister of bicultural Canada who declared—and sincerely meant it, 'A British subject I was born; a British subject I will die,' and yet, when he was asked by the British Government for help in the Sudan in 1885, shied away from what he regarded as 'no concern of Canada', and added, 'Our men and money would be sacrificed to get Gladstone and Co. out of the hole they have plunged themselves into by their own imbecility'. Yet Macdonald helped reluctantly in the Sudan, as Laurier would do in South Africa, finding an uneasy compromise between local independence and imperial loyalty, and when Britain was endangered the dominions rallied to it as the effective centre of the Empire. Isolation might, as a Canadian politician (Sir George Eulas Foster) first said, be splendid, but in practice it was always tempered by necessity.

Indeed, even while the settlement colonies knew that there were many areas in which their interests diverged from those of Britain, they had little desire to break all their ties with the imperial centre; for, having gained the right to rule their own local affairs, they realized that this could only be done—in an unashamedly expansionist age like the nineteenth century—if the aegis of some greater power extended over them. Independence would have put the Australasian colonies at the mercy of French or German adventurers, backed eventually by French or German arms; their situation would have been that of the Boers, enacted in a different region and with different imperial aggressors. For Canada in the 1840s independence could only be, as Elgin remarked to Grey, 'a means to the end, annexation'.

If the self-governing colonies in the mid nineteenth century chose something delicately balanced between independence and imperial federation, and if in the long run the inclination was towards the former possibility, one can find two excellent reasons for this tendency. Firstly, there was the natural desire, once a people had gained certain rights over its own existence: to extend those rights until it was free entirely of the demeaning relationship imposed by external tutelage. Secondly, there was the ambivalent attitude of Britain itself towards the self-governing colonies during the crucial period of growth towards political maturity between the 1840s and the 1880s.

For, until Disraeli and his followers refurbished the imperial idea in the 1870s, British statesmen of all parties were inclined to view the settlement colonies, and especially Canada with its extended American border, as embarrassments rather than assets. When Sir John Macdonald and other delegates from the Canadas went to London in 1866 to discuss the confederation of the North American colonies, they encountered tactless manifestations of relief rather than signs of active interest. 'I cannot shut my eyes to the fact that they want to get rid of us,' said Alexander Tilloch Galt, who had signed the Annexation Manifesto of 1849 but had since returned to the conviction that Canada should develop as a nation in close association with Britain. 'They have a servile fear of the United States, and would rather give us up than defend us, or incur the risk of war with that country.'

It was not entirely a matter of fearing the United States. A host of other factors contributed in the 1860s to the British desire to disperse responsibility—which meant responsibility for self-defence as well as for self-government—as widely as possible across the Empire. Gladstone and the Free Trade Liberals were anxious to reduce military expenditures. The seventy thousand British soldiers who had manned the colonial garrisons at the end of the Napoleonic Wars were reduced by at least a quarter by the early 1850s, and during the following decades the withdrawal of troops continued. On the other hand, partly as a result of this policy, there were alarming signs of British military weakness. When Disraeli wanted to make a gesture of strength on the eve of the Congress of Berlin in 1878, it was from India that he had to fetch the seven thousand troops he stationed in Malta. The stalemate of the Crimean War; Bismarck's cool and successful defiance of Palmerston over the issue of Schleswig-Holstein in 1864; the perils which Disraeli himself had so adroitly sidestepped at the Berlin Congress: all pointed to the fact that although Britain enjoyed a theoretical but untested naval supremacy, she was too weak in military terms to meet the European crises in which her imperial role might unexpectedly involve her. Britain had indeed abandoned temporarily the role as holder of the balance of power in Europe which had taken her armies to the continent repeatedly between 1689 and 1815 (and would do so again in the twentieth century), and Bismarck went from bullying Denmark to defeating Austria–Hungary and France and setting up the German Empire, with Britain watching powerlessly from across the Channel. But even if—except for the Crimea—Britain kept its armies out of European wars for ninety-nine years, there was still the danger that France might start some adventure in the Levant, or Russia make some move towards India like that which later happened in the Pendjeh crisis on the borders of Afghanistan in 1885, and in such circumstances Britain would have difficulty assembling quickly enough the necessary men and equipment, because they were scattered over the long seaways and vast spaces of empire. These apprehensions were completely justified. Britain was never, from Waterloo onwards, prepared for rapid victory in any sizeable war; that would be demonstrated in South Africa in 1899, and again when Britain finally got involved in Europe in 1914 and 1939. The slow bleeding of these successive long-drawn-out conflicts did as much as any other single circumstance to bring about the eventual end of the Empire.

Because of this combination of a desire for military economy with a consciousness of the dwindling of military power, Britain was anxious to encourage the colonies to take up their own defence so as to give greater mobility to her small professional army, and since the Canadian colonies were those whose weakness involved the greatest danger, it was natural that Britain should wish to see them standing as soon as possible on their own political feet. But in the nineteenth-century world the political options for independent nations were somewhat different from what they are in our own day, when minute and economically unviable territories can sustain political independence partly because world public opinion supports such proliferating sovereignties, and partly also because the tensions between the great powers in a nuclear age provide a kind of umbrella of inaction within which small States can flourish. In the nineteenth century small States survived sometimes as clients of larger ones, as Luxemburg and Monaco did, or because their neutrality was convenient for the larger powers, as in the case of Switzerland. But generally it was a matter of security demanding size. In Europe itself the last important clusters of petty sovereignties—in Germany and Italy—were moving towards unity and as soon as they did join together into large nation-states, the whole structure of European political life was changed.

Neither the Canadians nor the British imagined that a State as important as either Germany or Italy could be created north of the United States, but at least it might be possible to establish a new political combination within the Empire that would be large enough in size and in population to give pause to potential expansionists along its borders. The initiative in creating it did not come from Britain. Theoretically, changes in colonial constitutions were among the areas reserved for the imperial Government, but it was already tacitly understood that nothing should be altered unless the colonies requested it, though it clearly lay within the rights of the Governors to make known to local politicians Whitehall's opinions on such issues.

There were of course abundant reasons within the North American colonies to seek a change in their political condition. In some ways they were too little united; the change in transport patterns created by the appearance of the railway suggested a need for greater co-ordination between Canada and the Atlantic colonies, as did fear of the United States, which increased during the Civil War when the Confederates used Canadian soil to mount raids on the northern states and Washington reacted truculently by unilaterally terminating in 1865 the Reciprocity Treaty covering trade between the two countries.

Yet there were also ways in which at least the two Canadas were too tightly united. At first there had been considerable harmony between French and British reformers, and the Baldwin–Lafontaine ministry worked as smoothly as any coalition could. As time went on, however, it became evident that even the reformers in the two provinces had divergent aims. The Orangemen and Scots Presbyterians who gained influence in Canada West were anti-Catholic, and increasingly anti-French. That assimilation had failed to materialize seemed a cause of grievance to them; they saw Canada's progress held back by the presence of a people who clung to their antiquated farms and resisted economic modernization as obstinately as they resisted accepting the English language and the Protestant religion.

The truculence of the Grits—as the Liberals of Canada West called themselves—was aggravated by the system of electoral parity. Because of massive immigration, the English-speaking population of Canada West now exceeded the French-speaking population of Canada East, and if one included the English settlers of the Eastern Townships in Quebec and the English-speaking residents of Montreal, the French were now outnumbered to such an extent that even their celebrated war of the cradle would never enable them to catch up. Under the slogan 'Rep. by Pop.', the Canada Westers stridently demanded an electoral reform that

would give them a representation proportional to their actual
voting strength; realizing that this would submerge them politically, the French Canadians insisted on clinging to the parity
system which they had previously denounced as inequitable.
Various devices were tried in the hope of reconciling the differences between the two peoples. Each Government had two
leaders to represent the two language groups, and for a while this
leadership-in-tandem was combined with an even more bizarre
double majority system, by which no law was considered acceptable unless it was approved by a majority of the members for
each province. Such clumsy expedients were bound to fail, and by
the middle of the 1850s it was clear that a new political form must
be evolved. The idea of a federation, suggested in the past by
Roebuck and Ellice in England, was revived, and now, for the
first time, Canadians began to show an interest in this political
remedy for their cultural ills.

Once the hope of a solution had emerged, there was an un-
expected drawing together of the opposing groups, French-
speakers and English-speakers, Conservatives and Liberals, and
in 1864 a coalition headed by John Macdonald, Georges-Étienne
Cartier and the formidable Grit editor of the Toronto *Globe*,
George Brown, was created to explore the prospects of a confederation of the British North American provinces. After discussions with the Maritime Provinces, an agreement was reached
on the outlines of a federal constitution. This would redivide
Canada into its two provinces, each enjoying control over all
purely local affairs; the two provinces, with the remaining
colonies, would come together in a federation that would assume
the name of Canada and would shed colonial status, achieving that
strange half-state, no longer a dependency, not yet a nation, for
which the title of Dominion was chosen. Britain accepted the
proposals and Parliament passed the British North America Act
which, considerably amended, is still the constitution of Canada.

Debate has ranged, almost ever since modern Canada was
sketched out in 1867, regarding the exact intentions of the Fathers
of Confederation. Macdonald seems to have favoured giving
decisive power to the centre, but there have been persistent efforts
to assert the rights of the provinces, and French Canadian constitutional theorists have even talked of a 'compact' between the
two cultural nations, French and English, on which confederation

was based; they imply that undue centralism, operating in the interests of English-speaking Canadians, has broken this compact. It is an interesting Rousseauish idea, and it fits a concept of loose confederation with considerable local powers which would undoubtedly be the best form of government for an immense and loosely connected country like Canada. But in historical terms it is impossible to find any documentary evidence that supports the existence of such a compact.

The British Government in power at the time of confederation was a Liberal administration more or less controlled by Gladstone and Bright, both inclined to be continentalist in their attitude towards North America; with unprophetic vision, they seem to have believed that American manifest destiny was a force not to be resisted, and that eventually Canada would fall away from the Empire and be dismembered into states of the Union. As for the Americans, they obviously hoped for the same eventuality, but contented themselves for the time being with a couple of threatening gestures. Congress expressed its consternation at the establishment of a new monarchical State north of the border, and the State Department purchased Alaska, which the Hudson's Bay Company had been foolish enough to decline when the Russians offered it at a bargain price.

The Canadians, however, recognized a destiny of their own which, if not exactly manifest, could at least be attempted. The people of Canada West, now transformed into Ontario, were running out of available land, and even before confederation they had been looking speculatively at the rich prairie lands along the Red River. As part of the arrangement with Britain, the Government in London bought out the rights of the Hudson's Bay Company in Rupert's Land, and transferred the title to Canada. West of the Rockies the colony of British Columbia, spawned in the Cariboo Gold Rush, had been in existence since 1858, and it was induced to join the confederation with the bribe of a railway to link it with eastern Canada. The railway was completed and Canada physically united by 1885, but already formal occupation had been made of the prairies by the creation of the North-west Mounted Police and the celebrated ride to the foothills of the Rockies. By these tenuous means, and by the decisive effrontery with which a people three million strong laid claim to half a continent, the American bluff of manifest destiny was effectively called. Canadian unity was not achieved without tragedy and injustice. If the Indians were not killed in large numbers, their great cultures on the prairies and on the Pacific coast were destroyed, and the way in which the *métis*, who had created their own frontier pattern of existence, were twice goaded into rebellion and suppressed remains one of the deeper scars on Canadian history.

Yet in terms of the history of the Empire, and of its decline, the success of the Canadians in creating a nation in the face of considerable American hostility and of difficult natural obstacles is extremely important, for had Canada not proved viable as a dominion the whole character of the epoch that saw the Empire reach both its apogee and its end might have been profoundly different. Sir John A. Macdonald and his associates must rank high among the conspirators against the Empire; they would have rejected such roles with indignation and loud protestations that their loyalty to the imperial connection was far more sincere than that of such lukewarm custodians of Britain's inheritance as the Gladstonian Liberals. They would have been right, yet in the long perspective the ultimate consequences of their actions speak more loudly than their words.

In 1883 the British historian Sir John Seeley delivered the Cambridge lectures, which were eventually published in a celebrated book entitled *The Expansion of England* that came to be regarded as one of the seminal works of imperialist theory. Seeley argued that despite the present strength of the European powers, even the newest and most vigorous of them, even Imperial Germany itself, would inevitably be eclipsed by the sheer physical gigantism of Russia and the United States, whose resources of territory, raw materials and manpower, and hence of both industrial and military strength, were bound eventually to bring them to the lead in the coming struggle for world power. It was not an entirely new insight; the Russian writer Alexander Herzen had made the same prophecy earlier in the century. But Seeley gave it a new perspective by suggesting that Britain, alone among the western European powers, might be able to challenge the new giants.

He pointed out that because circumstances had allowed Britain to keep relatively free from European commitments, and to concentrate on building a large navy rather than allowing herself to

be drained by the maintenance of immense conscript armies, she
had forged ahead of her rivals in the competition for empire. In
North America, in Africa, in Australasia, she had established
communities of British race and language that were developing
into political entities in their own rights, bound by ties of tradition
and common interest to the mother country. The resentments that
destroyed the First British Empire had been avoided by the reasonably prompt granting of responsible government. And now, if the
British all over the world were willing to come together again
voluntarily into a federal union, into a 'Greater Britain', of which
the dominions would be integral parts, then London might still
be the capital of a world power—the only world power that would
have no need to fear Russia and the United States because it would
always exceed the stronger of them in population, in territorial
extent and in industrial potentialities.

Seeley introduced a new element into imperial thinking. Hitherto the open imperialists like Disraeli and the crypto-imperialists
like Gladstone had seen the Empire as primarily a matter of Britain
and India; to sustain that axis even Gladstone had turned to his
military adventures in the Levant. Gladstone had regarded the
settlement colonies as dispensable and Disraeli had treated them
with suspicion, since for him the essential imperial relationship
was one of authority and dependence, and a self-governing colony
was a contradiction in terms. Seeley had perceived that a generation of responsible government did not appear to have produced
the separatist inclination which most British politicians had expected when Canada was created in 1867. For him the dominions
were a more important element in the future of the Empire than
the Crown colonies or even India, for he believed that continued
rule over peoples who would not accept British culture must
eventually be weakening to the Empire.

From the viewpoint of England, Seeley's arguments appeared
reasonable and practical and, under their inspiration the Imperial
Federation League was founded in 1884 as a non-partisan body.
Among its most fervent supporters were the Liberal imperialists,
led by Lord Rosebery. Imperial Germany rather than the United
States was the model whose startling recent success inspired the
imperial federationists. They talked of a joint defence system, of
a federal parliament, of a system of federal taxes, of a diplomatic
service federally operated, of a customs union. The last proposal

was to have a much longer life than the rest, for as Empire Free Trade it was still being advocated by Lord Beaverbrook as late as the 1930s.

Seeley's ideas seemed in the 1880s to be riding the wave of events. As the Empire steadily expanded it seemed indeed that only proper co-ordination was needed for such assembled might to be irresistible. But, as the succession of Colonial and Imperial Conferences after 1883 was to demonstrate, Seeley had really come too late; the pioneer dominion, and the self-governing colonies which aspired to the same status, became with every gathering decreasingly amenable to the idea of imperial co-ordination.

If Seeley had spoken at the beginning of the 1860s, before the confederation of Canada, it is possible that the idea of a federal union, under which they would be represented according to population in an imperial parliament, might have appealed to the colonists of Canada, Australasia and the Cape; but Seeley made his proposals not only after most of the colonies populated by British immigrants had received self-government. He did so after the confederation of Canada had established the conception of dominion status as a step on the road towards national self-sufficiency. And already by 1883 Canada had advanced too far along that road for a change in direction to be brought about by anything short of physical force, which by now was unthinkable. The territorial unity of the dominion had been achieved and would shortly be made effective by the completion of the great railway from ocean to ocean. The prairies were ceasing to be empty spaces on the map as immigrants flocked to them not only from Britain but also from continental Europe and the United States. The North-West Rebellion would shortly provide an opportunity to deploy a Canadian army across the prairies, and the minute rising of the *métis*, who at no time had more than two hundred fighting men in the field, was treated as an opportunity for a display that Canada was now a self-sufficient nation. In 1870, at the time of the earlier rising along the Red River, British soldiers under Wolseley had gone with Canadian volunteers to Fort Garry to show the Americans that Canada's autonomy did not mean the end of Britain's concern. But, that gesture once made, most of the British troops departed from Canada in 1871, and in 1885 Macdonald was able to show that in any ordinary emergency his country could stand on her own. American expansionist senators from mid-Western states were expected to take note.

It was appropriate, even if no more than a coincidence, that in 1871—the year the British regiments sailed away—the earliest Canadian nationalist movement, 'Canada First', emerged, with its barely submerged anti-Americanism and its stress on the need to lessen hostilities between the various cultural, linguistic and religious groups that made up the Canadian people. The Canada Firsters recognized that unity was essential before Canada could achieve national maturity. Their movement never attained massive proportions, but it is significant of the wide appeal of nationalist sentiments that in 1878, after having been defeated in 1873 through the revelations of Tory graft in the financing of the Canadian Pacific Railway, Sir John A. Macdonald was returned to power on a 'National Policy', which included tariffs to protect nascent Canadian industry as well as railway projects and the encouragement of immigration. The fact that Canadian tariffs were imposed on British as well as American imports amounted to an open rejection of the British imperial policy of Free Trade.

Canada quickly developed its own social and political character. The presence of the French Canadians as an obstinate island of cultural conservatism rendered the kind of assimilative process that had developed in the United States impossible. Canada remained a cultural and regional mosaic; its people were differentiated by place of residence as much as by language, and they tended to think of themselves—as they do today—as *Québecois* or Nova Scotians or British Columbians first and Canadians afterwards. The retention of the monarchical system was paralleled by a tendency to perpetuate a hierarchical society which a recent Canadian author, John Porter, vividly described as a 'vertical mosaic', and yet, if the ways of British gentry lingered, the militancy of British labour rebels also came in on the immigrant ships, so that the Canadian provinces have provided the only socialist Governments in America north of the Rio Grande. Canadian political life has remained British in form.

Inevitably, Canada was affected not only by the proximity of the United States, with its resultant similarities and resentments, but also by the relationship between Britain and that country, which led in turn to a sharpened realization of the divergence of Canadian and British interests. Dominion status, as it was originally understood, carried no connotations of diplomatic freedom. Diplomatically the Empire was still regarded as being undivided; the Crown could speak to the extra-imperial world through one oracle only, the Foreign Office in London, and any international negotiations affecting Canada had to be carried on by Britain. At best, a Canadian might be allowed to sit on the British negotiating team when Canadian interests were discussed.

It was not long before Canadians learnt that their interests on such occasions were treated in terms of general British policy, which often meant that they were lukewarmly defended. In 1871 Macdonald was allowed to participate as one of the British team in the negotiations leading to the Treaty of Washington. He signed under protest a treaty in which the Americans paid no compensation for allowing the Fenians to raid over the border into Canada, and almost no compensation for the rights Britain gave them to fish in Canadian waters. In 1903, in the discussions over the boundary between British Columbia and Alaska, the British representatives accepted a solution that deprived Canada of the access it had enjoyed to the sea during the Russian occupation of Alaska. Even direct relations between Britain and Canada were conducted on a somewhat inegalitarian basis. In 1880 Canada appointed its first High Commissioner in London. Britain not only refused to appoint a counterpart, on the grounds that the Governor-General represented imperial interests in Canada, but also refused to grant the Canadian representative the recognition that would have been accorded an ambassador. Again it was a point on which the precise role of the Crown came into question. How, in terms of Victorian political reasoning, could the monarch accept the credentials of an ambassador purporting to be her own representative, even though he came from another nation within the Empire?

For the time being, however, these matters of external policy were less important to the rulers of Canada than ensuring that internal authority was consistently Canadian. In some directions it was inevitably limited, and yet from the beginning Canadian leaders sought to overcome these limitations.

For example, the ultimate court of appeal for the whole Empire was the judicial committee of the Privy Council, a gathering of British judges. Canada set up its own Supreme Court in 1875, but this proved to be only one additional hurdle in the process of litigation, and persistent cases continued to find their way to the

Privy Council until this avenue of appeal was finally closed in 1949 and Canada became judicially self-contained.

Because Canadian confederation itself stemmed from imperial legislation, the judicial committee of the Privy Council even played its part—and more persistently than any Colonial Secretary would have dared attempt—in deciding how the Canadian constitution would operate in practice.

Parliament in London had passed the British North America Act, and until the Statute of Westminster there was no legal way it could be prevented from repealing it and returning Canada to the status of a group of Crown colonies. There was never any likelihood of such a bizarre eventuality, but Britain's position as the guardian of the Canadian constitution was on at least one occasion forced on the attention of the Dominion Government by direct intervention. This happened in 1874, after the Liberals, led by Alexander Mackenzie, deliberately slowed down progress on the Canadian Pacific Railway. Into the resulting dispute with British Columbia stepped the Colonial Secretary, Lord Carnarvon, and the Governor-General, Lord Dufferin, who listened to complaints from the Pacific coast and offered arbitration. Mackenzie first rejected, then appeared to accept, arbitration, but the fact of intervention was resented and led to a sharp inquiry about the Governor-General's rights in such matters. In fact, it could be interpreted that a dispute between the two levels of Canadian government was a point at which, in its role as guardian of the Canadian constitution, the British Cabinet had a legitimate right to intervene. But Whitehall learnt its lesson, and the Cabinet did not again directly intervene in Canadian internal politics.

Yet the Privy Council remained a means by which, without offering intervention but merely by considering pleas, Britain could continue to shape Canadian political life. The 1880s were a time of high regional feeling, when the provincial Governments grew restive under Macdonald's attempts to create a centralized nation-state. Macdonald's surrender to Ontario Orangemen, when he allowed the execution of Louis Riel for his part in the North-West Rebellion, played into the hands of the fiery regionalist Premier of Quebec, Honoré Mercier. Ontario, Manitoba and the Maritime Provinces all had their grievances against the federal Government and the powerful dominion-wide corporations with which they suspected it to be too closely linked. The Nova Scotia legislature actually passed in 1886 a series of resolutions which declared the right of the province to secede from confederation unless its grievances regarding taxation were placated.

This time the Colonial Office did not intervene, nor did Nova Scotia leave the confederation. But as a result of petitions from the disaffected provincial Governments following on the first Inter-provincial Conference called by Mercier in 1887, the judicial committee of the Privy Council interpreted the British North America Act in the direction of greater provincial autonomy, thus moving the political structure of Canada away from the concept of Ottawa supremacy on which Macdonald had based his policies, and establishing an equilibrium between the central and the local Governments which, with oscillations of emphasis (more centralization during wartime and more localization during peacetime), has continued to this day. The central Government learnt that it had either to reach agreement with the local administrations or to face the distasteful alternative of having its actions directed by a tribunal in London, and the result was a system of consultations in which, even if the federal and provincial Governments were often in disagreement, they sought compromises that would render external arbitration unnecessary.

By 1896, when Wilfrid Laurier became Prime Minister, Canada had finally established in practice the non-intervention of Britain in any internal affairs except the rare cases that found their way by the initiative of Canadian institutions or individuals to the Privy Council. As a French Canadian continually under pressure from the Quebec nationalists led by Henri Bourassa, Laurier was concerned to establish the freedom of Canada within the Empire, which circumstances forced him to interpret mainly in terms of military independence. Laurier's belief was that the Empire should be a 'galaxy of free states', and it was certainly in this sense that at the Diamond Jubilee he interpreted his role and those of his fellow colonial prime ministers; they were there, he believed, to represent nations that came voluntarily to offer their tribute to a common queen.

The core of Laurier's attitude was that there should be no obligation for a dominion to follow the policies of Britain, though this did not obviate a voluntary participation in any action that might follow from such policies. It was the right of choice that he wanted to retain in Canadian hands, and though he had to follow a difficult path between the extravagant loyalties of some English Canadians and the extreme isolationism of some French Canadians, he succeeded in establishing this voluntarist principle, and in the process contrived to take into Canadian hands many of the necessary attributes of independent nationhood.

Laurier fought his battles for independence largely at the colonial and imperial conferences, where he had to contend not only with the imperial centralization that the British Government tended to favour between the 1890s and the First World War, but also with the unquestioning Anglophilia of some of the Australian and New Zealand delegates.

Even at the colonial conference that celebrated the Diamond Jubilee, Laurier refused to be carried away by the euphoria of the occasion, and rejected as contrary to the spirit of the colonial constitutions the setting up of a permanent Imperial Council with power to regulate Empire tariffs, and to set the contributions of the various colonies towards imperial defence in terms of men, money and materials. 'Canada is a nation, Canada is free, and freedom is nationality', he remarked on this occasion.

In later conferences of 1902 and 1907 Laurier firmly rejected any arrangement that would imply a commitment to action on Canada's part though he had assisted Britain in a war of which he did not altogether approve by arranging for Canadian volunteers to be sent to South Africa; he did so on the strict understanding that Britain pay the entire cost of this limited participation, so that it might not be said that Canadian money was being used to fight an imperial war against the Boers, whose stand many French Canadians admired.

Laurier not only resisted military commitments for the future. He also brought national defence into Canadian hands by dismissing the British commander of the Canadian militia in 1904, and by arranging for Canadian forces to take over the garrisoning of Halifax and Esquimalt, so that the last remaining British troops left Canada in 1906. In 1909, when the Imperial Conference discussed a unified naval command for the Empire, Laurier argued that this would mean control by the Admiralty of ships and men paid for by Canada, and instead proposed a small and separate Canadian navy whose assistance could be offered in any crisis in which the Canadian Parliament found it necessary and appropriate to act. Laurier's Naval Services Bill was passed by the Canadian

Parliament in 1910 after a bitter struggle in which the strength of the Canadian imperialists, led by the Maritime Conservative Sir Robert Borden, was clearly demonstrated.

Laurier's triumph was a hollow one; he was shortly defeated by an attack which exploited an inconsistency that has constantly haunted Liberal politics in Canada. It was usually during Liberal administrations that decisions were made that contributed to the loosening of imperial ties, but during Liberal administrations also the greatest favour has been shown to the kind of co-operation with the United States which political enemies can easily interpret as continentalism, aimed at replacing British influence by American influence. Laurier followed his Naval Services Bill by calling an election in which the main Liberal proposal was a new agreement with the United States on reciprocity in tariffs. This enabled the Conservatives to fan the double fires of imperialism—directed against a party that had ruined the prospect of a great Empire navy—and anti-Americanism, encouraged by the catchy slogan 'No truck nor trade with the Yankees'. Laurier was defeated and his plans for a Canadian navy were not fulfilled for a number of years.

Laurier's political career was finally destroyed by the First World War, when he stood by his promise to the French Canadians to resist conscription and led the Liberal Party to a shattering defeat over this issue in the elections of 1917. This was ironical, since it was Laurier's firm policy over Canadian military commitments that enabled his successors during and after the First World War to establish Canada not only as a completely independent nation within the Empire but also as a recognized international entity.

When war was declared in 1914, there was no doubt in the minds of Canadians of any party, except for a few French Canadian nationalists and even fewer international socialists, not only that Canada was legally at war, but that this was a war in which she was morally and politically obliged to take part. Canada, like the other dominions, accepted that whatever the disagreements between the parts of the Empire in times of peace, in war it presented a united front; Britain's declaration of war bound them automatically. There were of course other contributing factors, including strong impulses of sentiment; colonials of British birth tended to volunteer early and in large numbers. And there were strong political reasons for each of the dominions to enter the war. Australia and

New Zealand were anxious, for their own safety, to preserve British power in the Levant so that the Suez Canal would be unendangered. These dominions and South Africa wished to eliminate the German colonies in their vicinities, and were not averse from a little imperializing on their own account. And even Canada, though it had nothing territorially to gain from the war, and faced no immediate perils from a German victory, was aware that the destruction of Britain as a world power and the disruption of the European political pattern would lead to an international anarchy whose consequences would be incalculable.

But there were always reservations in the Canadian mind, because it was a divided mind, and the French Canadians did not feel the same urge as their English-speaking compatriots. Many French Canadians in fact volunteered, and some Quebec regiments gained a formidable fighting reputation. But Quebec had been detached from Europe more than a hundred and fifty years before, and the French Revolution had deepened the gulf, so that despite the French language and the vestiges of antique Europeanism that lingered in the villages along the St Lawrence, the French Canadian was more North American in his detachment from European concerns than other Canadians, apart from the Indians and the Eskimos. The war revived flagging imperial sentiments in English-speaking Canada; it had the reverse effect in French-speaking Canada. The bitterness that ensued when the English-speaking Conservatives imposed nation-wide conscription is a fact of Canada's inner history and belongs only peripherally to an account of imperial decline. Yet precisely because the French Canadian attitude to an imposed imperial loyalty was a disturbing internal factor, it strengthened externally the progress towards Canadian nationhood, since it forced Canadian leaders to demonstrate at each step that they were acting independently of British dictation. Among other things it led them to insist that their troops should form a separate Canadian Corps under Canadian command, a precursor of the Canadian Army that fought in the Second World War.

In 1917 an Imperial War Cabinet was created at whose intermittent sittings the dominion prime ministers attended; this dealt with the immediate issues involved in fighting the war. For the wider issues that the war's termination would bring into focus, the Imperial War Conference was created. In one way these were clever devices invented by Lloyd George to give the dominions a sense of intimate participation in decisions relating to war and peace that substantially were made by a small inner group of British leaders. Nevertheless, it was a case in which shadow became almost as important as substance, for Resolution IX of the 1917 Imperial Conference described Britain and the dominions as autonomous nations within the Imperial Commonwealth, and declared that they must all have an adequate voice in the formulation of foreign policy in so far as the Empire was concerned. This resolution did not go so deeply into issues of dominion sovereignty as the discussions of the Imperial Conferences of 1926 and 1930, and it did not have the binding legality of the Statute of Westminster, but it laid the foundations for the advances in national status that the dominions achieved at the end of the war.

Here again the initiative rested largely with Canada, for it was Sir Robert Borden's protest that led Lloyd George to agree that all the dominions, together with India (but excluding Newfoundland), should be represented at the Versailles Peace Conference on an equal footing with such lesser powers as Belgium, and that in addition the British delegation itself should include one of the dominion prime ministers, serving in rotation. The dominions signed the peace treaty, and became founding members of the League of Nations, where—at first regarded as extra mouth-pieces of British policy—they slowly attained stature as independent sovereignties, until in 1927 Canada was elected to a non-permanent seat on the League Council.

The period between 1919 and 1927 represented the real watershed in the winning of diplomatic independence and international recognition on the part of the dominions. The policy pursued by Canada was a rather ambivalent one, since the Canadians were willing to interfere with British foreign policy where it suited their ends, but asserted their independence where that seemed more desirable. At the Imperial Conference of 1921, for example, it was Arthur Meighen, the Canadian Prime Minister, who persuaded Britain to abandon the treaty with Japan. The same conference accepted the fact that Britain could no more than hope to equal the single largest rival navy, and it was on this basis that the dominions took part in the British delegation at the Washington Conference of 1921; so far as the Canadians were concerned, it was of little consequence whether the American or the British fleet were larger, so long as both exceeded that of the Japanese, whose rising power across the Pacific was increasingly feared by western Canadians.

Later in 1921 the Liberals returned to power, and William Lyon Mackenzie King, grandson of the rebel of 1837, took up Laurier's nationalist role. King had neither his grandfather's fiery impetuosity nor Laurier's urbane charm, but he combined with some extraordinary private superstitions a shrewd political instinct. The experience of the war had taught him that the delicate balance between the various peoples of Canada was easily disturbed by external complications, and he proceeded to act firmly on this conclusion. The occasion to demonstrate his view that diplomatic independence was essential for national survival came in 1922, when Mustapha Kemal's Young Turks were threatening the British occupying troops in Chanak and Lloyd George sent out appeals to the dominions for supporting contingents. Mackenzie King refused to regard Canada as automatically bound, and ignored the repeated British attempts to elicit Canadian aid. 'I am sure the people of Canada are against participation in the European war', he noted in his famous diary, and he also remarked more pointedly, 'If membership within the British Empire means participation by the dominions in any and every war in which Great Britain becomes involved, without consultation, conference or agreement of any kind in advance, I can see no hope for an enduring relationship.' The Chanak crisis passed without actual conflict, but Canada refused to ratify the Treaty of Lausanne, which, in 1923, settled the differences between Britain and Turkey, and two years later, with the other dominions, declined to take part in the Locarno Conference or to be bound by the treaty that resulted.

Not only were the dominions determined to be uninvolved in the international complications into which Britain was led by its interests in Europe and the Middle East; they began to seek a more active diplomatic life of their own. Canada had established its Department of External Affairs as early as 1909, but it did not set up any diplomatic missions abroad until 1923, when with Ireland it led the dominions by appointing consular representatives in the United States. Also in 1923 Canada independently signed its first treaty—an agreement with the United States relating to halibut fisheries—without British participation. Washington prudently checked with Westminster before actually signing the treaty, but the British Foreign Office indicated its approval, thereby terminating a policy of diplomatic subordination formulated in 1895 when the Colonial Secretary ruled that the negotiation of any treaty with a foreign power must be in the hands of a representative of the imperial Government acting in association with a representative of the dominion or self-governing colony in question. In 1927, when it appointed its first ambassador to Washington, Canada attained full diplomatic maturity; shortly afterwards it established missions in Paris and Tokyo.

When the Imperial Conference of 1930 accepted the diplomatic as well as the legislative pretensions of the dominions, and the Statute of Westminster gave them legal form, these were in fact little more than ceremonial acts, of understandings already accepted. By 1914 the internal autonomy of the dominions had been secured; the last effective channel of imperial interference, the judicial committee of the Privy Council, was used with increasing scarcity for matters of constitutional importance. Before the end of the 1920s, the contributions in men and materials which the dominions made during the First World War, and the diminution of Britain's stature which victory paradoxically brought, had combined to make nationalism in the white settlement colonies and in Ireland a fact that needed only formal acceptance. But even formal acceptance was important; it signified Britain's dawning realization that the imperial era was drawing towards a close.

X Variant Dominions

In many ways the evolution of the other dominions towards the point of independence represented by the Statute of Westminster was similar to that of Canada. Yet there were significant differences, and the relative rapidity and eagerness with which the emerging nations detached themselves from the tutelage of Whitehall was closely related to their past histories and to their particular socio-political situations in the early twentieth century.

In differentiating Canada's role as pioneer in this development we have had to consider not only the fact that it had a past in another Empire, which left a hostage population, but also the constant changes taking place during the century since confederation in its relationship with the United States. If Canada showed almost truculent independence in its foreign relations between 1922 and 1925, this was not merely because the wartime troubles between French and English Canadians had made Mackenzie King nervous about accepting European commitments. It was also because, in becoming more isolationist towards Britain, Canada had become temporarily more continentalist towards the United States.

This was partly a result of King's personal inclinations and of his experience as a student of American industrial relations, which led him to overvalue the links between American and Canadian industrial and labour corporations. But there were deeper economic reasons. The United States had long been Canada's leading customer in international trade. But, owing to the financial strains which Britain underwent during the First World War, a shift in economic relations on a much deeper level had taken place by the early 1920s. In 1900 Britain controlled 85 per cent of all foreign investment in Canada, and the United States only 14 per cent. By 1922 the Americans controlled already 50 per cent of such investment and Britain had dropped to second place with 47 per cent. This was an unreversed progress, and by the end of the Second World War, which forced a massive selling of British overseas investments, American interests would control 72 per cent of foreign investment in Canada and Britain's stake would be negligible.

But the change in Canadian attitudes was more than a matter of economic relationships, which are always slow to affect the surface of political life. Canada was the first of the dominions to realize that henceforward she could not rely on Britain alone for protection in time of war. The economic imperatives that had forced Britain to the negotiating tables in Washington in 1921 had ended for ever her title to command the world's oceans. It was only certain seas she would now be able to patrol effectively, and because of the primacy of her interest in India, the main naval concentration outside British waters would be in the Mediterranean, the Red Sea, the Indian Ocean and the South Atlantic. Similarly, because of a new focusing of British territorial and oil interests in the Middle East after 1918, the main British air strength outside England would lie in Iraq, Jordan and Egypt. In the Pacific, British naval activity, once commanding, was reduced to coastal and riparian patrol duties, and the Americans and Japanese ruled the deep waters; even in the North Atlantic Britain was no longer all-powerful.

In any crisis, the Royal Navy would concentrate first on keeping open the Suez Canal, and Canada's most immediate protection from attack by sea would be the American navy. There were, at this time, no mutual defence agreements between Canada and the United States such as exist today. Indeed, during the 1920s the secret war plans to which the Canadian General Staff gave the highest priority envisaged a hypothetical American invasion, but no Canadians, except a few brass-hats oriented to 1812, took the possibility seriously. Most Canadians believed that the United States would, out of sheer self-interest, come to their aid in the event of invasion. The lingering fear was not of American inaction, but that Canada might be chosen—under the guise of protection—as a battleground to save American soil.

No other dominion, with the exception of Ireland, could afford to be as confidently independent of Britain as Canada began to feel in the 1920s. And Ireland was perhaps the only dominion which

accepted the Statute of Westminster at the time of its promulga-
tion as merely a temporary convenience, for Ireland was the one
participant in the discussions leading to the Statute whose leaders
attached no importance to the idea of dominion status. For them
it was merely a stage in the progress towards a complete independence which they intended to secure as quickly as they could. The
Irish were not greatly troubled with the problem of defence;
they believed that there was no need for a formal alliance with
Britain, since in its own interests that country would protect them
from a potential invader. And Britain, whatever the formal
relationship between the two countries, would always have a need
for Ireland's farm produce. Ireland could thus combine actual
dependence with a fine illusion of independence.

The situations of the three other dominions were somewhat
different, since none of them lay close to a country that would
automatically protect it in time of crisis and all were lightly
industrialized, dependent on foreign trade, and especially British
trade. More than 70 per cent of New Zealand's exports and 55
per cent of South Africa's exports went in 1930 to Britain; more
than 50 per cent of Australia's foreign trade was with other parts
of the Empire. Such countries clearly had a vested interest in
sustaining the great imperial trade routes. If Britain thought Suez
was essential to keep open the seaway to India, Australia and New
Zealand thought it must be protected to sustain their lifeline to
Britain, and thus soldiers from both dominions fought in the
Levant during the two World Wars. Similarly, South Africa was
as concerned as Britain to sustain the Cape route, and the presence
of the British navy at Simonstown was accepted with little
question until after the Second World War.

Among these dominions New Zealand stands at the point of
virtually diametrical opposition to Ireland, for it was almost reluctantly that this most distant of dominions accepted her independence, as if it were an imposition of destiny rather than a
gift. Though New Zealand took part in all the discussions leading
up to the Statute of Westminster, not until 1947 did its Government take advantage of the Statute's provisions; this decision was
reached only after the events of the Second World War had convinced New Zealanders that they could no longer rely on Britain
for protection in their Pacific remoteness.

The ANZUS pact of 1951, by which the United States guaranteed the integrity of both Australia and New Zealand without Britain's participation, was the logical end of a shifting of power relations that began in formal terms with the Washington Treaty of 1921 and the withdrawal of British naval power from the Pacific, but which went virtually unrecognized in the southern part of that ocean, until the shock of 1941, when Pearl Harbor was bombed; when two of the great British capital ships on which the Australasians had relied for protection were destroyed off Malaya; when Malaya itself fell and Japanese forces swept south-eastwards as far as the Solomons, where they were held not by the armies or warships of the British Empire but by those of the United States. The New Zealanders were not happy about this change in protectors, for it portended an imperial Götterdämmerung which they did not want to acknowledge. And despite ANZUS New Zealand has been as little inclined to accept American as she always was to accept Australian leadership. Once, in 1890, New Zealand and the six states of Australia conferred on the question of a local federation, but the discussions were predictably inconclusive, and when the Commonwealth of Australia came into being New Zealand did not join it. The present century has seen no real shift in New Zealand's basic choice, to sustain the British links as long as possible, in economic if not in political terms, and then to make the adjustments that will combine a fair degree of economic and political security with genuine independence.

The unemphatic nature of New Zealand's part in the events that led up to the metamorphosis of Empire into Commonwealth reflects the smoothness of her earlier progression towards independence within the Empire. The only period when there was any marked strife between the New Zealanders and the imperial Government was comparatively early, between the 1850s and the 1870s, and even then it was distinguished by nothing so dramatic as Canada's small but violent rebellions or even Australia's Eureka Stockade. That early situation in New Zealand was complicated by the presence of the Maoris as a large and warlike indigenous population and by the fact that at the celebrated meeting of Captain Hobson with the Maori chiefs at Waitangi in 1840 sovereignty was ceded on condition that the land should remain the property of the native people except where it was sold to the Crown.

Wakefield's New Zealand Company had already acquired lands

before the 'treaty' of Waitangi was made, and the disputes over these and other deals provoked warfare between the Maoris and the settlers, so that it was several years before Sir George Grey, the third Governor, could achieve even a temporary pacification. Grey resisted demands for a representative assembly and even persuaded the imperial Government not to implement an Act passed in 1846 for that purpose, since he feared the consequences if a few thousand settlers were allowed to legislate the fate of a majority of Maoris in a somewhat truculent mood. Only when he had brought some order into the country was a further law enacted, the New Zealand Constitution Act (1852) under which the first Assembly met in 1854, and responsible government was granted in 1856. The imperial Government temporarily reserved Maori affairs and land sales in the hands of the Governor. In 1862 this field was handed to the New Zealand Cabinet, and the islands became internally self-governing in every respect.

The immediate result was a Native Land Act authorizing direct purchases by settlers from the Maoris. This led to a recurrence of disputes followed by warfare, in which the Maoris were led by millenarian prophets who combined customary Polynesian beliefs with chiliastic elements from the teachings of the missionaries and a rather grotesque parody of European ideas of sovereignty, expressed in the so-called 'King movement' and in sects like Ringatu, which continue to influence Maoris even in the late twentieth century with their strange amalgam of pagan concepts and Christian dogma. The later Maori Wars began sporadically in 1860, and assumed such serious proportions by 1863 that considerable numbers of imperial troops had to be employed, supported by gunboats on the rivers, by settler volunteers and by levies from among the Maoris who were traditionally hostile to the rebels.

The situation bred dispute between the colony and the imperial Government, which, after the extravagances of the Crimean War, was intent on reducing military expenditures and had hoped that on gaining responsible government New Zealand would assume the cost of maintaining internal order. In 1865 London reduced the military establishment to four regiments, and decreed that the New Zealand Government must pay for them at the rate of £40 per soldier per year. This created resentment among the settlers at what seemed a petty-minded economizing on the part of Britain's rulers, and in 1870—for the first and only time in New

Zealand's history—there was broad and loud talk of secession and even of annexation to the United States. The Americans, who had recently ignored an offer of Fiji by its paramount chief Cakobau, showed no signs of response, and the movement quickly fell away when New Zealanders realized that, now the Maori threat had passed, the British navy was a better protection than the British army from the foreign powers who successively seemed to threaten isolated Pacific nations. (Russia was the favourite bogy in the 1870s, as was Germany in the following decade.) A decade later the relationship between New Zealand and Britain was transformed by the successful development in 1880 of the first refrigerated ship.

This revolution in ocean transport meant that the great pasturelands of New Zealand, whose exports had hitherto been restricted almost entirely to wool, could now find foreign markets for their meat, butter and cheese, and from this point a symbiotic trading pattern arose between New Zealand and Britain that inevitably affected political relationships. For the past ninety years Britain had been the leading importer of New Zealand produce; once it took more than three-quarters of the dominion's exports, and even recently, on the eve of entry into the Common Market, it has been taking between 35 and 40 per cent.

From 1880 onwards New Zealand became a relatively prosperous pastoral country with a considerable urban life that depended on the products of the farms. Changes in the political structure had already taken place in the 1870s when the ten provincial Governments were abolished and a single centralized administration created in their place. The result of these parallel developments was a surge of New Zealand nationalism, under leaders like Joseph Seddon, accompanied by strong imperialist sentiments. New Zealand was economically supported by her British markets and protected by the British navy. After the Maori wars came to an end, Britain interfered little with internal affairs, and the Governors she sent were mostly bland, inactive men. Since most New Zealanders were British by descent and few had convict ancestors, there was never any sense of the British Government representing an alien race or a detested class, and New Zealanders were generally content to leave the wider imperial issues to whoever ruled in Westminster without much thought that their interests might be mishandled; they were fortunate in having no neighbour like the United States whose relations with Britain might adversely affect their own.

As early as the first conference of colonial premiers, New Zealand agreed to contribute to the expenses of the Royal Navy; not until 1913 did she decide to set up her own minute naval force. New Zealand riflemen fought against the Boers in South Africa, and in neither World War was there any doubt that New Zealand should support Britain to the utmost; indeed, at the critical point of the Second World War, when Japan entered the conflict, New Zealand did not follow Australia's example of withdrawing its forces from the Middle East to the Pacific, but accepted Churchill's persuasions and left its troops to take part in the Italian campaign rather than recalling them for home defence.

Given such a record of imperial loyalty, in which the labour movement hardly differed from the more conservative elements, it is hardly surprising that New Zealand leaders tended to be interested in imperial federation, which they saw in terms of a partnership in which the juniors would have a growing voice. This view became sharper after New Zealand acquired dominion status in 1907, and at the Imperial Conference of 1911 the Prime Minister, Sir Joseph Ward, proposed that the dominions be regularly consulted in the shaping of foreign policy. Asquith coldly replied that imperial foreign policy was British policy and could only be made in Britain. The fact that such a remark could not possibly have been made after 1918 illustrates the accelerating changes that took place in imperial attitudes from the beginning of the twentieth century.

There were, after the 1870s, only two issues on which New Zealand tended at times to differ sharply from Britain. One was the question of the Pacific islands. New Zealand shared both Australia's fears of French and German penetration into the Pacific and its ambition to enhance its own national status by the creation of a micro-empire. In the 1890s Joseph Seddon actually spon- sored—to the great annoyance of the Colonial Office—an agitation among planters in Fiji to get the administration of the group transferred from Whitehall to Wellington, and there was great indignation in New Zealand when Germany was allowed to annex Western Samoa. In compensation, New Zealand was allotted the Cook Islands and other small Pacific possessions; Samoa, how- ever, continued to be a source of patriotic anguish, and as soon

as war was declared in 1914 a New Zealand force set off northward
and captured Apia; Samoa became the first addition to the British
Empire during the First World War.

New Zealanders were also inclined to be unashamedly racist in
their imperial views; most of their leaders, irrespective of party,
believed firmly in the innate superiority of the Anglo-Saxon race,
and the Yellow Peril—that late-nineteenth-century nightmare of
invading hordes of Chinese and Japanese—seemed so real to them
that they created immigration codes which virtually restricted
entry to Europeans. Such a policy aroused disapproval in the
Colonial Office, which paid at least lip-service to the idea of an
empire in which men of all races and colours were potentially
equal, but New Zealand was hardly out of line with the other
dominions, for Australia's policy was equally restrictive from an
early date, Canada closed its frontiers to Asians early in the twentieth century, and South Africa refused the privileges of citizenship not only to the native black population but also to Indians.

The Australian implants so different an image on the mind from the
New Zealander that one is tempted to overemphasize the divergent
roles of these two southern dominions. By the early nineteenth
century the convict-heritage had created in Australia a class of
native-born residents who inherited the grudges of their fathers,
oppressed as prisoners or discriminated against as emancipates.
This type of Australian inclined towards a nationalism that was all
the more strident since those who held it had to recognize a con-
tinual dependence on Britain for naval defence and for commercial support as the world's great wool market.

The strong trade union movement in Australia, the Labour
Party which rose early to a position of influence, and the Nationalist Party were all projections of these frustrated social emotions,
aggravated by the strong Catholic Irish element in the population
and by the curiously stratified form that Australian society—
despite much lip-service to democratic forms—assumed in
practice, typified in the gentry who still appear in grey toppers
and frock coats for the annual social rite at the Melbourne race-
course.

Like New Zealand, Australia was early preoccupied with the
establishment of its own subsidiary empire, and like New Zealand
it developed a racist orientation expressed most blatantly in the

White Australia policy of the Nationalist Party, with which the Labour leaders tacitly agreed. Indeed, the Australians went even further than the New Zealanders in their views of white supremacy, for where the latter eventually gave full civil rights to the Maoris and encouraged their assimilation into the general life of the country, the policy of the Australians towards the aborigines varied from extermination in Tasmania to condemnation to helotry in the rest of the country. Australian nationalism was directed exclusively towards building and giving stature to a country of Europeans and their descendants, and even the democratic social manners that developed in Australia projected this feeling, for they were based on the concept of a society that was not only equal but also homogenous; a coloured skin was as unacceptable as a display of patrician manners.

Australia's imperial policy can be seen as a magnification of the national ideal of 'mateship', a concept that had arisen partly from the need for mutual aid in the bush, and partly from the insistent demand for equal treatment on the part of the sons of the convicts. Mateship lay at the very basis of the Australian Commonwealth: of the fact that it was a federation of equal states rather than a centralized legislative union such as New Zealand became; of the fact that it had to be confirmed by a referendum in which every man in every state could vote; of the fact that no state's capital could be allowed precedence, so that Canberra was built in the bush as a neutral centre of government. And it explained the attraction which the idea of a federal empire, in which all the partners would have an equal voice, exercised over Australian leaders until the most critical point of the Second World War.

Yet the idea of mateship was inseparable from the idea of personal pride. Ideally, it could be conceived in Kiplingesque terms as a meeting of strong men for mutual advantage. Arguments of the need for common defence at a time when the Germans were menacingly active in the South Pacific persuaded the Australian colonies to give up the passionately separatist loyalties that had divided them for almost half a century since the first responsible Governments were created on the island continent. And the somewhat uncritical willingness to accept imperial bonds which the Australians displayed in one Whitehall gathering of prime ministers after another was combined at times with emphatic and not very subtle manifestations of nationalist dissent.

The difference between the Australians and New Zealanders on one hand and the Canadians on the other was shown very clearly at the Imperial Conference of 1911. Australia strongly urged that the British Government consult the dominions before it signed treaties that bound the Empire. Wilfrid Laurier, however, was opposed to the motion, not because he agreed with Asquith's view that Britain was necessarily the dominant partner in the Empire; he believed that if a dominion gave advice on an imperial treaty, then it was bound to support the British Government in any action consequent on the advice being taken, and he did not want to tie Canada in moral bonds of this kind.

Canada tended, as did South Africa and Ireland, to take a somewhat legalistic view of the imperial links that remained after dominion status had been achieved, seeking constant definition and narrowing, and the difference from Australia and New Zealand was shown in the dominions' varying reactions to the Statute of Westminster. Canada worked hard for the Statute and immediately accepted it; the Australians regarded it with suspicion that verged on alarm. Robert Menzies thought that those who demanded and framed it had done 'a great disservice' to the Empire, and that it had been a mistake to reduce to an explicit formula something that should have been observed in the spirit, not recorded in the letter. He was almost echoing Churchill's view of the Statute as 'a repellent legalism'. The difference in views arose from the fact that by 1931 Canada already believed it had other viable options than unquestioning acceptance of the Empire, while the Australians and New Zealanders still believed that they needed the British navy and the Suez Canal; even as late as 1956 they would vote with Britain in the United Nations on the Suez question. With the Statute of Westminster the Canadians felt they had been given the front-door key; the Australians feared they had been locked out.

Yet Australian national pride grew strong and demanded its occasional gestures of independence. At the time of the South African War, the state Parliaments debated freely before they agreed, with proper show of reluctance, to send troops to fight beside the British. In 1908, first of all the dominions, Australia established its own naval squadron. At the end of the First World War the Australians and the New Zealanders were not only truculently insistent on retaining the possessions they had seized

from the Germans, but also objected successfully to an attempt
to institute free immigration into the mandated territories, which
W. M. Hughes, the Australian Prime Minister who took a
pugnacious role in the Versailles Peace Conference, feared would
mean a mass infiltration of Japanese into New Guinea. And,
strangely, it was Australia that, by raising a difficult constitutional
question, precipitated the discussions at the Imperial Conference
of 1930 which led to the Statute of Westminster.

In 1930 the time came to appoint a new Governor-General to
Australia. In accordance with the tradition that had obtained in all
the dominions since Canadian confederation, the retiring
Governor-General was a British peer, Lord Stonehaven. But the
Government of Australia was in the hands of the Labour Party,
and the Prime Minister, James Scullin, was an obstinate democrat,
who decided that his country no longer needed an effete English
aristocrat as its acting head of state. According, he proposed a man
who on two counts would break with precedent; for Isaac Isaacs
was an Australian and a commoner. King George V, who had
strong ideas on constitutional propriety, did not object openly to
Isaacs as a commoner, but he did contend that a Governor-
General, as his representative, must be British. Accordingly, he
refused to accept Scullin's nominee. The Labour Government in
London was highly embarrassed, and finally, when Lord Passfield
could find no Fabian way out, it passed the matter on to the
Imperial Conference later in the year, which decided that in such
cases the King should act according to the advice of his ministers
in the dominion concerned. George V made a final effort to persuade Scullin to abandon Isaacs, but the Australian Prime Minister
was obdurate, and his man became Governor-General. The discussion of constitutional principles in the case of Isaacs prepared
the way for the Statute of Westminster, and left the Australians
somewhat appalled at the consequences of Scullin's obstinacy.

The adjustments in allegiance which Canada made in the 1920s
did not really begin in Australia until the Second World War
brought the Japanese threat into the centre of the country's vision.
Australians had not been unaware of that threat as the Japanese
moved aggressively into China in the 1930s, but they had been
divided in their views of how to meet it. The United Australia
Party, then in power, believed in supporting an imperial system
of defence, and, with as little regard for its weakness by land as the

British General Staff, looked to Singapore as their bastion of defence. The Labour Party stressed the need for non-involvement in the British defence system and advocated the building up of a massive independent air force to sink an invading navy.

In the crucial year of 1941 the Labour Party came into power, and early in 1942 John Joseph Curtin made the decision one can regard as the first Australian declaration of independence. When Malaya fell to the Japanese, he recalled the Australian Seventh Division from the Near East to safeguard the homeland. On February 17th he categorically refused a request from the Pacific War Council in London to send the division to Burma, and in the next few days resisted the urgent appeals of both Churchill and Roosevelt; the Seventh Division returned home and shortly afterwards began clearing the Japanese invaders from New Guinea. From this point, with the growing realization that if any power could help to protect her it would be the United States and not Britain, the attitude of Australia began to approximate to that of Canada. Autonomy became yearly more extended, and 1951 marked the symbolic emergence of Australia into national independence with the signing of the ANZUS pact as an alliance outside the dying imperial partnership.

I have left South Africa and Ireland to the last among the white dependencies of the Empire partly for chronological reasons. The Union of South Africa was just over twenty years old and the Irish Free State had been in existence less than a decade when the crucial discussions leading to the Statute of Westminster took place. But there is an even better reason for ending with these two late dominions; their history illustrates most clearly how complexly and often paradoxically interrelated were the various aspects of the Second Empire's disintegration.

On the surface there is little evident relationship, for example, between the Boer Republics and the South Africa they later dominated, and the Asian countries which gained autonomy a quarter of a century after South Africa, and which in the end were largely responsible for South Africa's departure, not from the Empire, but from the Commonwealth. Yet it is a notable fact of imperial history that Gandhi developed in South Africa, and against white South Africans, the strategy of non-violence known as *satyagraha* which he later used with terminal effect against the British in India.

By the peculiar combination of non-violent resistance and moral blackmail at which he was so adept, he forced Smuts into negotiation, and out of negotiation emerged the Indian Relief Act, which removed a number of legal disabilities inflicted on Indian immigrants. But the Indians were never accepted as full citizens of South Africa, and in recent decades their situation as a marginal people has steadily worsened.

The question of racial relations within South Africa is a tortuous one. But it is fair to say that, though there have been profound disagreements between the two white peoples, the Afrikaners and the English have not differed profoundly in their racist inclinations. Even before the South African War, it was mainly the British Government, embarrassed by the urgings of humanitarians and radicals at home, that was concerned for the rights of the Bantus and other native peoples in Africa. With few exceptions, the British in South Africa were convinced that the Africans were potentially dangerous and must be kept resolutely in what the whites decided should be their place; they must in no circumstances be granted political equality. White manual workers—who were mainly British—closed their unions to blacks, and insisted on the maintenance of racially differentiated patterns of wages. Even Gandhi was concerned only with the rights of the Indians; while he was in South Africa he had very little to say on behalf of the native peoples, and most of his fellow Indians shared the racial prejudices of the whites.

The creation of the Union of South Africa in 1910 was a triumph for the Afrikaners, achieved because the Boer leaders Smuts and Botha adopted a technique of moral pressure not unlike that which Gandhi had deployed against them. The British were so appalled by the military difficulties of the South African War, and so sensitive to the harm it had done to their imperial image, that they were resolved to avoid a repetition of armed conflict. The only way they could do so was by taking the Boers into the imperial partnership, which they did in two stages: by granting responsible government to the Boer provinces in 1907 and by establishing three years later a Union in which the Afrikaners were in a permanent majority among the white population. When Milner remarked bitterly from his imperialist point of view in 1908 that the granting of responsible government to the Orange Free State and the Transvaal meant a return to 'government by the commandos', he was undoubtedly correct. But Campbell-Bannerman was also correct when he said in 1903, 'The truth is, we cannot provide for a fighting Empire, and nothing will give us that power.' The price for the deal that had to be made with the Boers for the perpetual occupation of Simonstown and the guarantee of the long route to India was the abandonment of the native peoples in the four colonies.

Smuts and Botha accepted the union on the justified assumption that from this point there would be no opposition from Britain and little from the British local residents to the perpetuation of a colour-stratified society. Under the agreement reached by the national convention of representatives from the four colonies in 1908 and 1909—and confirmed by the British Parliament when it passed the South Africa Act in 1910—the franchise was to remain as at the time of union in each of the colonies. This meant that only a small number of non-white residents—the Cape Coloured people, who were completely Europeanized in culture—were ever allowed to vote, and even they were removed in 1933 from the common roll and forced to vote separately for whites to represent their interests in a Parliament uncontaminated by the presence of coloured men.

Yet at the time of the union, South Africa was not so far removed from the other white dominions in its racial attitudes as the dimensions of the situation might suggest. Until after the Second World War Britain was the only country of the Empire—with the special exception of the Maoris in New Zealand—in which a man not of European ancestry could enjoy full civil rights; an Indian or an African who was a British subject could vote as soon as he had established residence in Britain, and as early as 1892—in defiance of Lord Salisbury who asserted that Britons would never elect a 'black man'—the voters of the London borough of Finsbury sent as their member to the House of Commons the Indian leader Dadabhai Naoroji; this, incidentally, was the first sign of a susceptibility among ordinary Britons to the kind of appeal to their sense of fairness on which Gandhi was to rely so heavily at a later stage in imperial history.

What the example of South Africa showed very clearly was that the process by which imperial power was devolved among local states on the peripheries of empire was no guarantee of internal freedom within the self-governing units which were thus created.

No more than in other historical settings did national independence guarantee either social justice within the independent territory or the liberation of 'inferior' groups from discrimination. The liberation of the United States had already demonstrated this fact; while slavery was abolished in the British West Indies in 1838, it survived in the southern states until 1865.

Once dominion status had been achieved by South Africa in 1910, the aim of the dominant Afrikaner group was to gain the complete freedom of action that would enable them to establish the domination over the black Africans which they felt was necessary for their material prosperity and their safety alike. On this question the differences between Smuts the imperialist, Hertzog the nationalist and Malan the extreme nationalist were differences only in tactics, not in ultimate objectives. Smuts and Botha believed that most was to be gained by infiltrating the British imperial ruling class; they showed their loyalty during the First World War by suppressing a rebellion of their former comrades in arms and by seizing German territory in Africa. Then Smuts proceeded to London, where alone among colonial politicians he was admitted to the centre of policy-making, the British War Cabinet—an instrument of power quite different from the Imperial War Cabinet, which was devised mainly as a forum for the expression of dominion views.

Smuts was careful to limit his imperialism to the areas where collaboration was beneficial to white South Africa. He opposed the imperial federation which conservative Australians favoured, since this would have imposed limitations on too many local interests, and he was always ready to presume on the trust his charm and intelligence had aroused among British statesmen to state home truths about the relative status of Britain and other units of the Empire. He reminded the representatives of the dominions at the Imperial War Conference in 1917 that, whatever they might think, 'we are subject provinces of Great Britain'. At the Washington Conference in 1921 he remarked that the presence of dominion prime ministers did not mean that they had yet been recognized as 'international persons', since they had not been invited to represent their own countries, but merely to swell the United Kingdom delegation and make it appear more impressive. Whatever immediate advantage might be gained from membership of the Empire, Smuts preferred to think in the looser terms of a Commonwealth, a term he tended to use freely before most other imperial politicians; he conceived it in the nebulous shape of an inspirational association, a form which it would actually assume.

The active support which South Africa gave the Canadian delegation at all the imperial conferences between the two World Wars was directed entirely to establishing such a legally recognized mastership over South African affairs that the Afrikaners would be able to do whatever they wished internally without having to pay attention to British public opinion. A first step was achieved when the South African command of the British army was terminated in 1921 and the last imperial troops departed; it was done with a great appearance of good will, and the day seemed distant when English crowds had roared their hatred of the Boers on Mafeking Night and Swinburne had chanted, 'Strike, England, and strike home!'

In 1929, following Canada's example, South Africa began to develop an independent foreign policy, establishing embassies in Washington, the Hague and Rome, and concluding a trade treaty with Germany. Once the Statute of Westminster had been secured, Smuts became noticeably less ardent in his imperial sentiments, and in 1933 he and Hertzog came together to form the United Party, leaving in isolation both the extreme Afrikaner nationalists led by Daniel Malan and the extreme British loyalists of the Dominion Party. Yet it was Smuts and Hertzog who passed the laws that provided the foundation on which the heirs of Malan built up *apartheid*. The Status Act and the Seals Act complemented the Statute of Westminster in 1934 by declaring South Africa's internal and external independence and making it in all but name a republic. (It had already been the first dominion to choose in 1927 a national flag that eliminated all British symbolism.) Then by a series of restrictive acts, confirming electoral disabilities, strengthening the reserve system, and providing for the segregation of blacks in towns and cities, the Smuts–Hertzog regime established the pattern on which later Afrikaner nationalists would create a society so divergent from the general post-imperial trend within the Commonwealth that further association would and did become impossible.

The struggle for the independence of the white-dominated State of South Africa has obviously no direct links with the struggles of the subject colonial peoples that began to move into the foreground during the 1930s. Though they exchanged some curious courtesies, it is hard to imagine two attitudes more opposed than those of Smuts and Gandhi—and Smuts was the most polished of South African racists. But history creates strange indirect relationships, and just as life in South Africa taught Gandhi to be a rebel, so also events there in the long run militated in favour of those colonial liberation movements whose parallels the Afrikaners have always suppressed. The South African War, for example, was the first war in which Britain's military vulnerability was demonstrated. If the numerically weak Boer commandos could so paralyse the great British army, what might not other rebels with much vaster manpower resources do? And then there was the policy of conciliation which produced the strange result— at least in terms of known imperial precedents—of two defeated provinces being granted internal self-government five years after they had been overcome. Admittedly, this had happened in a situation where the rival white peoples could not afford to remain long in discord if they wished to retain control over the black majority; still, it showed that there were occasions in which Britain might be blackmailed into making concessions for fear of the consequences of doing otherwise, and in the internationally tense world of the dawning twentieth century such occasions might become more frequent. Finally, there was the fact that in pressing for the Statute of Westminster, South Africa had played its part in gaining full self-government for all the territories dominated by white populations which had formerly been colonies subject to imperial decree. What had been won by Europeans within the Empire, it did not seem inconceivable—to those who had read the English writers who spoke so eloquently of freedom—that others also might win. And so the record of South Africa cannot be taken as an isolated history; it is a significant strand in the great tapestry of imperial triumph and decline.

Among those who learnt from South Africa, as they learnt from every other situation of imperial unrest while producing a kind of rebellion inalienably their own, were the Irish. Ireland's case was in fact so extraordinary in terms of the British imperial record, and so different in its historical background from that of any other dependency, that one is tempted—though the temptation must be

resisted—to regard it as a situation *sui generis,* a unique conjunction
of two peoples joined eventually by language and by blood, yet
divided by irreconcilable traditions and by memories of violence
too dark for oblivion.

For Ireland, we have seen, was a remnant of that Anglo-
Norman system of the Plantagenet kings by which England had
sought to establish herself as an imperial power on the continent
of Europe. By the time Ireland shook free of British domination
to the extent of gaining dominion status in 1921, the relationship
had existed for more than seven centuries. It had never been an
easy relationship, though it had gone through productive phases
and produced a few glories of the imaginative life through the
interaction of English and Irish cultures. Today, fifty years after
the atrocious intimacy of their relationship came to an end with
the creation of the Irish Free State, one is conscious of the ways
in which the life of both England and Ireland has been impoverished by the parting. Certainly this had been the case in
literature and in the drama. There had not been another Shaw in
London—or another Synge in Dublin; no second Joyce had
surfaced in Trieste or its late-twentieth-century equivalent, because there were no longer any Joyces being born in Ireland to
take the plunge. The whole story of the cultural decline of Ireland
after its liberation, and the corresponding weakening of English
creative life, is a problem for the cultural historian to consider with
an extensiveness that the limits of this book do not permit. But it
is, as well, a problem that through its very existence demonstrates
that England's relation to Ireland was not—at least since the great
cross-cultural process began at the end of the seventeenth century
—a simple matter of colonial tyranny.

Even England's relation to India was never as simple as that.
The ending of the Raj was a traumatic episode for the British, but
even more traumatic for those Indians who were politically aware
enough to understand what was actually happening as the mould
of government within which their society had been hardening for
a century was removed; perhaps the really dramatic story in India
was not how the British reconciled themselves to departing, but
how the Indians, recognizing that the democratic forms which the
British had left were indeed better than anything they had endured
in the days before Warren Hastings, painfully set out to make such
apparently alien patterns work, and miraculously did so.

But the case of Ireland was more complex than the case of India because here the hypocrisy that enters into all imperial relationships, and obscures that transitional area where illusions of trusteeship merge into realities of power, was compounded by the fact that while in India the British had never stayed to form an immigrant ruling caste, in Ireland they did precisely this. Ireland was a dependency in the medieval, not the modern style; it had been colonized not by merchants concerned with the profits of fugitive trading or administrators completing a career that would end on a pension in Brighton, but by feudal lords whose interest was in the land. From the twelfth century, wave after wave of English and Scots settlers—lords and yeomen—were transplanted to Ireland, and an amazing number of them became as Irish as the Moghuls became Indian. Yet they retained their status in the English ruling class, so that the Fitzgeralds, for all their medieval recession into the Celtic fastnesses of bogs and mountains, emerged by the eighteenth century, like so many other old Anglo-Norman-Irish families, to take their part in the spread of empire. There were few families among the Victorian English gentry who did not have slightly raffish Irish cousins, just as there were few British regimental messes, or English public schools, or clubs in India or Natal that lacked their contingents of imperial Irishmen.

This close social and even familial relationship between the gentry of England and Ireland made it easy for the less imaginative of the Victorian ruling class to deny that Ireland was or could possibly be a nation on its own. For such people Ireland was a land of country houses whose owners ruled over a race of barefooted colleens and of slyly charming peasants with a gift of the gab and an inclination to be violent when fired with poteen. It was the English who held such a view of Ireland and nurtured it into sentimental poignancy with Tom Moore's *Irish Melodies*, that allowed their comfortable doctrines of *laissez faire* to blind them to the needs of Ireland in the 1840s and to allow millions of Irish to die in the great famine that was brought about because the potato crop failed after the peasants' corn had been taken to pay the rents and exported to Britain.

The sentimental view of Ireland complemented grotesquely the brutal realities of English rule. For there was no country in the whole history of their various empires in which the British committed so many atrocities as in the land that—apart from Wales—

was nearest to them, a land inhabited not by primitive barbarians
but by a people who had preserved the ancient learning of the
West when the remainder of Europe lapsed into the chaos of the
Dark Ages. There was nothing in the history of the Second
Empire, for all its vast spread of dominions and colonies, that
compared with what was done in Ireland during the six centuries
before the Second Empire ever came into existence. The famous
massacre of Amritsar, which played so crucial a part in the decline
of British rule in India, and all the lesser Amritsars of the nineteenth and twentieth century, were insignificant compared with
the oppressions perpetrated in Ireland by Cromwell and by
Mountjoy before him. And after the age of violent massacres and
repressions had ended, there were the generations of economic
repression, of exploitation by landlords absent in England, which
Swift denounced and which led to the great famines and migrations of the nineteenth century. If any country provided an object-
lesson in the follies of imperial economic policy during both the
First and Second Empires, Ireland was it; the mercantilist system
destroyed Irish industry and made the country an agrarian dependency relentlessly exploited by Britain, and the doctrines of the
Manchester Liberals prevented any effective remedial action when
the consequences of such a policy led to universal distress.

On top of the memories of military brutality, landlordly exploitation and administrative neglect was superimposed the
spectacle of cynical constitutional manœuvres by which Ireland
was given its own Parliament in 1782, on the theory that it was a
separate realm under a common Crown (dating from Henry VIII
who created the Kingdom of Ireland). In fact, the Parliament was
picked from the Protestant minority and the executive power was
in the hands of a viceroy appointed from London. After a series
of rebellions between 1795 and 1798, inspired largely by the
French example, even this lame pretence of independent government was unacceptable. The Parliament of Ireland was bribed to
vote itself out of existence, and to vote in the Union, by which the
United Kingdom of Great Britain and Ireland was established and
Ireland ceased to have even the degree of separate identity that
was accorded a Crown colony. It was not even a dependency with
its own assembly like the Isle of Man or the Channel Islands; it
became an integral part of the British kingdom, and at least one
region of Ireland, the Protestant enclave of Ulster, wished to

maintain that status. So did enough of the gentry and of the Dublin Ascendancy—mainly Protestant in religion—to produce among the late-Victorian ruling class of England itself the feeling that while political concessions might have to be made to settlement colonies across the Atlantic or in the far Pacific, merely to prevent their following in the wake of the United States, Ireland was a part of the physical and cultural entity of Britain, bound to England in a unique symbiosis, and that to see Ireland governed in any other way than from Westminster via Dublin Castle would vastly diminish British world stature and hence British power.

Emotions, inevitably, were as strong on one side as on the other. Yet by the second decade of the twentieth century Ireland had in fact advanced so far towards the goal of self-liberation that the violence which erupted on Easter Day, 1916, and marred the country for nearly a decade afterwards, was induced as much by nationalist romanticism as by political necessity; its goal would certainly have been otherwise achieved in accordance with the general drift of disintegrative change within the Empire. In fact, after the famines of the 1840s and the abortive risings of Young Ireland in 1848 and the Fenians in 1867, the condition of Ireland improved slowly but steadily. There was no way of mitigating the bitterness which the years from 1845 to 1847 had left in Ireland or—worse for the Empire—had transplanted to the United States. But relief could be given to those who survived and stayed, and in two Acts of 1870 and 1881 Gladstone granted the main demands of the Irish Land League—fixity of tenure, fair rents and free sale of the tenant's interest; while in 1903 the Land Tenure Act enabled the farmers to buy their land on easy terms which were usually less than their existing rents, with the result that in a very few years the great estates of the absentee landlords were liquidated and a new class of peasant landowners was created throughout Ireland. Already in 1869 Gladstone had disestablished the Anglican Church in Ireland, so that Catholic farmers no longer were forced to pay tithes to clergy they regarded as heretics.

The political situation was more difficult to solve than the agrarian, largely because of disagreements among the Irish themselves, between the Anglo-Irish gentry and the Catholic lower classes in Southern Ireland, and between the Catholics everywhere and the Ulster Protestants of all classes. Irish self-government first became an issue in 1870 when Isaac Butt created the Home Rule

Association, based on the belief that only self-government could cure Ireland's ills; Home Rule—by which was then understood internal self-government—became the aim of the Nationalists led by Parnell and later by Redmond, and it not only gained the support of Gladstone and a large section of the Liberal Party, but aroused widespread sympathy in the United States and—more important in imperial terms—in Australia and Canada.

Questions of national dignity and military security, however, aligned many Englishmen against Gladstone, not only among the Conservatives but also among the Liberals; a large group of Liberal Unionists, led by Joseph Chamberlain, found that the Irish issue led them eventually into the Conservative ranks. Gladstone's first Home Rule Bill was defeated in 1886; his second passed the Commons but was heavily defeated by the landed magnates in the Lords in 1893, and this setback led Arthur Griffith to found in 1900 a new party called Sinn Fein—'Ourselves Alone'—which bore some resemblance to the Indian National Congress at certain phases in its career, since Sinn Fein declared that the Irish should rely not on an English Parliament but on themselves; Griffith called on the Irish Nationalist Members of Parliament to withdraw from Westminster and set up their own national convention. The original programme of Sinn Fein called for passive resistance, since it was thought that the violence of the Fenians had led to no good result. The return to violence was, as we shall see, actually provoked by the more extreme advocates of continued union with England.

In 1909 it had seemed as though the gaining of Home Rule was virtually assured. A Liberal budget had been defeated by the House of Lords, and Asquith decided to precipitate a showdown with the peers, for which he needed the voting support of the Irish Nationalists; Redmond's price was Home Rule, and after the Lords capitulated and the Parliament Bill was passed in 1911, it looked as if the promise would be kept. The Home Rule Bill passed the Commons in 1912, and though the Lords rejected it, the Parliament Act would allow it to become law in 1914 if the Commons passed it again.

At this point a combination of imperialist elements intervened to exploit and inflame the fears of the Ulster Protestants that in an independent Ireland they would be at the mercy of the Catholic majority. Bonar Law, the Canadian who had recently succeeded to the leadership of the Conservative Party, was involved in the plot, but the principal open leader was Sir Edward Carson, a Dublin Protestant M.P. whose other claim to celebrity was his sadistic hounding of Oscar Wilde. In September 1912 Carson proclaimed a Covenant of Resistance to Home Rule, which many thousands of Ulstermen of all classes signed, and shortly afterwards an Ulster Volunteer Force was raised and equipped with arms smuggled in with the connivance of the army. The extent of military participation was shown by the fact that Field-Marshal Lord Roberts and General George Richardson placed themselves at the head of the Ulster Volunteers, who were pledged to resist, by violence if necessary, the imposition of any attempt to make Ulster subject to a Home Rule Government in Dublin, while there was a technical mutiny in the cavalry base at the Curragh, where fifty officers, led by General Hubert Gough, declared that they would resign their commissions rather than use force to impose Home Rule on Ulster. The result of this activity among the Unionists was the formation in 1913 of the nationalist Irish Volunteers, pledged to enforce Home Rule once it became law. If the Ulster Volunteers were manipulated by high-placed reactionaries in England, the Irish Volunteers were under the control of the Irish Republican Brotherhood, the remnant of the old American–Irish Fenian movement, and orders from the secret I.R.B. headquarters in New York played an increasingly important role in the nationalist movement from this time onwards.

The I.R.B. extremists provoked in April 1916 the celebrated Easter Day rising, when a small group of insurrectionaries seized the centre of Dublin and proclaimed the Republic of Ireland. The rebellion was suppressed after several days of fighting. The British authorities made the mistake of executing sixteen of the leaders, and gave the nationalist movement sixteen martyrs.

> O but we talked at large before
> The sixteen men were shot,
> But who can talk of give and take,
> What should be and what not
> While those dead men are loitering there
> To stir the boiling pot?

So Yeats expressed the sentiment of Ireland, which had been against the Easter Day rising itself, but now swung away from the moderate Nationalists under Redmond and gave its support to Sinn Fein, the party that preached the defiance of English legality. Sinn Fein contested the British elections at the end of 1918, and returned 73 M.P.s out of 102 in all Ireland. They refused to attend in Westminster, and boycotted Lloyd George's attempts to reach agreement on an appropriate formula of government. Instead they proclaimed again the Republic of Ireland, and set up their own assembly, the Dail Eiraan, which they ordered the Irish people to treat as the true Government. There followed the years of guerrilla fighting between the Volunteers, transformed into the I.R.A., and the British forces, and though the loss of life was small— probably about 1,500 people killed on both sides in three years of fighting—the people of Britain were appalled by this lingering conflict coming at the end of the First World War. Eventually in 1921, under pressures from Smuts and other dominion leaders, Lloyd George offered a truce to De Valera, leader of the I.R.A., and in December 1921 the treaty was signed by which Ireland became the Irish Free State and a dominion equal to Canada; six counties of Ulster were excluded to become Northern Ireland and a bitter problem from that time onwards to both Ireland and England. The Plantagenet conquest of Ireland was annulled at last; the seven centuries of dependency were ended, and the British withdrew except from their naval bases and left the new Irish Government to carry on two more years of internal warfare against the republican extremists.

In fact, all the Sinn Feiners were republicans. It was merely a matter of how quickly Ireland should go on her way to independence. Ireland attended the imperial conferences and always appeared by the side of Canada and South Africa in pressing for extensions of dominion autonomy, leading to the Statute of Westminster. Once the Statute was attained, and De Valera returned to power in 1932, Ireland would move ahead of the other dominions in severing the imperial links. An important step was De Valera's new constitution of 1937, in which he implemented his concept of Ireland as a state in 'external association' with the British Commonwealth, turning Ireland into a quasi-republic by replacing the office of governor-general by a popularly elected president. In the following year the British abandoned their naval bases on Irish soil, and in 1939 Ireland displayed the effectiveness of its independence by declaring itself neutral in the Second World

War, a stand no other dominion took. Finally, the goal of complete detachment from the British Empire was achieved in 1948, when Ireland became a republic and left the Commonwealth; by the Republic of Ireland Act of 1949 the British Government accepted this termination of a long, unhappy, passionate attachment.

Ireland, the nearest geographically of the dominions, was the first to detach itself formally from the Empire-Commonwealth; the greening of that spot of red on the map so close to England's shores was a clear portent of the constriction of imperial power. Yet Ireland was not the first British possession to leave the Empire; Burma had preceded her a few months before, not even waiting for dominion status. The process of change was accelerating, and the nationalist movements of the non-European colonial countries, to which Irish Home Rule and Nationalist movements had long given the encouragement of example, were at last catching up with those of the white dependencies. The principal role that Ireland had in this drama of the death of empire was surely its ancient and consistent standing on the ground that the imperialist idea of ruling another people even for its own good was without moral foundation. Most other colonial peoples had at one time or another accepted, or at least passively acquiesced in British rule; the Irish, as a people, never acquiesced.

Interlude

XI The Year of No Return

I have referred in an earlier chapter to 1930 as 'a year of omens'. It could also be called 'the year of no return', for it was a time when decisions were made that—though few people then recognized it—marked the beginning of an irreversible process by which the Empire shrank and diminished from its greatest magnitude during the decade after the First World War.

The present chapter I have shaped in the form of an interlude, since it marks a necessary break in the chronological continuity of the narrative. 1930 was the year in which the long struggle of the white dominions for self-government and nationhood came to a head in the negotiations that led to the passing of the Statute of Westminster. But it is impossible to talk of the dominions as if they were the only dependencies of the British Crown when at the same time equally important developments were emerging elsewhere in the Empire. 1930 was also the year of Gandhi's salt march and the surrender of Weihaiwei, and these episodes were as crucial in their effect on imperial history as the events leading up to the Statute of Westminster. Thus in dealing with this critical year I have jolted time a little out of the chronological pattern of my remaining narrative so that these events can be viewed in mutual proximity, as people reading the morning newspapers in London undoubtedly became aware of them; in the next chapter I shall step backward to sketch out the events that led up to the incidents in India and on the China coast.

The events I am about to describe stand out all the more strikingly when they are viewed from our point in the future, because 1930 was also a year in which the activities of the colonial rulers became streamlined as never before. Throughout the period of great colonial acquisitions, the administration of the Empire had been haphazard in every way. Ireland and India had their own

Secretaries of State with appropriate departments. The Channel Islands and the Isle of Man came under the Home Office. Egypt, Sudan and the Chinese concessions were ruled from the Foreign Office. Since 1925 relations with self-governing territories had come under the Dominions Office. (The Colonial Secretary at first doubled as Dominions Secretary.) The rest came under the Colonial Office (with interference from the Admiralty and the War Office in the case of Gibraltar, Malta and St Helena) but the arrangements for recruiting colonial servants varied from colony to colony. Only Malaya, Hong Kong, Ceylon and the Western Pacific High Commission held competitive examinations and the remaining colonies recruited rather haphazardly on the basis of personal contacts; not even all colonial servants were recruited by the Colonial Office, for a further department, the Crown Agents for the Colonies, acted as a kind of collective high commission in London for the colonial territories and recruited all their technical personnel.

The untidiness of this pattern did not appear to cause alarm among the classic architects of the Empire. Disraeli constructed the imperial myth, Salisbury doggedly expanded the Empire, Chamberlain elaborated the constructive aims of imperialism, without being concerned about such anomalies as the fact that Sudan was the responsibility of the Foreign Office and neighbouring Uganda of the Colonial Office, or that officials in Burma belonged to the Indian Civil Service and officials in Ceylon did not, or that cadets in Ceylon were chosen by examination and their counterparts in Mauritius got in by influence. It seems to have been felt in Whitehall—if it was never said—that each colony had been acquired under special conditions and evolved in its own way, and that the sleeping dogs of empire should be let lie. And the lack of co-ordination had its advantages. It encouraged those rare Governors who had the talents needed for their task; Lugard, for example, would never have carried out his spectacular experiments in administration if he had not enjoyed a freedom in the choice of his subordinates as well as in the formulation of his policies.

But the kind of open organization that may be appropriate to a dynamic imperialism is no longer effective when the expansive stage is past. By 1930 the rulers of Britain knew that the economic limitations which forced their country to abandon its role as the world's leading sea power had by that very token declared an end to further territorial gains. At this point even the most optimistic imperialist could not see the future as more than, at best, an era of consolidation. But even among those who foresaw the eventual break-up of the Empire, few realized that they stood at the point where the downward path actually began, the point beyond which any decision relating to the Empire would contribute to the complex of forces encompassing its end.

Thus, among other things, 1930 was a year when an unprecedented reconstitution of the imperial administrative machine took place. Haphazard recruitment was brought to an end by the creation of a uniform Colonial Service to be entered by competitive examinations administered by a Colonial Appointments Board. During the same year the separation of the Colonial and Dominions Offices was completed by the appointment of a Secretary for the Dominions.

These changes took place under the second Labour Government, and specifically under the old Fabian stalwart, Sidney Webb, now, as Lord Passfield, Colonial Secretary. Webb had never been an anti-imperialist. Like many other Fabians, he held the view expressed eloquently by Bernard Shaw in *Fabianism and the Empire* (1900) that a well-administered colonial system can be a powerful instrument for promoting social reform and education. Webb himself had worked in the Colonial Office for ten years, and one of his close associates in the Fabian Society, Sydney Olivier, had served from 1907 to 1913 as Governor of Jamaica and had made a genuine effort there to improve the conditions of small independent farmers. It could be said fairly that Olivier, Shaw and Webb all believed in the superiority of Western civilization, and especially of British political traditions as modified by the Fabian Society. They subscribed to the doctrine of the white man's burden but aimed at creating devices to make that burden easier to bear. It is in this light that we must see Passfield's unification of the Colonial Service; he was seeking to create an effective mechanism for a gradual Fabian programme of reform and education in the colonies. It is doubtful if he or any of his fellow Fabians thought colonial independence an important goal, or a desirable one in the near future. They were more concerned with social than political ends; they saw politics mainly as means and were therefore always political relativists.

In a sense, then, we can regard the reform of the Colonial

Service in 1930 as a neutral act so far as wider imperial policies were concerned. Passfield merely felt that a tidying up of the service might make Fabian approaches to reform somewhat easier, but he was not interested in major changes in the structure or direction of the Empire, and most of his colleagues shared this approach. Thus one can say fairly that if the three crucial decisions of no return which I am about to discuss were made under the second Labour Government, its responsibility amounted to very little more than a virtual inability to understand the ultimate consequences of acts to which, as Britain's rulers in that vital year, its members gave their assent.

The first was that which marked, with the negotiations leading up to the Statute of Westminster, the end of the long political evolution in the self-governing colonies inhabited by people of European descent. It was also the culmination of the cycle set in motion at the Imperial Conference of 1926, when the differences of opinion on foreign policy that had emerged between Britain and some dominions led to pressure, from Canada, South Africa and Ireland especially, for a clearer definition of their political status. Discussion concentrated largely on a symbolic issue with wide implications. What was the actual role of the Governor-General in a dominion?

In Crown colonies a Governor directly embodied the power of the imperial Government, and implemented its policy through his executive officers except where specific powers were transferred to local legislatures. The Viceroy of India held similar power and responsibility. And until 1926 it was assumed that the Governor-General in a dominion, though he had lost executive power, was still the representative of the imperial Government. Yet if the dominions were to be accepted as self-governing, the Governor-General had no right to embody the power wielded by the British Parliament. What he could embody was the headship of state that Britain and the dominions shared, and it was accordingly decided that he should represent the Crown and not the British Government; in other words, he would become a surrogate constitutional monarch, bound to accept the advice of the local Government to which he was accredited. The British Government would now be represented by a High Commissioner—a kind of inter-imperial ambassador.

To give an aura of principle to this practical arrangement, the old philosopher-statesman Arthur Balfour, author of *The Defence of Philosophic Doubt*, was called in at the conference of 1926 to head an Inter-Imperial Relations Committee, which drew up the document since known as the Balfour Draft—as distinct from the Balfour Declaration, which promised a Jewish homeland in Palestine. The Draft declared that the dominions were 'autonomous communities within the British Empire, equal in status, in no way subordinate to one another in any aspect of their domestic or external affairs, though united by a common allegiance to the Crown and freely associated as members of the British Commonwealth of Nations'.

This was vague enough to please all parties; it acknowledged in principle the equality between Britain and the dominions which the Canadians, South Africans and Irish demanded, while it placated the Australians and New Zealanders by stressing allegiance to the Crown, and finally it removed the stigma of imperial subordination so far as the dominions were concerned by giving official cognizance to the concept of a British Commonwealth of Nations. The phrase had been given currency more than forty years before when Lord Rosebery, discussing before an Australian audience the possibility of nations evolving within the Empire, had remarked that this need not imply separation, 'because the Empire is a commonwealth of nations'. It was a commonwealth, nevertheless, in which some were still regarded as more equal than others. India, like the colonies and protectorates, was recognized as bound in a relationship of subordination to Britain. There was nothing in the Balfour Draft or in the general proceedings of the Imperial Conference of 1926 to suggest that those who subscribed to it contemplated extending the rights they had been assured to the non-white peoples of the Empire; indeed, the South Africans were sharply opposed to the very idea of such an extension.

But the very vagueness of the Balfour Draft created situations that demanded definition. The Governor-General might take the advice of the dominion Government relating to the laws it passed, but whose advice should the King-Emperor take in appointing the Governor-General? And how far should dominion legislation conform to imperial legislation? The Colonial Laws Validity Act of 1865 still remained on the statute books; it decreed that colonial legislation which was inconsistent with imperial legislation could

be held *ultra vires*. This was at variance with the spirit of the
Balfour Draft, at least as interpreted by Prime Minister Hertzog in
South Africa and Prime Minister King in Canada, and in 1929 a
Committee on Dominion Legislation was set up to consider these
questions. It reported to the Imperial Conference of 1930, and this
conference accepted its recommendations.

In outline, the most important were that the King should act
always on the advice of his ministers in the dominion concerned,
which meant that each dominion would be a separate entity and
in formal terms all that united them would be acceptance of a
single symbolic headship of state; that the clauses of the Colonial
Laws Validity Act that might affect dominion legislation should
be repealed; and that dominions should not be bound by any past
or future British legislation unless they specifically requested it.
Any provisions in British Acts serving as constitutions of the
dominions that might limit their freedom should be repealed at
request, and any changes in the royal titles or succession should
receive the consent of dominion Parliaments as well as that of
Great Britain.

The acceptance of these recommendations by the Imperial
Conference of 1930 represented the point of no return so far as
the dominions were concerned; their embodiment in the Statute
of Westminster, passed by the British Parliament in 1931, made it
clear that the links between the mother country and the dominions,
where they were more than symbolic, had become voluntary
matters of loyalty and common interest. Canada, South Africa and
Ireland accepted the Statute immediately; Australia and New
Zealand postponed for more than a decade their requests for its
application to them.

Ultimately the most important decision of the Imperial Conference of 1930 to be embodied in the Statute of Westminster was
the provision that dominion laws should be recognized as having
extra-territorial validity. Up to now the international status of the
dominions had existed mainly in token form; they had signed the
Versailles Treaty, they were members of the League of Nations,
but they still for the most part conducted their foreign affairs
through Britain. Now they could become internationally recognized States and they began slowly to build up their own foreign
services. There was no real possibility from this time onward that
they would develop into less than nations in their own right or

that they would fail to take independent positions in world politics.

Events in India in 1930 led to a result that in appearance was much more modest a break with the past than the Statute of Westminster, but in terms of its consequences was even more important. India held a special and anomalous position within the Empire. It was not a colony, but a separate monarchy ruled by the British king in his role as Kaiser-i-Hind. Up to the time of the Mutiny, while the Moghuls still ruled nominally it had been administered by a Governor-General theoretically representing the East India Company but in practice appointed by the British Government. After the Mutiny the Governor-General became also the Viceroy, acting on behalf of the King-Emperor as head of state. Not only was there a Secretary of State for India, but this minister was directly responsible to Parliament and enjoyed a great deal of discretion in making decisions relating to India; he was advised by a Council for India in London, but in matters requiring secrecy he could act independently. The Government of India in Delhi conducted its own foreign relations with neighbouring countries, ruled its own dependencies, and was a member of the League of Nations, while its representative—always a British official—attended the Imperial Conferences. Thus India was always recognized as a political entity on its own, and under British rule it became a far more unified country than it had ever been before, both in administration and in national sentiment. The problem therefore in India's case was not admitting that a nation existed, since no one denied that fact, but determining how far and how soon Indians would govern their own land.

It was a complex question, since in Indian minds it involved not only the belief that they should be allowed a greater share in the government of their country, proceeding quickly to Home Rule, but also the conviction that they should be consulted in any move towards the transfer of power.

Over fifty years a series of piecemeal and paternalistic reforms had shown Britain moving with the monumental slowness of a Japanese No player towards responsible government in India. In 1882, under the Viceroyalty of the radical Lord Ripon, a start was made with elected Municipal Councils. In 1909 the Governor-General's Legislative Council and the provincial Legislative Councils were modified so that a minority of members in the former and a majority in the latter would be elected on a franchise closely restricted by property qualifications. In 1919, under the Government of India Act, provincial Governments with a measure of responsibility were established; the celebrated system of dyarchy provided for certain fields of government to be transferred to elected provincial ministers, while others were reserved for the local Governors. The central Government, however, embodied no principle of responsibility to the electorate; the Governor-General remained responsible through the Secretary of State to the British Parliament and people.

All these reforms, seen by the British as tending to prepare Indians for a steadily greater measure of responsible government, were presented in a typically paternalistic way; at no stage did Indians themselves play any part in their formulation. This was perhaps the most important factor in Congress opposition to taking any part in provincial administrations created under the 1919 Act. They demanded instead immediate Home Rule—i.e., complete internal self-government—but there seems little doubt that if they had been allowed to negotiate directly with the British Government they would have accepted less. For their part, the British realized that once they granted the principle of consultation on an equal footing with Indians, they would admit the justice of the Indian claim to complete autonomy, and this in the 1920s they were not prepared to do.

Out of this impasse the events of 1930 emerged. In 1927 Lord Irwin, the incumbent Viceroy, had summoned Gandhi and the other Indian leaders to meet him in Delhi. They were invited not for consultation but to be informed that the British Government had decided to send a commission, led by Sir John Simon, to investigate in India the possibility of further constitutional change. The commission had been appointed without consultation with any Indian representative, it would be responsible only to Parliament in London, and it would include no Indian members. Indians would be invited to offer opinions and evidence, but the commission was not asked to take their wishes into account in framing its recommendations.

Not only Congress, but all Indian parties, including the Muslim League, boycotted the Simon Commission; educated Indians were united in regarding it as a denial of their right to decide their own destiny, and since the events of 1919, culminating in the massacre of Indian protestors at Amritsar at the orders of General Dyer, they had begun to regard this right as precious and not to be denied. In December 1928, after the Simon Commission had done its work, Congress passed a resolution demanding independence within a year. When Labour came into office in 1929 Ramsay Macdonald hinted obliquely at the possibility of dominion status being granted, but nothing was done. In December 1929 Congress therefore resolved on immediate severance from the Empire, called on all Indians to resign from official positions, and deputed Gandhi to lead a nation-wide civil disobedience campaign.

Gandhi opened 1930 with an Indian Declaration of Independence; it was not dominion status, but *Purna Swaraj*, or complete independence, that he demanded. The Government and the Indian people waited for him to act, and Gandhi—with characteristic chivalry—carefully warned his opponents beforehand of his intention to embark on a campaign of peaceful law-breaking. His acutely prophetic sense of the forces moulding the future of the Empire was shown in a single sentence of the letter he sent to the Viceroy: 'My ambition is no less than to convert the British people through non-violence, and thus make them see the wrong they have done India'.

Gandhi chose a simple but effective means of drawing attention to India's grievances. He led a march from Ahmedabad through the Indian countryside to Dandi, 241 miles away on the sea-coast, and there he plucked salt from the seashore, thus technically breaking the law that forbade anyone to be in possession of salt produced under the Government salt monopoly. The salt monopoly was extremely unpopular, and in choosing such a means of law-breaking Gandhi was able to let loose a campaign of defiance so broad that no less than a hundred thousand people were arrested, including all the important leaders of Congress. Non-co-operation went into full swing across the country and many of the towns were virtually controlled by committees of Congress workers who replaced the paralysed local Governments. Finally, the Viceroy decided to break the deadlock by releasing Congress leaders and acceding to Gandhi's request for an interview. It was an unprecedented act, not only in India but in the whole Empire; a rebel leader was freed from prison to confer as an equal with the King-Emperor's representative.

Apart from the release of prisoners and an agreement that salt might be made for personal use, the discussions had no great immediate consequences. Gandhi agreed to represent Congress at the Round Table talks in London in 1931, but as we shall see relatively little came out of that. Yet the long-term implications were enormous, for at last the principle had been accepted that Indians should have a hand in determining their own destiny as a nation, and one man at least apprehended the consequences of what, in a celebrated harangue, he termed 'the nauseating and humiliating spectacle of this one-time Inner Temple lawyer, now seditious fakir, striding half-naked up the steps of the Viceroy's palace there to parley on equal terms with the representative of the King-Emperor'. Winston Churchill clearly perceived that the ultimate meaning of Gandhi's meeting with Irwin could be the loss of India, and with India lost he knew that Britain would be reduced to a minor power.

To do him justice, Churchill was not concerned merely with the matter of British glory; he saw the whole incident as a breach of the firmness needed for effective trusteeship. As he said in February 1931,

At present while the Government of India is responsible to the British Parliament, which is the oldest, the least unwise and the most democratic parliament in the world. To transfer that responsibility to this highly artificial and restricted oligarchy of Indian politicians would be a retrograde act. It would be a shameful act. It would be an act of cowardice, desertion and dishonour. It would bring grave material evils, both upon India and Great Britain, but it would bring upon Great Britain a moral shame which would challenge for ever the reputation of the British Empire as a valiant and benignant force in the history of mankind.

The faithful discharge of our duty in India is not only a cause, but a symbol. It is the touchstone of our fortunes in the present difficult time. If we cannot do our duty in India, be sure we shall have shown ourselves unworthy to preserve the vast Empire which still centres upon this small island. The same spirit of unimaginative incompetence and weak compromise and supine drift will paralyse trade and commerce and prevent either financial recognization or economic resurgence. What we require to do now is to stand erect and look the world in the face, and do our duty without fear or favour.

One may not accept Churchill's imperialism, one may consider that what he termed 'unimaginative incompetence and weak compromise' was on Irwin's part imaginative courage, but there can be no doubt that in this speech, delivered six days after Gandhi's first meeting with Irwin, he showed an accurate grasp of the consequences if the trend represented by the Delhi talks could not be reversed. And in fact it was too late for reversal. The first meeting between Gandhi and the Viceroy was a point of no return for India and for the colonies, since once the possibility of equal discussion between rulers and rebels was allowed, an admission had been made that the wish of the subject people must in the long run determine their destiny, and such an admission must eventually erode the whole structure of the Empire.

The third crucial event of 1930 was the surrender of Weihaiwei. It was not the first incident that had shown the shift against Britain in the balance of Far Eastern power. During the 1920s the civil wars that swept over China, accompanied by Communist-led riots in the cities where industry was becoming established, created a precarious situation in some of the inland ports. In 1927 the British decided to withdraw from their concessions in Hankow and Kiukiang, places far up the Yangtse in the heart of China, where it would have been difficult to defend the trading areas even if the intruding nationalist troops had been expelled. The Navy continued to patrol the Yangtse with its gunboats to protect British shipping, and the withdrawal from trading concessions which were not parts of the territorial empire caused little concern in Whitehall. But China hands recognized that it meant a loss of face and would be interpreted by the Chinese—as the nationalists intended—as a sign of the weakening power of the British in the Far East.

The implications of the abandonment of Weihaiwei were more complex; it meant giving up a territory that had been governed as if it were a colony ever since the British leased it from China in 1898. The immediate function of Weihaiwei, to balance the Russian naval base at Port Arthur, disappeared after the Russo-Japanese War, but it was retained as a supply station; there was a convalescent home for naval officers from ships stationed in the

Pacific, and Weihaiwei's temperate air brought many British residents from Shanghai during the summer to relax on its beaches. It became a rather useless possession, but Britain kept it on Queen Victoria's principle of never giving up what one had gained. The Chinese wanted it back, but they also wanted Hong Kong, which the British had no intention of abandoning, and Weihaiwei was eventually surrendered, not because of the wishes of Chiang Kai-shek, but because Japan and the United States had exerted pressure on Britain to abandon the place ever since the Washington Naval Treaty in 1922. Both these powers had motives other than sympathy for Chinese nationalist aspirations; the United States was anxious to promote in every way the reduction of British imperial power, and the Japanese—already dreaming of the hegemony of the China Seas—were themselves planning to seize Weihaiwei, which they eventually did.

The surrender of Weihaiwei was the third point of no return in that fateful year of 1930. The abandonment of the concessions at Hankow and Kiukiang might be explained away as a mere retrenchment of commercial enterprises that had ceased to be profitable. But the surrender of Weihaiwei meant that Britain for the first time since the American War of Independence had surrendered actual territory which it ruled to a nationalist Government; for the first time also it had surrendered territory because of political pressure applied by other imperial powers.

It is when one considers these three events together that their final significance emerges. It is a significance at which Gandhi hints when he talks of converting the British people and which Churchill clearly perceives when he speaks of the 'spirit of unimaginative incompetence and weak compromise and supine drift' that he detects at work in British imperial policy. In all three incidents Britain was responding as she would not have done before 1918 to external pressures: to the wishes of the dominions, to the rebelliousness of the Indians, to the nationalist ambitions of the Chinese, to the rival imperial intents of the Japanese and the Americans. The significant point is that in each case the response, if not exactly a surrender, was a stepping back from power. 1930 was the year in which the weakening of the British will first become clearly perceptible. Such developments mature long before they find expression in action, and the preceding chapters have shown their ripening in the growth of dominion freedom towards the crucial point when that freedom becomes virtually complete. But at the same time the next stage, the attainment of Indian and colonial freedom, becomes active and inevitable, and in the remaining chapters I shall relate what happened in 1930 to the events in Asia and Africa and the other continents which brought the final end of the Empire.

Part III
The Brightest Jewel Lost

XII The Brightest Jewel
Imperilled

... the British Empire in India was both iniquitous and
beneficent; it was founded by violence, treachery and in-
satiable avarice, but also by incomparable daring and sustained resolution: it united India; it partitioned India; it
industrialized India; it stunted India; it served India; it rav-
aged India; it created modern India; it was selfless and
selfish, ruinous and constructive, glorious and monstrous.

(John Strachey, *The End of Empire*, 1959)

So wrote a rebel scion of one of the classic Anglo-Indian families,
the highest aristocracy of the Empire. John Strachey's ancestor
had been present when Clive cut his throat; later members of the
family had served faithfully on innumerable missions in Victorian
India; John Strachey himself, like the author of *Eminent Victorians*
who was his close relative, rebelled against the family tradition,
became a Marxist in the 'thirties, and later took part in a Labour
Cabinet as Minister of War. In the record of his family all the
British attitudes to the Raj were embraced, from total loyalty to
total rejection, but what most strongly emerges from John
Strachey's writings, and from those of all who were directly or
indirectly involved in India during the nineteenth and the early
twentieth centuries, is the centrality of the experience of ruling
India to the life of the British middle and upper classes during the
century of the Pax Britannica between 1815 and 1914.

If Ireland was regarded by the Victorians as Britain's back
garden, India was its country estate. Many families, like the
Stracheys, felt that they belonged to India as thoroughly as any
Moghul prince, though the Moghuls stayed, while the Stracheys
always went home to England if they survived enough monsoons.
It is mainly to people like this, who regarded themselves as

servants of India—or perhaps rather as servants of the Raj—that we must turn for our views on what India meant to Britain; even their views of what Britain meant to India are worth considering, since few unattached outsiders took the long journey there, and those who talked of India without seeing it were rarely as perceptive as Karl Marx, who understood something of Britain's double role there, as destroyer of the dying civilization of the past and agent of a modernizing regeneration.

It was in relations with India that the imperial attitudes of the British were shown in most variety, and with most emphasis. For those who saw the Empire in terms of power and pride, India was a fortress whose retention was a matter of life and death. 'India is not much thought of or understood at home', said Curzon to Balfour in 1901. 'But it is out and away the biggest thing the English are doing anywhere in the world. If we lose it we shall drop straight away to a third-rate power.' It was a theme Curzon repeated often with proconsular emphasis, and from the grand imperial point of view his sentiments were impeccable. None of the dominions—not even Canada with its vast territorial expanses and its barely exploited natural riches—was as essential to the imperial image and the imperial fact as India, for the dominions remained within the Empire only so long as the will of their inhabitants kept them, and none of the dominions provided an instrument of power comparable with the Indian Army, which was mobile enough to control almost everything that was important to Britain between Suez and Malaya.

On the other side to those who thought in terms of power (sometimes it was the other side of the same mind and mouth) were the Indian administrators who saw their presence as a great thust under which the Indians would be developed to the point where they could govern themselves within the perils of a modern world. Introducing his educational reforms in the years just before Victoria's accession, Macaulay raised the possibility that 'the public mind' of India might outgrow the institutions which Britain provided for its protection, that Indians would some day demand the democratic institutions of Europe; that, he believed, would be 'the proudest day in English history'. Mountstuart Elphinstone, perhaps the greatest of all Indian administrators in the days of the Company, looked forward to a future—very much like what actually happened—in which British power

would vanish for good and positive reasons. 'The most desirable
death for us to die should be the improvement of the natives
reaching such a pitch as would render it impossible for a foreign
nation to retain the government.'

Today the idea of trusteeship is in odour almost as bad as that
of imperial power. Many territories that are now duly accredited
members of the United Nations came hurriedly into being during
the 1960s, when it became unfashionable to plead that primitive
peoples needed a period of tutelage before they could accept
responsibility for their own destinies. And undoubtedly in the
final stages of transition from imperialism radical difficulties arose
from the idea that some men needed guidance and others were
equipped to guide. Doing what externally seems good for a
people may in fact mean violating a great deal that is culturally
vital to them. And once the pattern of trusteeship is established,
the time of release from it is liable to be extended indefinitely, on
the grounds that the trustees are always more capable or knowledgeable than the people whose affairs they hold in trust. But
such problems were barely evident to administrators like Elphinstone and the Lawrences when they developed the idea of government as a trust dedicated to advancing the subject peoples; they
acted with a consciousness of evangelical rectitude, and some of
their works were good.

Yet perhaps the greatest gift that Britain made to India by the
time Gandhi set out on his great salt march in 1930 was one that
had come about less through thoughts of trusteeship than through
the conveniences of government and the needs of power. For its
own purposes of control, Britain had superimposed on India a
unity far closer than the country had known in the days of its
ancient emperors, bringing under the aegis of its power and the
writ of Delhi territories which neither the ancient Maurya
emperors nor the Moghuls had ever governed.

So far as the British were concerned, the unity was important
mainly in administrative terms, but it was achieved by physical
means—by the great trunk roads and the railways, by a common
postal system—and by an English lingua franca that enabled
communication to pass between the educated among India's many
language groups. Foreign merchandise, unfamiliar manners,
above all new ideas spread in India as they had never spread
before. And among the new ideas was the notion that India could

be free and that this new-found unity was one of the prerequisites of that freedom.

What the generations of English rule had meant for India in this respect can be seen as one compares the failure of the Indian Mutiny in 1857 with the success of the seventeen years of campaigning that began with Gandhi's salt march of 1930.

The Mutiny was not an uprising on behalf of the freedom of the Indian people, since the Indians at that time did not think of themselves as a people; it was an uprising to resist suspected attacks on traditional patterns of behaviour. Within a considerable area of the Gangetic plain and the hill regions of northern Madya Pradesh it appears to have been well prepared, and the need for some sort of co-ordination seems to have dawned vaguely on the sepoy leaders; they sought to acquire it by resurrecting the dead symbol of Moghul power. But outside the north-central region of India the Mutiny made no appeal; nobody rose in support of it in the Dravidian south or in Orissa or Gujerat, nobody in Punjab or Sind, nobody in Bengal proper or Assam; nobody in the military principalities of Rajasthan; none of the three commercial cities which the British had established, Calcutta, Bombay or Madras, was affected except by panic among the box-wallahs.

But when Gandhi marched through the Gujerati countryside to pick up his salt on the beach at Dandi, the Indian people were aware of it from one end of the country to the other, because the British had united them physically by telegraphs and postal systems, united them intellectually by providing a common system of education, a lingua franca and a grounding in Western liberal ideas, and united them in intent by giving them a single alien domination which they could identify and unite to resist.

Without the British administration there would have been no Indian unity, as there had been no unity in the past; had there been no unity among Indians, the campaign that sent the British more or less peacefully from India could not have been devised; had the British not gone peacefully from India the whole story of the disintegration of the great empires would have been different and probably far more violent. One could put the matter as simply as that, and bring in an immediate verdict of *felo de se* against the Empire. But of course it was not so simple. The British provided the opportunity, but there were many possible ways of using it, and it was not immediately that Gandhi's essentially psychological approach, based on the inducing of shame rather than the terror which is the violent revolutionary's aim, came to dominate the tactics of Indian liberationists. But Gandhi's tactical psychology was aimed as much at the Indians as at the British. He sought to shame them both—the Indians into making themselves worthy of a life of freedom and fit for a struggle based on moral rather than physical pressures, and the British into making their own decision that the white man's burden was not worth carrying.

To do so he chose his symbolism carefully. Nothing could have been more simple and yet more dramatic than the illegal picking of salt from the sea shore. It seemed absurd to the whole world that such an act should be illegal, yet ever since the days of Clive the salt tax had been one of the most onerous impositions in India. Thus in one act Gandhi gave the Indians a simple but just cause for which they could practise *satyagraha*—the art of non-violent struggle—while he placed the British in the invidious position of ordering bloody police charges and imprisoning tens of thousands of people for an offence that seemed paltry and yet would cut away the whole foundation of autocratic rule if it were allowed to continue and multiply. Gandhi was a master of the art of creating dilemmas for his enemies (though he always called them friends) to solve.

But if Gandhi made an inspired use of the Indian love of symbolism and the British cult of fair play, he had to work with the political instrument that was to his hand. This was the Indian National Congress; by 1931 it had been welded, like Sinn Fein in Ireland between 1919 and 1921, into something in the nature of an alternative government to the British administration. It was able to order public servants to resign, to call strikes and boycotts that paralysed great cities, and at times—as in the great civil disobedience action that followed the salt march—to provide shadow administrations which, in such places as Bombay and Peshawar, actually took over the functions municipal bodies found impossible to continue. In 1939 Congress was able to show its strength as a counter-government by causing the resignation of all the provincial ministries because Britain would not agree to an immediate grant of independence.

Congress had come to this stage of militant authority from a curious beginning. Its actual founder was not an Indian, but an English amateur ornithologist named Allan Octavian Hume, a former Indian Civil Servant who believed that the rather remote autocracy which had developed in the decades after the Mutiny should be tempered by some form of democratic representation, and who called together the first meeting of Congress in 1885. Hume's fellow Anglo-Indians, who knew him as the author of the best guide to Indian game birds, can hardly have suspected in this kindly, eccentric man one of the assassins of the Empire, and yet if we are to impute responsibility to accessories before the fact, Hume could hardly be acquitted. For it is clear that Hume intended Congress to be a parliament where no parliament existed, and if eventually that parliament proceeded from discussion to action, this was in the nature of the kind of body he had set out to establish. Only seventy-two delegates assembled to Hume's first call in 1885, but more than twelve hundred arrived for the meeting in 1888, and from this point Congress became a true unofficial parliament in the sense that within its gatherings the various Indian philosophies of reform and rebellion fought for ascendancy and shaped the progress towards independence.

There was little in the early record of Congress or of the rival independence movements that foreshadowed the kind of campaigns which would emerge under Gandhi's leadership. In its beginnings, Congress was reformist and constitutionalist, but round about 1905 a polarization began to take place within the movement. On one side were the moderates, led by Krishna Gokhale, whose furthest aim appeared to be the slow gaining of self-government under British auspices. Gokhale was the product of the century of immersion in the doctrines of British liberalism which had produced such movements for purifying Indian life by following Western examples as Brahmo Samaj, founded in the early nineteenth century by the pioneer reformer, Ram Mohun Roy. Opposed to Gokhale in competition for the leadership of Congress and of the Indian independence movement was Balghangadhar Tilak, a Mahratta inspired by the martial traditions and the Hindu loyalities of his ancestors. He believed that in the traditions of Hinduism the forces that would regenerate India must be discovered, and he went so far in his resistance to Western influences as to oppose the abolition even of such distasteful practices as child marriage.

Gandhi—at least until he developed his distinctive philosophy of action—seemed to stand somewhere between Gokhale and

Tilak. Like Gokhale, he took much from the West, borrowing ideas from Tolstoy and Ruskin and incorporating the Christian sacrifice into his synthetic religion, and he acknowledged that Hindu behaviour needed drastic reform if India were ever to be worthy of her freedom. Yet he agreed with Tilak that the forces to regenerate India could be found in Indian society. Where he disagreed with him most profoundly was on the question of violence.

Both men were devotees of the great Hindu moral poem, the *Bhagavad Gita*, and both accepted as a guide to living its central doctrine that men must live in action without regard for its fruits—recognizing in this a nobler teaching than the Buddhist exhortation to non-action. But they disagreed profoundly on the kind of action that the dialogue between Krishna and Arjuna was meant to justify. Tilak, seeing the poem as part of the *Mahabharata*, and taking literally the battlefield setting in which Krishna makes his exhortation to Arjuna, assumed that it was a justification of violent action, and took it as a text to preach the expulsion of the British, if necessary, by terrorist acts. Gandhi, with less evident justification, devised a highly unorthodox interpretation of the *Gita*—and indeed of the whole of the *Mahabharata*; he contended that the entire epic must be taken as an allegory devoted to preaching the idea of victory by spiritual, not physical force.

During the early years of the nineteenth century, Tilak's teachings had a considerable effect on a minority of Indian nationalists; between 1907 and 1914 the terrorist movement spread from the Poona region to Bengal and Bihar. Not only was Tilak's influence at work among young orthodox Hindus, but there was also an infiltration of left-wing theories of propaganda by deed as developed by the anarchist groups of the time in western Europe.

Gandhi was politically fortunate in that his sense of responsibility to the Indians of South Africa kept him outside his own country during the whole of this critical period, which he devoted to developing his theory and practice of *satyagraha*. The term *satyagraha* means literally 'truth-force', and Gandhi argued that its real aim was not the moral coercion of the opponent but his conversion; one's antagonist must be won unharmed to accepting the rightness of one's aims. In actuality, there was always a strong element of coercion on successful *satyagraha*, and in later years

when Gandhi would practise it in the form of highly publicized
'fasts to the death' it came very near to being a kind of non-
violent terrorism which aroused much disguised resentment
among those whom it placed in intolerable moral dilemmas.
Nevertheless, as a tactic for a people with no other form of
effective resistance to colonial tyrannies it was extremely effective,
and by a dramatic use of it Gandhi gained a series of limited
successes in South Africa, so that when he went home to India in
1915 it was like the return of a general who has created a legend
on some remote frontier.

He came at an opportune time. The pre-war wave of violence
had failed, and the First World War itself created a kind of interlude. Of the great rivals for leadership in Congress, Gokhale died
in 1915 and Tilak in 1920. By this time Gandhi had already moved
into the centre of the stage, largely through a highly successful
satyagraha campaign in 1917 aimed at removing injustices in the
indigo plantations of Bihar.

At this time Gandhi still believed that justice might be established in India under British rule; he even helped to recruit Indian
soldiers for the support of Britain in the 1914–1918 War. Indeed,
in his most passionate campaigns against the Raj Gandhi never
abandoned his admiration for the finer aspects of British political
tradition, and often in later years he contended that he was merely
turning against the British their own libertarian principles. He
was encouraged at this time by the success of the Home Rule
League which had been established in India under the leadership
of Annie Besant; it had provoked the first statement from Whitehall which suggested to Indians that their country might eventually follow in the way the white dominions had already taken.
In August 1917 E. S. Montagu, the Secretary for India, had stated
that the Government's policy was 'that of the increasing association of Indians in every branch of the administration and the
gradual development of self-governing institutions with a view
to the progressive realization of responsible government in India
as an integral part of the British Empire'.

The practical consequences of Montagu's statement, and of the
report which he and the Viceroy, Lord Chelmsford, prepared in
1918, were considerably less agreeable to Indians than the expectations they had aroused. Yet the Government of India Act of 1919,
with its celebrated dyarchical form of government and its too-

obvious intent of tutelage, might well have been more widely accepted as a basis for progress if it had not been for an ill-timed hardening of administrative attitudes in India following on a revival of terrorist activities at the end of the war. Early in 1919 the so-called Rowlatt Acts were passed, providing for the internment of persons suspect of subversive activities and for the trial without jury of political offenders. It was at this point that Gandhi committed himself finally to the struggle to end British rule. He rejected the Rowlatt Acts less for their authoritarian nature than because he felt that, coming after Montagu's statement, they revealed the essential hypocrisy of the British Raj, which promised self-government and shortly afterwards, without consulting the Indians, deprived them of their basic civil liberties.

Aided by the prestige of his success in South Africa and in the indigo-growers' *satyagraha* at Champaran, Gandhi moved at this moment of crisis and discontent into the leadership of Congress, and from now until the eve of independence in 1947, whatever his official position in the movement may have been, he remained its non-violent generalissimo, carrying on his two-fronted war to regenerate the decayed traditional world of India and to convert the British to the acceptance of their own demotion as its rulers. The strange assemblage of conservatives and radicals, of Hindu traditionalists and Westernized rationalists, of capitalists and socialists and agrarian populists, who found common cause in the Congress movement were by no means all convinced pacifists like Gandhi. Indeed, the flourishing military presence of post-independence India expresses much more faithfully than the tactics Gandhi devised the actual character of the nationalism that developed within Congress even before the country's liberation. As Gandhi, who combined with his idealistic eccentricity a great deal of shrewd psychological perceptiveness, once remarked, 'Non-violence is my creed. It was never the way of Congress. With the Congress it has always been a policy.'

The distinction between *way* and *policy* is important. And indeed, non-violence was not the *way* of Indians in general, as Gandhi discovered long before the frightful massacres of Indians by Indians that took place when the country was partitioned at the time of independence. He first became aware of it in 1919, when his earliest nationwide call for a non-violent demonstration of protest against the perfidy of Albion resulted in outbreaks of mob

violence that might well have discredited his strategy completely if it had not been for the inhuman stupidity of Brigadier-
General Dyer in perpetrating the massacre at Amritsar, an act
which intelligent imperialists like Churchill recognized with a
shudder of apprehension as a bell tolling the knell of the Empire.
Those three hundred people dead in a square of the Sikh holy city
were as damning witnesses to imperial rule as the tens of thousands
of Irish whom Cromwell and Ireton killed in the seventeenth
century.

The events at Amritsar strengthened Gandhi's position in two
directions. On the one hand, no action could have shown more
clearly the constitutional and moral irresponsibility of the rule that
Britain perpetuated in India; many who had been willing to give
the Montagu–Chelmsford reforms a chance were now disillusioned
enough to throw in their lot with Gandhi and the others who were
calling for Swaraj. On the other hand, the display of brute force
in Amritsar revived memories of the tragic failure at the time of
the Mutiny because of the greater military strength and mobility
of the British. Thus Gandhi's *satyagraha* appealed to the leaders of
Congress as a strategy which would not invite paralysing repression, which at the same time would appeal to the traditionalist
India masses by its quasi-religious flavour and its appeal to the
traditional way of *ahimsa*—the avoiding of harm, and which—as
the more astute of them recognized in common with Gandhi—
would draw to the side of Indian liberation the liberal elements in
Britain itself, where after all the power of granting freedom lay.
On many occasions in the coming years Gandhi's associates would
be exasperated with his punctilious standing on principle, and
in spite of the devotion that he inspired as a guru, with his loin-
cloth and his staff and his great turnip watch, there were many
Congress leaders who paid only lip-service at best to his innumerable moralistic fads, to his cult of spinning and his love of cleaning
latrines as a sign of service to his fellow men. But they learnt to
respect and rely on his unerring tactical instinct, his sense of the
symbolic as well as the practical value of a particular line of action.

Many even among Gandhi's closest followers were especially
puzzled and disappointed when, after more than a decade of inconclusive struggle, he based what everyone expected to be a
major challenge to the British Empire on so simple a device as the
salt march. We have already considered how this led to Lord

Irwin's invitation to Gandhi, which, ending in the Gandhi–Irwin pact, represented an irrevocable step towards abdication on the part of the British Raj in India. But if we now observe the events of that time from the point of view of Congress and its campaign for Indian liberation, it is clear that here too a series of decisions was taken which set the compass for the last phase of struggle leading to the end of British rule.

By 1930, it must be remembered, Indian society had changed considerably from what it was in the earlier years of the century. Not only was the proportion of Western-educated Indians higher among the generation that was now coming to the fore, but they had absorbed—often under H. J. Laski at the London School of Economics—the left-wing ideas that were boiling up in England as the 'twenties turned into the 'thirties. In many cases—the Nehru family was one—the children eventually radicalized the parents. And women were becoming conscious not only of the need to struggle against a foreign oppression, but also of the need to change the conditions Indian society had traditionally imposed upon them. One of the most striking features of the great civil disobedience campaign of 1930 was the vast number of women of all classes who spontaneously joined the work of resistance and in doing so began to liberate themselves. This was true not only in the Malabar region, where the matrilineal system had always given women a measure of freedom and status, nor did it apply only to the comparatively rare women who at this time had gained some degree of higher education. The majority of the women who joined the campaign in 1930 came from regions and castes where their sex had traditionally been despised; many even broke out of purdah and came for the first time unveiled into the streets to join the *satyagraha* campain. Undoubtedly they were seeking freedom from much more than the British Raj.

Though the British were moving in the direction of some kind of self-government for India, their idea of progress completely failed to keep pace with Indian desires and expectations. As a counter-move to the visit of the Simon Commission in 1928 — which was boycotted because of its failure to include Indian representatives—a committee headed by Motilal Nehru (who unlike Gandhi had collaborated with the dyarchical system set up in 1919) prepared and published a report calling for full responsible government to be granted immediately 'on the model of the

constitutions of the self-governing dominions'. Motilal Nehru
and his associates had in mind the terms of the 1921 treaty with
the Irish rebels, and it is likely that, like the Irish, they saw
dominion status merely as a step towards total independence, since
after the events of 1919 there were few politically conscious
Indians who any longer set value on association with the British
Empire; that was left to the native princes, whose political survival
depended on the continuation of British rule. At its annual meeting in December 1928 Congress requested the implementation of
the Nehru recommendation within a year; Motilal's more famous
son Jawaharlal Nehru led a radical faction which demanded that
India become immediately a completely independent nation. It
was the kind of ultimatum that Congress leaders were in the habit
of issuing to encourage their followers rather than in the hope that
they would do more than hasten a little the tortoise pace of British
departure.

Yet when the second Labour Government came into power in
Britain in 1929, even though it enjoyed only minority rule, there
were great hopes in India that progress would be real and rapid
under a ministry at least some of whose members were avowed
opponents of imperialism and the Empire. But when Lord Irwin
returned in October of that year from conferring with the new
Cabinet, all he brought was an assurance in terms too general to
meet the growing impatience of the Indians, too vague for a time
as late as 1929, three years after the status of the white dominions
had been defined in at least general terms by the Balfour Draft. All
Ramsay MacDonald in fact committed the Labour administration
to was a statement that on the basis of the Government of India
Act of 1919 (which Congress had in any case rejected at the time)
'the natural issue of India's constitutional progress' could be
be regarded as 'the attainment of Dominion status'; he added a
promise to invite Indian representatives to a 'round-table conference' to discuss the difficulties arising out of the report of the
Simon Commission, which had further aroused Indian indignation
by expressing a doubt whether India would ever take to parliamentary government and which the Labour ministers themselves
were inclined to agree was not entirely satisfactory.

In its own way, MacDonald's statement was a momentous one,
since it was the first explicit admission by a British Government
that dominion status could be applied to any of the non-white

dependencies of the British Crown. But it was too late and too indefinite to meet the mood of Congress, and too imperially remote to satisfy Gandhi's desire for the kind of direct and human discussions which he later achieved with Irwin. There followed, almost automatically, the 1929 resolution of Congress demanding complete independence; the salt march; and the ensuing campaign with its innumerable arrests and its spectacular manifestations of non-violent discipline, which were amply reported in the British and American press, arousing widespread sympathy in the United States and for the first time bringing home to the British public the issues involved and creating admiration—often unwillingly given—for the courage of the *satyagrahis* who would endure brutal police attack without either faltering or countering with violence.

XIII The Beloved Antagonists

Gandhi improved on the opportunity which publicity had given to his cause in Britain, when, after his meetings with Irwin in 1931, he agreed to attend later that year the second of the Round Table Conferences. So far as the conference was concerned, his journey was wasted, since he was the sole representative of Congress in a gathering filled with the spokesmen of minorities varying from pariahs to princes, and from Muslims to Saint Thomas Christians. These delegates of divergent interests represented the latent disunity of India, and it seemed that the British, with their show of elaborate care for the rights of minorities and communities, were encouraging this fissiparous tendency in order to remain in power, while Gandhi, paradoxically, by claiming to speak for all the peoples of India, was defending the very unity which was the Raj's greatest creation. Throughout his life Gandhi was a great synthesizer, a great believer that apparently conflicting beliefs and interests could be brought together, and the extraordinarily heterogenous character of the Congress movement encouraged him in his view that even the most contradictory standpoints could be reconciled. But because he believed in reconciliation, and was so successful in achieving it in the actual situations in which he was involved, he failed to pay sufficient attention to the divisive tendencies that were constantly rising up with renewed vigour in India, a land of many religions and languages and local ways of life which had come together for the first time under the hand of an alien conqueror.

Certainly the famous Gandhian charisma failed to work at the Round Table Conference. The Muslims showed a growing inclination to go their own way under the able and powerful M. A. Jinnah, one of the few men who personally detested Gandhi, but the Congress leaders, including the Mahatma himself, were so caught up in the momentum of the movement they had created that they never really assessed the possibility that a powerful counter-movement might develop among their compatriots. If Gandhi had listened more closely to the babel at the Round Table in 1931, Congress might have coped more adequately with the divisive forces that arose in India as the Raj weakened, and the vast disorder by which the country emerged into independence as two mutually hostile nations might have been avoided. There was a strain of intellectual arrogance under Gandhi's seeming humility that gave him the inner power to carry on to the end the struggle against the Raj, but at the same time made it difficult for him to understand his Indian rivals; strangely enough, though, he developed into almost a science his understanding of his beloved antagonists, the British.

And if the Round Table Conference provided few opportunities of understanding with the representatives of the sectional interests of India, or with the British Government, which had shortly before changed its form from a vaguely sympathetic Labour Government to a National Government in which MacDonald was the prisoner of his imperialist allies, Gandhi used the opportunity of his visit to England to form a constituency for himself among the ordinary people of the country. Throughout the conference he insisted on staying in a poor quarter of the East End of London; it was the nearest he could find to the untouchable districts which he was now inclined to haunt in India, and he aroused an extraordinary curiosity and sympathy among the working-class people he encountered there. Later he went to visit the mill-towns of Lancashire, and his trip was something of a triumphal progress, all the more astonishing since his campaign of *swadeshi*—the boycott of foreign-made cloth—had caused great unemployment among the weavers. To these simple people, who as yet had no say in how the Empire was ruled, Gandhi seemed rather like Charlie Chaplin, the little man up against all the forces that made their own lives a misery. They remembered him, and during the 1930s Gandhi developed in the British consciousness from an annoying agitator in a remote imperial possession into an absorbing if slightly droll personality, whose exploits were followed with sympathy or hostility but rarely with indifference, and whose place in the popular consciousness was reflected in the frequency with which he appeared in the drawings of the time's great caricaturists, David Low and, later, Vicky.

What Gandhi was beginning to touch, whether he discussed affairs with a pious and conscientious British aristocrat like Lord Irwin, or talked about their lives with mill-girls in Oldham, was a dawning sense among British people of all classes that perhaps their unprecedented imperial success had led them into paths which were not quite consistent with the self-image that they held deep within their minds. For the Empire was such a strange and un-imperial structure in any traditional sense that it was often hard to understand how it hung together, and harder still to understand how it was related to the political philosophy which the British had developed for their own governing.

The empires of the ancient world had been built up mainly for dynastic glory, or the glory of some city community like Rome or Athens or Sparta. The greater the empire, the nearer to divinity was its ruler; the Achaemenian monarchs of Persia had taken to themselves the title of King of Kings, and Alexander and his Hellenistic successors had elevated themselves to the rank of epiphanies, manifestations of deity; in Rome the concept of the re-public had been found too fragile to support the weight of empire and had been replaced by the Caesar merging into the divine emperor.

The identification of empire and divinity descended to the middle ages in that strange ghost of an imperium, the Holy Roman Empire; the same sense of holy awe haunted the Russian Empire until the disastrous day in 1905 when Father Gapon led his peasants into the square before the Winter Palace to attract the benevolence of the Empire's share of divinity and was met by a storm of rifle fire. Both Spain and Portugal regarded their im-perial adventures as crusades to convert the heathen. Even the kings of France stressed the holiness of their Catholic majesty when the French explorers set up crosses on the headlands of the Gulf of St Lawrence.

Up to the Reformation indeed, and beyond it in Catholic and Orthodox countries and in lands outside Europe like the Celestial Empire of China and the realm of the Lion of Judah at the head-waters of the Blue Nile, the identification of empire with divine instigation continued. Imperial conquerors were holy for the simple reason that God—whichever God they supported—had permitted them to succeed in acquiring territory, and they made sure of the continued benevolence of the deity by ruthlessly imposing their own idea of how he should be worshipped, so that when the Portuguese arrived on the Malabar Coast of India they lost no time declaring that the local Christians of the Syrian rite, who claimed conversion by St Thomas and had certainly been practising Christianity since the second century A.D., were heretics to be subordinated to Rome.

The world's first completely secular imperialists were the Dutch, who calmly interpreted their Calvinist doctrines to mean that those subordinate to them were fated to be so by the inscrutable workings of the grace of God. There was no point in trying to convert those predestined to be heathen. But the British became involved in the contradiction of being religious imperialists without believing in the divinity of empire, which in the end was to lead them into intolerable dilemmas.

Disraeli, doubtless, would have been delighted if he could have hailed Queen Victoria not merely as Regina Imperatrix, but also like Antiochus as a divine epiphany, or at least, like the Holy Roman Emperor, as a privileged champion of God. But even the title 'Defender of the Faith' had in practice been relegated to the coinage, where it still remains, ever since James II's attempts to interfere with the religious life of the kingdom had led to the involved and sordid political intrigue that had gone down in British history under the strangely inappropriate title of the Glorious Revolution.

There was nothing glorious or revolutionary about the bibulous Hanoverians who were the eventual beneficiaries of that event, and under whom the First Empire died and the Second rose from its ashes. But, despite a few attempts to establish Anglicanism as a State Church, mainly in order to assure comfortable livings for the surplus clergy of England, the British Empire was officially a secular undertaking. There was no attempt by any governing body within the Empire to impose conversion on the subject peoples, as the Spaniards and Portuguese had done. In the case of India the eagerness of the East India Company to harmonize with indigenous customs and beliefs reached the extent of participating in Hindu religious festivals by providing escorts and salutes of cannon for the images that were paraded through the streets; all this caused much scandal among evangelical

Christians in England, and the practice was finally abandoned, but there was still no official attempt to impose Christianity, either in India or anywhere else in the Empire. The English had learnt from their thankless attempt to turn the Catholic Irish peasants into good Protestants.

Still, there were from the beginning tensions at work in a virtually secular empire that had not existed in those assumed to be ordained by God as emanations of the superior quality of the peoples of cultures who created them; in such holy empires the ruling class, either from faith or from a sense of the self-protective value of unity, always maintained an unbroken front in its attitude towards subject peoples. But the nineteenth century was a time when even religion tended to be egalitarian, so that the inner assault on the imperial point of view began on two different fronts, one impelled by religious and moral scruples, the other by political doubts.

First of all there were the evangelical Christians, made confident at the beginning of the century by their notable victories over the issue of slavery. They believed fervently in the superiority of their creed, and this led some of them to assume authoritarian stances, like Shirley Baker who became the virtual dictator of Tonga, or the Scots missionaries who set up a quasi-political regime around Lake Nyasa in Africa; there were even, here and there, civil servants and military commanders who took advantage of their positions of authority to proselytize, and one of the lesser contributory causes of the Indian Mutiny was the zeal with which certain British officers in the East India Company's forces set about attempting the conversion of their pious Brahmin or Muslim sepoys.

At the same time, the kind of predestinarianism that enabled Afrikaner Calvinists even in the late twentieth century callously to assume that Africans are beings forgotten by God did not flourish long in England, and the Victorians who went out into the remotest parts of the earth in the hope of achieving universal conversion believed that they were saving souls that were equal in the sight of God to their own. This gave them a very divided attitude towards imperialism. They saw the peoples they went to convert as children to be kept from corruption and carefully educated in Christian ways until they acquired maturity and could be regarded as good imitation Victorian Englishmen; this made them inclined to resist any interference from other Europeans until the process of transformation was complete. On the other hand, they soon learnt that in the unclaimed regions of the world, in the forests of Africa and the islands of Oceania, some kind of interference was inevitable, since it was as easy for rapacious traders, for Arab slavers or Australian blackbirders, to operate as it was for them, and for this reason, having tried in many cases to set up Christianized native kingdoms under their own tutelage, they usually gave in to the necessity of calling for the imposition of imperial power. British missionaries in Africa, French missionaries in New Caledonia and Tahiti, American missionaries in Hawaii were all in this way the precursors of their country's gunboats. Of all the many Christian kingdoms which the mission Churches set up in the pagan regions of the world, only one survived to the present day—the kingdom of Tonga, a splendidly preserved miniature of Victorian Christian monarchy; but even Tonga had to accept British protection to remain in existence.

But the logical conclusion of the evangelical creed was that paternalism could not last for ever. The children would grow up, and then they would be accepted as equals. It was because they sensed this that many of the imperialists, particularly those who inclined towards a crude form of racism, disliked the missionaries, who were especially unpopular in India. For the time being it was possible to perpetuate a situation like that described by Orwell in *Burmese Days*, where the Europeans sat in the front of the church while the native converts slipped in at the back. But everyone knew that some day the converts would want to move up to the front, and the conviction that they should do so made some forms of evangelical Christianity a weakening influence on the will to empire.

In recent years many priests and pastors have distinguished themselves in South Africa and Rhodesia in the struggle against the gross forms of imperialism that have survived in those countries, and it was in his contact with evangelical preachers in South Africa that Gandhi first realized to the full extent the radical social implications of some of the Christian doctrines; already, in England, he had been impressed on reading the Sermon on the Mount, and Christianity, filtered through the religious anarchism of Tolstoy's *The Kingdom of God is Within You*, became one of the strands that went into the making of *satyagraha*.

But though there is always the temptation to argue that British Christianity played its most decisive role in dismembering the Empire through its influence on Gandhian tactics, this would be unjust to other aspects of evangelical religion as it played on the attitudes of the British themselves. There is little doubt that the egalitarian inclinations of nonconformist Christianity, which contributed a heavy 'Chapel' support first to Gladstone's more anti-imperialist campaigns and then to the Labour Party, did a great deal to mitigate the imperialist influence of the Fabians on British left-wing political attitudes during the 1920s; this inclination was increased after the right wing of the Party split away to form the National Government in 1931, and left Labour under the leadership of the Christian Socialist George Lansbury, whose anti-imperialism was as sincere and complete as his anti-militarism.

In India itself, moreover, especially after the First World War, there were many missionaries who were moved to encourage and assist the struggle for national liberation. One of Gandhi's most ardent supporters and most valued associates there was the missionary C. F. Andrews; another was the Quaker pacifist Reginald Reynolds who carried to Lord Irwin the message in which Gandhi announced his intention to embark on the salt march and the ensuing *satyagraha* campaign; while one of the ablest of British publicists for the Congress cause was Edward Thompson, who first reached India as an educational missionary in 1910, and after twenty years observing the workings of the British Raj became a strong though critical supporter of Nehru and the more radical wing of Congress.

Edward Thompson introduces another important aspect of the changing British attitude towards India, for he was both a historian of the country—though a somewhat tendentious one—and a novelist of unremembered ability. Literature is one of the most sensitive indicators of a country's state of mind, often showing trends of thought long before they begin to find expression in political life. Since the early days of the nineteenth century a considerable British literature on India had sprung into being: little of it was produced on the spot, under the strain of Indian life, but much was written after their return to England by Anglo-Indians impelled by strong recollections to portray the kind of existence they had alternately endured and enjoyed. There was also a great deal of mere popular fiction exploiting the adventure or the exotic interest of India, like the novels for boys written by Henty about British military exploits in the subcontinent and the genteel romances of Ethel M. Dell, Maud Diver and Flora Annie Steel. Many of these writers advocated stern imperial rule—Maud Diver went so far as passionately to defend Dyer's massacre at Amritsar —and most of them reflected in their novels the ambivalent relationship, corrupted by mutual distrust, that had arisen between British and Indians after the Mutiny. Only rarely did criticism of Anglo-Indian society appear in British writings on India before the First World War, though Kipling—the most powerful of these writers—did not fear to speak his mind on the snobberies and frivolities of Calcutta and the little shut-in cantonments of the provinces. Kipling also, in the breadth of his mystique of imperialism, portrayed as no other writer on India has done the richness of the country's life, and spoke loudly—notably in *Kim* and a number of his poems—on the need for people of all races to fulfil what seemed to him the interdependent greatnesses of Britain and India. And Kipling, alone among his contemporaries, dared to warn again and again of the fates of empires that became too rigid and too proud.

It was a later generation that began to show the effect which life in subject India might have on the consciences of the more sensitive and open-minded Englishman who found himself cast in an imperial role. In the late Victorian age men like Allan Octavian Hume and his friend Sir William Wedderburn, who were not entirely satisfied with what the British had achieved in bringing India towards political maturity, had been able to conclude that it was simply a matter of guiding the Indians into the position where they could help themselves. There was really no element of doubt in the minds of such men about the value of Britain's role. They merely felt the paternal hand should be indulgent rather than stern. The contrast between their generation and the succeeding one is perhaps most dramatically shown by comparing them with the last British president of the Indian National Congress.

This was Annie Besant, one of the most extraordinary personalities in the varied history of British radicalism: a militant atheist collaborator of Charles Bradlaugh in the 1870s; an activist socialist in the 1880s who gained fame by leading the dramatic strike of the women workers in Bryant and May's match factory; an ardent Theosophist in the 1890s; a zealous student of Hindu culture in the first years of the new century; and, returning to the militancy of her socialist days, an agitator for Indian liberation in the 1910s. What makes Annie Besant so significant a portent is that she was the first of the British in India—or at least the first who gained any celebrity—to immerse herself in Indian life, to regard that life as good in its own terms, and to approach Indian problems with something resembling an Indian understanding. She founded a newspaper, *New India*, which became very influential, and through it she advocated Home Rule. Ordered to cease her agitation during the war, she refused, was interned in 1917, and emerged to find herself hailed by the Indians as a martyr and elected president of Congress, where she found that events had already passed her by, for it was now more than Home Rule that Gandhi and his followers wanted, and she saw in their campaigns a danger of violence which, as a Theosophist, she could not condone.

Annie Besant remains a more or less isolated figure among the Anglo-Indians; no one else became so intimately immersed in both Indian religious life and Indian nationalist politics. Only Edward Thompson among the significant Anglo-Indian writers became involved in the Indian nationalist cause while he was in the country; yet the works of many of these writers show a growing distaste for the position of the British in India. The earliest book of this kind was written not about India but about Ceylon. It was a novel called *A Village in the Jungle*, written by a member of the Ceylon Civil Service named Leonard Woolf, who later married Virginia Stephen. The novel was published in 1913, and by this time Woolf had resigned, for the writing of the book convinced him that he wanted no part of an imperial system. During the 'twenties the idea that the time for departure had come was expressed in several novels which aroused attention in Britain, notably Edmund Candler's *Abdication* and Thompson's *An Indian Day* and *Night Falls on Siva's Hill*. But the important work in bringing to the British consciousness the embarrassing complexities of their involvement in India was E. M. Forster's *A Passage to India*, which appeared in 1924.

Critics have always been divided in their views of Forster's intent in writing *A Passage to India*; some have seen it as a manifesto against British rule, and others have suggested that it is a criticism of Western indifference to Indian spiritual life. The probability is that Forster in fact had little didactic intent of any kind, and was merely writing a novel which he felt would be true of his own experience and perception of India. But the effect was something different, and for many British people in the 1920s—and especially in the 1930s after *A Passage to India* gained wide readership as one of the first books affected by the paperback revolution —Forster's representation of encounters between Britons and Indians was a revelation of the corruption as well as the injustice involved in the relationship.

In the 1930s Edward Thompson published books even more sharply critical of the Raj, including his master work, *A Farewell to India*, and a group of younger writers emerged to take up the theme, notably Dennis Kincaid, a member of the Indian Civil Service, and Eric Blair, a former officer of the Indian Imperial Police in Burma, who was to gain celebrity under his nom-de-plume of George Orwell.

Orwell's bitter sketches, 'Shooting an Elephant' and 'A Hanging', appeared in the early 1930s, and his novel, *Burmese Days*, in 1935. They epitomized the complex feelings of those young educated British who found they could no longer justify involvement in the mechanism of Empire. 'Shooting an Elephant' is particularly impressive for showing the false roles into which the imperialist is forced so as to maintain the position expected of him by the subject people while he remains responsible for keeping them in order and—theoretically at least—for their welfare. Like most writers of this group, Orwell makes no attempt to idealize the Indians or the Burmese. Indeed, one of the points that he and his fellows seem intent on making is that British and Indians do not get on well because their relationship is necessarily a false one. We should not—the implication flows from Candler and Thompson through Forster and Kincaid to Orwell—expect the Indians to be other than they are. Thus a whole century of Victorian endeavour to improve the subject peoples into Westerners is rejected. The further implication emerges that the best thing we can do for the Indians is to leave them alone; in other words to depart and let the people of the country deal with whatever situation may arise from the act of liberation.

Such writers represented a minority in British opinion even in the 1930s. The public they reached, even in Penguin editions, was a restricted one, and by no means all their readers were convinced.

The heritage of evangelical Christianity was still strong; the conflict between the sense of responsibility for people we have conquered and ruled and the feeling that the doors of the cage should be opened immediately was a painful one for many idealistic Britons. It was a particularly painful one when they were political leaders, and had to think of the possible economic consequences of withdrawal. Experience was to reveal, once India was free, that the financial profit of retaining an Empire had become much less than the cost of continuing to rule unwilling subjects, but this was not yet evident in the 1930s, and the indecisions which afflicted even the most sympathetic of British political leaders, with their responsibility to heterogenous groups of interests, was shown clearly in a book by a Labour leader published in 1937.

> The Labour Party has always fully accepted the rights of the Indian peoples to govern themselves, but it has recognized that the problem involved in developing self-governing institutions in a great continent inhabited by peoples who differ in language, race and creed is no easy one. The long period of British rule has created a situation in which there have been many rights acquired by particular sections of the Indian people. It is not right to abandon control without taking care to see that these rights will be respected. 'India for the Indians' is a simple slogan, but it is necessary to see what it means in terms of human life. There is no particular gain in handing over the peasants and workers of India to be exploited by their own capitalists and landlords. Nationalism is a creed that may be sustained with great self-sacrifice and idealism, but may shelter class domination and intolerance of minorities as well as economic exploitation.
>
> Throughout all the enquiries into the constitutional position of India, and also of Burma, Labour members have always realized that nationalism was not enough. They have always sought to give to the Indian masses the potential power of bettering their economic condition by political action. They have recognized frankly that it is unlikely that a poor and illiterate population will escape exploitation at the hands of the rich, the privileged, and the educated classes, but they have stood firm for giving them the possibility of advance.

They have recognized also that it is impossible for an alien race to overcome the social and economic evils which are closely bound up with the whole conceptions of the Indian people. Only the Indian people themselves can work out their salvation. The sooner they have the full opportunity to do so the better.

(The Labour Party in Perspective)

The authorship of this passage, with its significant avoidance of specific promises, is particularly interesting in view of later events; it was written by Clement Attlee, who only ten years later, in 1947, considered as Prime Minister that British opinion had reached the point where it would be politically safe for Labour to follow the personal inclinations of many of its leaders and set India free.

A comparison of Attlee's statement with what Orwell was writing in the 1930s on the one hand, and what Churchill was saying in defence of imperialism on the other, gives a fair perspective of the state of British opinion regarding the Empire on the eve of the Second World War. Many of the intellectuals and a fair portion of the working class were highly sympathetic to the idea of immediately liberating India. They were still, however, far from a majority, as were the surviving imperialists who followed Churchill's lead or—particularly among the lower middle classes —were bemused by Beaverbook's crusade of Empire Free Trade with its lingering dream of greatness through imperial federation. But a growing middle group was represented fairly accurately by Attlee's argument that Britain might have a responsibility to ensure that the colonial peoples were fairly set on the path of progress (and progress in this context seemed to imply Westernization) before the links were finally severed. The events of the war were to shift the viewpoint of this large centrist group, and it was this shift of opinion transforming itself into moral power that, as Gandhi had foreseen, eventually moved the British to resign their Empire.

XIV The Brightest Jewel Lost

Before the end was reached, the interim of the 'thirties had to be passed, a time of slow progress hidden under a veil of mutual exhaustion. Gandhi withdrew into formulating his plans for a village India after liberation, and into his struggle to purify Indian society by eliminating the discriminations against untouchables incorporated into the traditional caste system. Sporadic civil disobedience campaigns continued through 1932 and 1933, but Gandhi called them off in 1934 and for the rest of the decade remained in retreat from political activity, leaving Congress a battleground in which younger leaders fought for control, led by Jawaharlal Nehru from the Left and Subhas Chandra Bose from the Right.

For the rest of the decade initiative rested with the British. Already by this time a considerable change had come over their administration in India. The localization of the Indian Civil Service was proceeding apace, and it has been estimated that, even if the British had not abandoned the government of India in 1947, no more than a quarter of that elite corps of guardians would have been Britons by the end of the decade. In all the less prestigious services the proportion of Indians was high before the end of the 'thirties, and even in the Indian Army, which the British feared most of all to let out of their control, a policy of commissioning Indians came into operation with the outbreak of the Second World War and the immense increase in the Indian armed forces.

It was not, however, merely a question of British being replaced by Indian officials, for effective imperialisms have been created by co-opting local elites, as Akbar and the later Moghuls did when they employed as generals and governors the warrior princes of Rajputana who otherwise would have been a source of perpetual unrest. The British themselves—and especially the middle class, that for a century and a half had provided recruits for the Indian services—were growing weary of the white man's burden. Members of old Anglo-Indian families, like John Strachey and George Orwell, rejected the service of the Empire. Even in the 'thirties, a decade of low employment among the educated, the number and quality of candidates for the services declined. The prestigious I.C.S. itself began to assume an aura of obsolescence. And among those who entered it in more confident days and who accepted its eventual Indianization as the logical and desirable end of their efforts, an unease had developed over the equivocal character their work had assumed now they were expected to exercise authority and judgment over men they often respected for seeking to give concrete expression to the very ideals of self-determination which the British themselves had imported into India through their educational system and through classic English writings that were freely available in the bookshops of Calcutta and Bombay.

There was a dramatic example of this dilemma as early as 1922, when Gandhi came into confrontation at Ahmedabad with a young I.C.S. magistrate, C. N. Broomfield. The incident struck the imagination of every witness as a kind of portent of the future, and it went down into the mythology of the Indian independence movement as 'the Great Trial'. Gandhi had been involved during 1921 and the early part of 1922 in a number of civil disobedience movements which had saddened him because he could not eliminate the sporadic occurrence of violence, and finally, as he was about to launch a great *satyagraha* which he hoped—as he hoped of several such movements in the 1920s and 1930s—would last until the British gave up their rule, a mob in Gorackpur had killed more than twenty policemen and thrown their bodies into a burning town hall. Gandhi called off the campaign he had planned, and was so disheartened by the tragedy that when the British arrested him he remarked, 'My removal from their midst will be a benefit for the people.'

There was no doubt that Gandhi was technically guilty under the sedition laws, for he had written a number of articles in *Young India* calling for the overthrow of the Government and 'a fight to the finish'; quite evidently he had done so with a deliberate thought of provoking the British to take action against him, which they did. This part of the scenario was now customary; Gandhi's almost compulsive offering of himself for martyrdom and the expected and almost ritualized reaction of the police authorities. It was the handling of the case by Broomfield that was novel.

There was no doubt in Broomfield's mind that if he were to carry out the duty he had undertaken to sustain the Raj, he must condemn Gandhi in accordance with the law, for the prisoner not only admitted but gloried in his guilt. Yet if there was ever a man on whom duty weighed heavily it was Broomfield on that day, for he recognized the stature and temper of the man who stood before him and the nobility of his cause. He sentenced him to six years' imprisonment, giving the verdict the air of a compliment by remarking that this was the sentence which Gandhi's predecessor Tilak had once received for a similar offence. He added that in passing sentence he had taken into account that in the eyes of many of his countrymen Gandhi was a great patriot and a great leader; even those who differed from him, Broomfield added — with the obvious implication that he was speaking for himself — recognized his high ideals and the nobility and saintliness of his life. 'If the course of events in India should make it possible for the Government to reduce the period and release you,' he added, 'no one will be better pleased than I.' Gandhi thanked Broomfield for his courtesy and judge and prisoner bowed solemnly to each other, Gandhi going joyfully off to prison and Broomfield returning to his villa with a troubled mind. Broomfield made no other notable contribution to the history of India; there was no need. He had stated memorably the dilemma of the Englishman of good will in the India that in those decades between the wars was lurching towards freedom.

The dilemma of which all Indian administrators were now conscious — the problem of where paternal government should end and the masses of India be given into the control of their largely self-appointed leaders — dominated the British legislation which in turn set the pace of events in India during the middle years of the 1930s. After yet another Round Table Conference at the end of 1932, from which Gandhi was absent for the simple reason that he was imprisoned in India, and after extensive deliberations by parliamentary committees, the Cabinet finally produced the Government of India Act, which passed through both Houses and became law in 1935. It was a cumbersome hybrid measure, intended to satisfy as many Indian interests as possible, and, under the guise of completing the British achievement of Indian unity, to bring the native states into the political structure of the country. This was to be attained by creating a federal political framework. British India would be divided into eleven provinces, in each of which there would be local self-government. The native states would remain locally autonomous, and for the time being at least under the absolute power of their rulers, modified by constitutions in the rare cases where these had been granted. But there would be a federal legislature, partly elected by the voters of British India (on a range of qualifications which now gave the franchise to at least thirty million people) and partly nominated by the princes, and this would control all matters of national concern through responsible ministers, except for foreign affairs, defence and the amending of the constitution, which would remain in the hands of the British authorities.

Contrary to British expectations, the federal proposals pleased nobody. Congress objected because the native states were not required to guarantee responsible government or civil liberties. The Muslim League objected because the majority of princes were Hindu and this would weight the federal structure even more heavily against them than the proportions of population might justify. In the end the princes themselves killed the scheme because they were unwilling to accept the loss of sovereignty it implied.

The clauses of the Act that provided for responsible provincial government in British India could, however, go into operation immediately, and the Government planned to hold elections early in 1937. It was an interesting test of the flexibility of Congress policy. Should the organization, having so loudly and so often demanded complete independence, now accept the kind of local home rule which the Canadian colonies had achieved almost ninety years before? There were few of the leaders who did not wish to enjoy, after the years of struggle, the first taste of power. They asked advice of Gandhi, who had no intention of participating. 'India is still a prison,' he told them, 'but the superintendent allows the prisoners to elect the officials who run the jail.' Adopting a line that events showed to be of dubious honesty, Congress candidates ran on an election manifesto that pledged them 'not to co-operate in any way with the Act, but to combat it and seek to end it'. When Congress gained a majority in six of the eleven provinces and emerged as the largest single party in three others, that promise was quickly forgotten and, after some face-saving negotiations about the residuary powers of disallowance vested in the Governors, Congress took office in seven provinces.

There was a brief interlude of co-operation and relative peace-fulness, when the Indians felt for the first time that they were controlling their own destinies, and the British felt that they had at last neutralized Congress by incorporating it into the power structure of the Raj. Congress ministers enjoyed giving instruc-tions to British civil servants and ordering British police officers to deal with rioters, who began to appear in the streets again as soon as they discovered that Indians were not much different as rulers from Englishmen. The most serious negative effect of the situation was undoubtedly the polarization of interests which power and the prospect of further power induced. The Muslim League, which had not done very well in the elections, began to talk of a separate Muslim State, and riots between Hindus and Muslims, and between Sikhs and Muslims, became more frequent. Factions hardened within Congress itself. The Communists, growing in strength, skirmished around the edges of the political battlefield, and embarrassed the new Congress Governments by fomenting strikes which destroyed the appearance of universal support.

Perhaps the most significant development was the way in which the Congress leaders who had assumed office turned away from Gandhi's programme of a decentralized village society with minimal government and minimal administration. The more dy-namic leaders, whether they were capitalistically or socialistically inclined, envisaged a free India that would not only adopt the governmental structure evolved in Britain, but would also move towards industrialization and a general Westernization of educa-tion and social attitudes. Some Gandhian ideas, such as prohibition and the promotion of handicrafts and village industries, were encouraged, but this was done mainly as a gesture to the past of the movement and to its most distinguished member.

Looking back, one can indeed see these early Congress minis-tries as a model of the India that was to emerge after liberation, with its adept manipulation of a genuine democracy to produce one-party rule, its ministerial arrogance, its emphasis on indus-trialization as a panacea for an agrarian society, its nominal tribute to the Gandhian tradition, its hypersensitivity to criticism, its sanctimonious tone, and its reliance on a bureaucracy taken over from the British and little adapted.

By 1939 Congress was settling down fairly efficiently to the business of ruling. There seemed every reason to suppose that in India, as in the settlement colonies, this was the first stage in a graded progress towards freedom and that in a decade or so the country would reach dominion status, after which the Indians could choose what kind of independence they wanted to adopt.

The possibility of this leisurely development was destroyed by external events which revealed to the Indians that what they had grasped as substance was only shadow. In September 1939, without consulting the provincial ministries or the leaders of Congress or the Muslim League, the Viceroy, Lord Linlithgow, proclaimed that India was at war with Germany. He was moving carefully within the constitutional limitations of the 1935 Act. The provincial Governments had no legal right to be consulted over all-Indian affairs, the province of the yet uncreated federal legislature. And even the federal legislature, had it existed, would have had no legal grounds for protest, since the declaration of war involved precisely those areas of responsibility—foreign affairs and defence —reserved to the Viceroy. All imperial precedents taught that internally self-governing territories, which the Indian provinces but not India as a whole had become, must still accept imperial decisions on all matters of external policy. Until the Statute of Westminster this had applied even to the dominions. And India was not yet a dominion.

The leaders of Congress were faced by a situation made complex by their own divided feelings and loyalties. For the pacifist Gandhi the situation was very simple: violence should be avoided, Britain and France should abandon military resistance to the Nazis and receive German invaders with a show of civil disobedience. For Subhas Chandra Bose, the right-wing nationalist, it seemed equally simple, as it seemed to many of his kind in Europe; he believed that he could use the totalitarian dictators to displace the British and emerge free of both in the end. Nehru did not share Gandhi's refusal to acknowledge the existence of evil, nor did he imagine, like Bose, that he had discovered the right kind of long spoon to sup with the devil. He harboured no illusions about the dictators, and he welcomed the fact that Britain had taken up the struggle against them. But he was unable to accept the idea of India fighting beside Britain in what purported to be a fight for freedom if her own freedom were denied. The situation created by the Viceroy's declaration was made all the more bitter since it defined very clearly her difference of status from the white dominions. All of them had declared war separately, in South Africa's case only after acrimonious debate; Ireland had even declared neutrality instead of war, and yet had been allowed to remain within the Commonwealth. It was intolerable that India should not have the same choice.

The leaders of Congress, presuming on their influence over the provincial Governments, issued a statement declaring their abhorrence of Nazi crimes against humanity but refusing to associate themselves with the war effort unless India was declared an independent nation. This was beyond the Viceroy's power, or even that of the Cabinet in London, under present legislation. Linlithgow, who was anxious to reach a compromise within existing possibilities, announced that the British Government envisaged dominion status as an ultimate end and undertook that as soon as the war was ended the 1935 Act would be modified after consultation with Indians of all parties and communities. He invited the leaders of the various interests to co-operate in forming an advisory council so that the Government should be in touch with Indian opinion.

It was as much as Linlithgow could do, but it was not enough for the leaders of Congress, who assumed that the responsibilities of Britain in Europe and the Far East provided them with a unique opportunity for applying the pressure of non-cooperation. Accordingly, they ordered all the Congress-dominated provincial Governments to resign. The Governors assumed emergency powers, and the net effect of the exercise was to strengthen the Muslim League. Jinnah pledged allegiance to the British cause, and the Muslims continued to enlist in the Indian Army, so that in spite of Congress non-cooperation, almost three million Indians joined the British colours. It was the largest volunteer army in the world's history, serving in East Africa, Egypt, Iraq, Burma; 65 per cent of those who enlisted were Muslims. Jinnah exacted his price. In March 1940 he denounced the federal provisions of the 1935 Act and declared that the Muslim League aimed at the establishment of an autonomous State in the areas where Muslims were in the majority. It was an obligation which the British were forced in the end unwillingly to honour.

Meanwhile, further communications between Linlithgow, who continued to offer dominion status after the war, and the Congress leaders, who called for immediate independence and a constitutional assembly elected by universal suffrage, led to no conclusion, and Gandhi was called out of his political retirement to organize another *satyagraha*. Indian politics seemed to have returned to another of its customary impasses, when the situation was changed by the resounding collapse of British power in the Far East.

Long before December 1941, when the Japanese set out deliberately and successfully to destroy British power in the China Seas, perceptive observers had foreseen that the British position on the China coast would be imperilled in the event of another world war, though few of them can have expected so rapidly dramatic a collapse.

As we have seen, the mere increase in responsibilities which the spread of empire entailed had convinced the British Government even before the First World War that it was no longer possible to defend single-handed the City's interests on the China coast; the alliance with Japan had been initiated in 1902 to offset the threat of Russia, and it had shown its further uses in the First World War.

By weakening the British economy, that war virtually destroyed the British position in the Far East. By abandoning the treaty with Japan and accepting the American conditions for limitation of navies embodied in the Washington Treaty, Britain lost an ally without immediately gaining a friend. At a time when Chinese nationalism was gaining in audacity and Japanese imperialism in strength, Britain was forced to withdraw its capital ships from the Far East, and to rely on small ships and small garrisons, supported by the hollow but expensive gesture of the Singapore naval base.

The withdrawals from Hankow in 1927 and Weihaiwei in 1930 were interpreted by the Chinese and observed by the Japanese— and perhaps also by the Americans—as signs that the old lion was at last losing its teeth. It is arguable that the Japanese might not have so lightly begun their adventures in the Far East if these incidents had not convinced them that Britain was no longer a real power on the China coast. Their invasion of Manchuria began significantly in the year after Britain withdrew from its northern Chinese outpost of Weihaiwei, and it was followed in 1932 by a Japanese landing at Shanghai, as a result of which the International Settlement was so closely threatened that the race-course became a battlefield between Chinese and Japanese. At the time, indeed, the English *taipans*, who controlled Shanghai's commerce and virtually ruled the International Settlement through its Municipal Council, were so blinded by their anger over British concessions to the Chinese that they favoured the Japanese, much as English Conservatives at the same period favoured Mussolini and a little later favoured Hitler. An imperialist National Government was back in power in Westminster, and face was temporarily saved when Britain managed to send soldiers from India and ne-gotiate a truce which established a demilitarized zone around the International Settlement.

In 1937, five years on in economic recession, when the Japanese and Chinese again fought on the outskirts of Shanghai, the British were able to send fewer men than the French and no more than the American contingent. These ten thousand or so troops which the Western powers together assembled seemed a puny defence force in comparison with the two hundred thousand troops which the Japanese brought in to occupy the region surrounding the city, once accepted without dispute as a British sphere of influence. The Japanese gave emphasis to their triumph by holding a vic-tory march through the International Settlement. They also chal-lenged the British control of the Chinese Maritime Customs, and forced changes in its administration. The onset of war in 1939 brought a further weakening of the British position on the China coast; in August 1940 the last of the imperial land forces were withdrawn, and the young men who had formed the backbone of the Shanghai Defence Force departed for service in England. Only American marines and a British gunboat remained as un-impressive defenders of European interests. The Japanese took the opportunity to challenge the British control of the Municipal Council, and they demanded and gained equal representation. In November 1940 even the American marines departed. In Decem-ber the Japanese set about destroying all manifestations of Anglo-Saxon power, whether British or American, in the Far East.

It is unnecessary to go into the details of that sensational *débâcle*, for they have been often described and discussed. It is sufficient for present purposes to note the rapidity with which events followed each other, and the way in which they revealed the void of power that lay behind the mask of British prestige. On December 7th, the day of Pearl Harbor, the Japanese sank the British gunboat and occupied the International Settlement; British concessions in Japanese-dominated parts of China were simultaneously seized. On December 8th Hong Kong was attacked; despite its garrison and a display of foolhardy valour on the part of the clerks and shopkeepers enrolled in the Hong Kong Defence Force, it was reduced by December 18th. Sarawak, Brunei and North Borneo were overrun by January 8th. In Malaya the attacks began on December 7th and after nightmare weeks marked by civilian panic and military incompetence, the British troops retreated into the island stronghold of Singapore on the last day of January. Disaster followed on disaster. Two of Britain's greatest capital ships, the *Prince of Wales* and the *Repulse*, sailed out to defend Singapore without proper air cover and were immediately sunk by Japanese planes. And the impregnable Singapore, which no known navy could have breached, proved all too vulnerable by land. It surrendered on February 15th. Meanwhile the Japanese had swept into Burma and down into Oceania. One by one the British possessions fell: the Gilberts, the Solomons, most of New Guinea. But there the impetus of the great wave of invasion slowed and died. The Japanese never took Port Moresby, they never reached the New Hebrides or the Ellices, they did not cross from Burma into India. But it was not by its own power that Britain halted and turned back the flood. The Australians and the Americans held the Japanese in the South Pacific, and of the million troops who were needed to fight them in Burma, no less than 700,000 were Indian.

The British have traditionally taken a pride in losing battles but winning wars, and in the past their doggedness had often enabled them to conceal under the glory of victory the early defeats that came from a chronic inclination towards unpreparedness. But the victory over the Japanese in the Second World War carried so much less of glory than of relief for Britain that the defeats were remembered and the lessons drawn. A century of British arrogance and exploitation in the China Seas from the scandalous days of the Opium Wars had been brought to an end by non-European people. The audacious bluffs by which handfuls of British soldiers had defeated great disorganized armies of Asians would work no more; the strange charisma by which a single Englishman could rule unarmed over half a million subjects had been dissipated for ever. Not only had it been shown that Asians could fight the white man's kind of war as efficiently as the white man; it had also been shown that as white men went the British were not even very efficient in their military arrangements, and that self-satisfaction and a century of unchallenged security in the Far East had made them unalert in a perilous world. Such sweeping defeats inevitably lowered their standing, even among peoples who later found the experience of 'liberation' by the Japanese unpleasant enough to welcome a return of the British, as the Malays and the Gilbertese did. And the extent to which they owed their return in the mid 'forties to massive American aid did not enable them to regain more than a semblance of their former prestige. The days were gone when Indian or any other Asian boys would chant, as Gandhi and his friends did in childhood:

> Behold the mighty Englishman.
> He rules the Indian small
> Because being a meat-eater
> He is five cubits tall.

The Brocken spectre that Britain once cast over the East was dissipated, in 1941, for ever.

Yet the Brocken spectre is always cast by a real figure, and while the Japanese had swept away the insubstantial manifestations of British power in the Far East, that power still in 1941 remained solid in the old heart of the Empire; in the Near East, which, even when the invasion of Britain was feared, was defended so stubbornly that neither the Germans nor the Italians ever came dangerously near to Suez; and in India, where—even if Burma, which had become a separate colony in 1937, was mainly lost—the boundaries of the traditional Raj were always held. In these areas the British armies were far stronger, better equipped and more ably generalled than they had been in Malaya and Hong Kong, the only defended British strongpoints in the Far East. Hong Kong, except for the dispatch of two badly trained battalions from Canada, was left to its fate as virtually indefensible, and the hasty and ill-planned last-minute attempts to save Singapore—which merely resulted in tens of thousands of men being unnecessarily consigned to Japanese prison camps—contrasted with the elaborate and ably sustained plans to save Suez and the frontiers of India, made at a time when the British Government was seriously considering the possibility of Britain having to be temporarily abandoned and the struggle for the Empire carried on from headquarters in Canada.

It was this solid British presence that the Indian nationalists had to face at a time when the misfortunes of war had made the British disinclined to submit to political reverses as well. Nevertheless, the entry of the United States into the war had changed the situation, since Roosevelt made it clear that he did not wish American assistance to result in an increase in the British Empire, as it had done in the previous World War, and also pressed the point that it was inconsistent to fight for freedom in Europe and not in Asia. Even before America's entry into the war, Churchill had been forced, by Britain's need for economic aid, to accept the Atlantic Charter, which declared that the two countries 'respect the right of all peoples to choose the form of government under which they will live; and they wish to see sovereign rights and self-government restored to those who have been forcibly deprived of them'.

The Atlantic Charter did not refer specifically to the British Empire; nevertheless, its implications were evident, and it was in their spirit that Roosevelt pressed for British moves that would have the effect of diminishing the scope of empire. He was successful in the Far East, for early in 1943 the British and American Governments agreed that all special rights in the treaty ports of the China coast should be abandoned, so that the British control of the Chinese Maritime Customs came to an end. Only Hong Kong—retained in the face of American disapproval—would remain at the war's end, the last remnant of the structure of British power on the China coast, though the *taipans* would return for a brisk four years of trading before the Communist victory in 1949 and the final eclipse of the British presence in Shanghai and the satellite ports.

In India it was largely through Roosevelt's urging that Churchill in 1942 sent out Stafford Cripps to try and end the impasse between Congress and the Government. Cripps appeared to be well fitted for the mission; he was known as a left-wing socialist and an anti-imperialist. But Cripps was also a rather moralistic intellectual who would earn universal dislike in Britain during the later 1940s for the austerities he inflicted in his role of Chancellor of the Exchequer. And the proposals he carried with him differed in detail rather than substance from what had already been offered. Britain would still be responsible for the defence of India. Dominion status was still the limit of the British offer. It would still be granted only at the end of the war after a constitutional assembly consisting of representatives from British India and the princely states had decided its form. Any province or state that wished to keep aside from the union would still be free to do so. This did not meet the Congress demand for an independent national Government in a united India, and it did not meet the increasingly firm Muslim League demand for a separate Islamic State. Cripps went back without any agreement, and in August 1942 Congress passed a resolution calling on the British to quit India immediately and unconditionally. Gandhi came out of retirement to lead yet another great *satyagraha* campaign. He and the other Congress leaders were immediately arrested and interned in the Aga Khan's palace at Poona, and the agitation fell into the hands of obscure leaders of another kind, so that several months of violence ensued; the disturbances were relatively quickly brought to an end, and the British went about their task of holding on to and defending India.

But the years that followed were marred by a number of incidents whose cumulative effect was a great shaking of British confidence. Owing to a failure of distribution, largely due to the requisitioning of river craft for military purposes, a disastrous rice shortage in Bengal led to one of the worst Indian famines in sixty years. Conservative estimates of the number of dead start at 1,500,000; others run as high as 3,000,000. In political terms this was an immense blow to the reputation for efficient and humane administration by which the British had tried to justify their presence in India; even the most chaotic native administration could hardly have done worse. Furthermore, among the immense Indian armed forces there were signs of disaffection of a kind the British had dreaded since the days of the Mutiny. Subhas Chandra Bose, who had fled to Berlin in 1941, arrived in Japanese-held Singapore in 1943 to set up a puppet 'provisional Government of free India'. From among the Indian prisoners of war in

Singapore and Burma he formed an 'Indian national army' to fight beside the Japanese. Only a minority of the prisoners joined this organization, which played no significant part in the Burmese campaigns, but it was disturbing knowledge to the British that many of its members came from the Sikh regiments on whose loyalty they had previously relied. Then, early in 1946, ratings of the Indian navy mutinied in Bombay; in addition to these anti-British manifestations, there was a growing tension between Hindus, Sikhs and Muslims within the armed forces, which made the Indian regiments increasingly unreliable as an instrument for maintaining order. If, as the imperialists in Britain still argued, India should be held for another generation so that impartial administration could foster its real unification, then it would have to be held by British occupation forces considerably larger than had been kept there before the war. Such an army could only be sustained by conscription, and there were immense political difficulties involved in the use of British conscripts to defend imperial possessions indefinitely.

The difficulty of manning a continued administration of India was only one of the problems that faced the British Government when the war ended in 1945 and the status of India for the foreseeable future had to be determined. There was also the economic situation of Britain, with foreign investments almost entirely dissipated, and with financial obligations to the United States that forced Whitehall to give an ear to American opinion, which at that time, before the breach in the wartime alliance with Russia and the success of Communism in China, was critical of the continuing British presence as a power in Asia.

American opinion was only part of a general climate of anti-imperial thought in those first two or three years of peace, when people still took seriously the concepts of a just world that had formed the most effective aspect of Allied propaganda during the years of war. It was in this spirit that in the general election of 1945 the British people—who had accepted Churchill as the best man for fighting a war—decided to make a change when it came to organizing the peace, and for the first time elected a Labour Government with an absolute working majority.

The Labour Party was sensitive enough to the atmosphere of that time to recognize the mood of generosity in which the people had voted them into power. The British wanted a better life for themselves, but they wanted it also for others whose lives lay in their power, and there is no doubt that the idea of liberating India had the approval of the electorate. The new Government got quickly to work by sending out a Cabinet Mission, led by Lord Pethick-Lawrence, a great friend of India, and including Cripps. In association with Lord Wavell, the Governor-General, the Cabinet Mission worked out a plan for a federal India, with a union Government that would control only foreign affairs, defence and communications, and with subordinate groupings of provinces which could arrange between themselves how they might deal with local matters. This would allow the Muslim provinces to form themselves into a bloc enjoying a considerable autonomy. Both Congress and the Muslim League provisionally accepted the plan, and then, whether by design or folly, Nehru made a pronouncement that once India was free the constitution could be amended. This immediately aroused Jinnah's suspicions, wrecked the chances of the Cabinet Mission's plan, and made the partition of India inevitable.

From this point the main desire of Britain was to extricate itself from a situation that grew daily more chaotic, as fighting between Muslims and Hindus began in Calcutta and Bihar. It was too late now for the firm re-establishment of the Raj, and in any case the British Government had no desire for that kind of retrogression. Somehow Britain must contrive to withdraw with the least loss of face while leaving the Indians to work out the consequences of their own disunity. An Executive Council set up under Nehru's leadership to serve as a provisional cabinet failed to secure full Muslim co-operation, and the elected Constituent Assembly met in December 1946, only to be boycotted by the League. Wavell, an honest and able man who had done the best he could in a difficult situation, was made scapegoat and dismissed from the Governor-Generalship. This cleared the way for Lord Mountbatten, a great-grandson of Queen Victoria, to wind up the rule which she had assumed in an age of different concepts; deputed to arrange the transfer of power by June 1948, he succeeded in doing so nearly a year earlier by declaring almost as soon as he arrived in the spring of 1947 that the only solution was the creation of two separate independent countries in the subcontinent, India and Pakistan. Britain accepted this Herculean solution and on July 18th, 1947, Parliament passed the law granting independence.

It was in part a saving of face, since the Act granted both India and Pakistan dominion status, but on the understanding that they proceed thence at their own pace.

In mid August the last alien troops left India, but if the British had gone, their work largely survived, in systems of administration and education, in military traditions, in the language that remained the only effective lingua franca, in the strange Victorian slang that Indians and Pakistanis still use, and—in India itself at least—in a democratic system of a fundamentally British kind.

With the independence of India and Pakistan, the transformation from an Empire into a Commonwealth advanced by an important and formally recognized step. In July 1947 the Dominions Office became the Commonwealth Relations Office, and the Imperial Conferences were replaced by Commonwealth Prime Ministers' Conferences. The survival of a part of the British domain that could still be considered imperial was recognized by the continued separate existence of the Colonial Office until 1955. Yet though this colonial empire at the moment of India's liberation still loomed large on the world's map, the loss of India meant that the population of the Empire outside the dominions was reduced in one stroke by three-quarters. With the loss of India, Britain remained for another twenty years an imperial power of steadily decreasing importance, but in 1947 it ceased to be an imperial giant.

The liberation of India has been in great part the result of a shifting of the structure of power within Britain, due to the coming to political consciousness and political capability of classes to whom the Empire had no concrete meaning as a way of life, and whose imperial sentiments had existed only at times of jingo passion and then only in distorted forms. As the imperial rulers within India had decreased in numbers, their support at home had correspondingly shrunk. One may doubt whether—as some recent historians of India have argued—Macaulay and Elphinstone would have felt that their dream of an Indian future had come true, and certainly there were eloquent critics of what Churchill called 'the steady and remorseless process of divesting ourselves of what has been gained by so many generations of toil, administration and sacrifice'. But it was astonishing how little response such Jeremiahs evoked, and how gladly, almost indifferently, the British in 1947 witnessed the beginning of the end of empire.

Time, in truth, had transformed them; they were a different people from the Victorians and Edwardians who had created the Second Empire; not less courageous, as their solid and solitary defiance of an apparently all-conquering Germany had shown in 1940, but certainly less convinced of the innate superiority of the Anglo-Saxon and his consequent right to rule as much of the world as he could grab.

Part IV
Hustling to the End

XV   Imperial Masquerade

George Curzon was often regarded as the most pompous and imperceptive of all imperial proconsuls. As the doggerel ran,

> My name is George Nathanial Curzon,
> I am a most superior person,
> My cheek is pink, my hair is sleek,
> I dine at Blenheim once a week.

Yet Curzon's insights in terms of imperial power were often prophetically accurate. He was derided or condemned when he sent troops into Tibet to ward off the Russian danger and when he proposed to set up a protectorate in Persia in a similarly precautionary mood. Yet, from a purely imperial point of view, the ideas of annexing Tibet and Persia were not at all lacking in strategic wisdom; all that was lacking was the ability on Britain's part to sustain such conquests.

Curzon was certainly correct when in 1908 he cut through the talk of trusteeship that had accompanied the seizing of the African colonies and Egypt, and pointed out that all these possessions were really ancillary to the Empire in India, and that their fate depended on the survival of the Raj. The ultimate imperial consequences of the loss of India were clear to Curzon as they were to few men in his day or even in 1947. 'Your ports and your coaling-stations, your fortresses and your dockyards, your Crown colonies and protectorates will go too. For either they will be unnecessary, as the tollgates and barbicans of an Empire that has vanished, or they will be taken by an enemy more powerful than yourselves.'

In a world where the United Nations has acted as a kind of universal public opinion, and where the nuclear balance of power has led aggressors to move carefully and only near to home, Britain's imperial possessions were not forcefully taken away after

India was freed; indeed, some possessions already lost were actually returned to her in the attempt to re-create the *status quo ante bellum* after the defeat of Japan. But they were gradually found to be unnecessary, and when we look back in the 1970s at the dismantling of the Empire—hardly a year from 1954 to 1971 without a colony (sometimes two or three) leaving or a protectorate being abandoned—it has all the harmonious regularity of a planned progression.

The impression is heightened by the fact that, in spite of nasty brushfires in Kenya, Palestine and Cyprus, Britain never had to face disastrous colonial wars like those the French fought in Algeria and Indo-China or the Americans in Vietnam. This was partly due to the reluctance to put up a big imperial fight that developed after the South African War. Wilfred Scawen Blunt noticed this reluctance as early as 1913. 'If the lessons of history teach us anything, they teach us that a nation cannot retain other nations in subjection unless it is ready at all points to fight. The English nation is already overburdened with its dependencies and though everyone talks the language of imperialism, the will to defend the Empire is altogether lacking.'

This was not completely true, for in two wars after Blunt wrote the Empire off as an indefensible proposition, the British fought hard and successfully against their imperial rivals to preserve Suez and the confines of the Indian Raj. On the other hand, they showed a progressively growing distaste for internal wars of suppression against subject peoples; nobody in Britain gloried in a bloodthirsty police action against the Mau Mau in Kenya as their Victorian ancestors had gloried in similar actions against Afridi guerrillas or Ashanti warriors, and when the violence of Arabs and Jews grew too intense in Palestine, Britain gladly sacrificed the dubious strategic advantages of holding so turbulent a territory and returned its mandate to the United Nations. Only in Malaya after 1945 was imperial warfare carried out by the British with any zest, and that was almost a struggle against an alien rival, since the guerrillas were Chinese Communists and the indigenous people of the country—the Malays—opposed them.

Yet a reluctance to fight hard for what was left of the Empire did not mean that the colonial territories were easily abandoned or that there was a conscious plan of dismantling what was left of the Empire. Few of the British in 1947 were as imperially astute as Curzon, because few of them shared any longer his obsession with the destiny of Anglo-Saxon power, so that there was little real consciousness that in giving up India Britain was ceasing to control an Empire or even to be a major power. For its own political ends, America was anxious for the time being to sustain the myth of Britain as the third of the Big Three, and Britain in turn still believed that its status in the world was conditioned by its territorial holdings and its remaining spheres of influence, so that there was no immediate desire to jettison what remained of the Empire after India's liberation.

It is true that Ceylon, which had already attained limited self-government in 1931, and Burma, which had reached the same status in 1937 on its separation from India, had left the Empire shortly after Indian independence—Ceylon to remain within the Commonwealth and Burma to sever entirely its links with Britain and withdraw into the xenophobic detachment which in the last two decades has increasingly characterized its relations with the outside world. But these acts of liberation were inevitable, for both countries were neighbours of India, had been in advance of it in terms of responsible government until 1947, and, owing to the prevalence of the Buddhist religion, had a considerably higher literacy rate than any part of India except the strongly Christian Malabar region. With India gone, Burma was no longer needed to defend its eastern frontier, and the one point of strategic value in Ceylon, Trincomalee, was guaranteed to the British navy by the treaty of independence.

Otherwise, Britain seemed to stand secure in its main areas of power. Its influence in the Middle East was as yet little diminished. Iraq was still a client State; Jordan, though it had become a sovereign State in 1946, was still subsidized by Britain and its Arab Legion was still commanded by Brigadier Glubb; Aden and the outposts of the Persian Gulf were solidly held, and British garrisons still watched—though with increasing discomfort—over the Suez Canal.

It is true that Palestine had already, by 1947, become virtually impossible to govern, thanks to Zionist terrorism and American pressure to receive more Jewish immigrants, whose arrival automatically raised the temperature of Arab animosity. The Labour Government was initially sympathetic to the Zionist cause, but by 1947 even the British Left had begun to regret the Balfour

Declaration and the difficulties of keeping two rival peoples at peace within a small territory, particularly when each regards the other as an intruder. Accordingly, Ernest Bevin, then Foreign Secretary, announced that Britain would relinquish its mandate, and the United Nations was left to satisfy both sides. But though the British felt relieved to escape from the role of Levantine policeman, they did not avoid being blamed by the Arabs for having in the beginning encouraged the idea of the Jewish National Home, and in Egypt especially this resentment was added to all the other grudges accumulated against Britain in more than sixty years of unwilling association. None felt it more bitterly than the Egyptian officers whose forces had been humiliatingly defeated in the war that adjusted in Israel's favour the borders laid down by the United Nations.

Still, for the time being there seemed no one—and certainly not the Arab armies defeated by a handful of militant Jews—who could challenge Britain's role as leading power in the Middle East, a role which it valued not only for the prestige, but also for the concrete gifts of power through continued domination of the Suez Canal and the oilfields of Iraq and the Persian Gulf.

Apart from the Middle East, Britain retained undiminished its possessions in Africa, in South-East Asia, in the West Indies and Oceania; it kept Hong Kong and the Falklands and its fortress possessions in the Mediterranean. Nobody, even among the Labour ministers at that time, imagined that these possessions would be abandoned quickly. The idea of trusteeship was still strong, and under the guidance of the Labour Colonial Secretary, Creech Jones, a programme of colonial development was evolved, and sustained by the Conservative ministry that came into power in 1951. It was considered, even by socialists, that the immediate liberation of most of the African peoples would be an act of criminal irresponsibility. Decades, even generations of political education and economic development, it was thought, would be necessary before most of these peoples could be ready for independence.

The Colonial Service had traditionally been economical in both personnel and expenditures, never using two men where one might suffice, expecting officers in the field to attend to every aspect of administration, working where possible through indirect rule, and in general behaving as if the ghosts of Adam Smith and

William Ewart Gladstone were maintaining a perpetual audit on the extravagances of the colonial system. Colonies were expected to pay their own way, and the total expenditure on them out of British taxes in 1930 was approximately £3 million a year. By 1950 it had gone up to more than £40 million; the increase was devoted partly to paying the greatly expanded personnel of specialists and technicians, and partly to the activities of the Colonial Development Corporation, established to provide the various colonies with the necessary infrastructure of public utilities on which industrial systems could be built up.

As in most situations where outsiders move in to decide what is best for a country, there were some disastrous miscalculations, both economic and political. Sometimes, indeed, it seemed as though the Laputan Academy of Projectors had been resurrected to give a Swiftian absurdity to the last act of the imperial drama. The most celebrated and costly of these follies was the Groundnut Scheme, which was supposed to transform the economy of Tanganyika by turning three million acres of land into a vast peanut farm to provide Britain with an adequate supply of edible oils. Bulldozers cleared the brush, people were moved about the countryside, settlements were created, a railway was plotted out, and £36 million was spent before the experts departed, defeated by the soil and the pests, leaving a few barely productive plots among the returning bush.

The political schemes were hardly less impractical. Like British generals, who were said to be always ready for the last war, British colonial officials in the imperial twilight were anxious to repeat among the colonies of Africa and the Caribbean the feats of federation that had turned the old settlement colonies of Canada and Australia into nations large enough to be economically viable and to count as middle powers in the modern world. On the surface there was something to be said for a programme of federation. The West Indian island colonies, which lost their economic importance after the abolition of slavery removed cheap, reliable labour from the sugar plantations, would obviously benefit from a joint administration that could plan their common development. And the African colonies were from the beginning artificial territorial divisions that had been carved out during the later nineteenth century when the European imperial powers were dividing Africa between them. They brought together tribal groups of varying cultures and levels of sophistication, and since few such colonies had existed as political entities until their white conquerors united them, there seemed no reason why their boundaries should not be adjusted to turn them into countries of fair size and population.

The British colonies of West Africa were divided by intervening French colonies, and this made any kind of federation geographically difficult, but in Central Africa a territorially viable federation with about half a million square miles and a population of 7,000,000 could be created out of the three colonies of Northern Rhodesia, Southern Rhodesia and Nyasaland. In East Africa a similar federation might be made up of Kenya, Uganda and Tanganyika; it would be almost 600,000 square miles in area, and in the early 'fifties the population would have been round about 15,000,000. These East African territories had some faint tradition of unity in the past, since they had all been once under the suzerainty of the sultan of Zanzibar, though his power had been felt only in the Arab seaports. They had been given a degree of later unification when the Labour Government in 1947 set up the East African Commission to administer inter-territorial services, such as railways, harbours, telecommunications and airways.

The elitism of the trusteeship envisaged by the Conservative Government of 1951, which set on foot the experiments in colonial unification, is clearly visible in the plans for the Central African Federation, established in 1952. Southern Rhodesia, was, as we have seen, already internally self-governing, with a legislature elected on a franchise that kept all power with the whites, who numbered 8 per cent of the population. Out of more than 2,200,000 blacks, only 380 could vote. Northern Rhodesia and Nyasaland were both Crown colonies, with no element of responsibility in their government. Northern Rhodesia had a smaller but vigorous white minority of about 3 per cent, and in Nyasaland the number of whites was negligible. Altogether there were about 250,000 whites, with well-entrenched interests in land and minerals, against almost 7,000,000 blacks. The idea behind the scheme, as conceived by Oliver Lyttleton, the Conservative Colonial Secretary, appears to have been that the whites would provide a leadership that would ensure the efficient operation of the Federation until the Africans had become sufficiently educated in democratic ways to take their share in government. Given the record of the white settlers in governing Southern Rhodesia, it represented at best a naïve hope; a crude but not undescriptive image of the kind of society that would emerge was given by Godfrey Huggins, the Prime Minister of Southern Rhodesia, who described the relationship between whites and blacks as a partnership like that between a rider and his horse.

The whites greatly favoured the Federation. The blacks were apprehensive from the beginning; and justly so, for the record of Southern Rhodesia had shown that there was a vital difference— even in terms of alien rule—between white colonial administrators who endeavour to be impartial and white settlers who have a stake in retaining the best lands and in maintaining an ample labour corps of subservient blacks. Before 1939 the blacks might have accepted the situation in the hope that white paternalism would gradually mitigate their situation. But by the 1950s nationalism was reaching even into the remoter corners of Africa; the blacks within the Federation demanded more effective representation, but, though reforms were made, they still left the white settlers in effective control. Underground resistance movements spread throughout the Federation, and especially in Nyasaland under the leadership of Hastings Banda. Banda and several hundred other Africans were detained under emergency laws, but this did not stem the tide of protest, and in 1960 a review of the situation by Lord Monckton concluded that African opinion was almost unanimously against the Federation, and recommended that member colonies should be given the opportunity to secede. As soon as the local legislatures in Nyasaland and Northern Rhodesia secured black majorities under their amended constitutions in 1962, they left the Federation and resumed for the time being their status as partially self-governing colonies. In 1963 the Federation came to an end.

The Federation of the West Indies had an even shorter life, beginning in 1958 and dissolving with acclamation in 1962. The only deep loyalty of the West Indians outside their own islands had been to Britain; except perhaps for the Fijians, there were no non-European inhabitants of the Empire who were prouder of their status as British subjects, but they had no sense at all of a Caribbean nationality, and the attempt to create one foundered on the cultural differences between islands with English and French traditions, and also between islands like Jamaica with mainly

L*

black populations and islands like Trinidad which were intensely
multi-racial. The promise of freedom tended less towards the
promotion of unity among the former colonies than towards
increasing particularization, the most striking case being that of
Anguilla in the Leewards, with a population of 5,000 and an area
of 35 square miles, which in 1967 demanded independence of
St Kitts-Nevis (now an 'associated State' of the Commonwealth,
self-governing but defended and diplomatically represented by
Britain), to which it had been quite contentedly attached during
the colonial era; rule by neighbouring West Indians, its people
decided, was infinitely more irksome than rule by the British.

The East African Federation, last of the dreams of unification
fostered by the Tories of the 1950s, never came into existence,
though the 50,000 white settlers of Kenya were completely willing
to serve as its guiding elite. There were constitutional difficulties
over Tanganyika being a United Nations mandate, and the
scheme was finally abandoned during the period of heavy rule in
Kenya that was precipitated by the Mau Mau revolt. Yet, perhaps
because a close political federation was never attempted, the
three East African countries did enjoy—until the recent dissen-
sions created by the Amin dictatorship in Uganda—a greater
degree of effective unity than other formerly colonial regions,
owing to the smooth continuation of the East African High
Commission as the East African Community, which has acted not
only as a joint transport authority but also as a kind of common
market.

It is clear from what happened in these three instances that the
British politicians and colonial officials had allowed their ideas of
trusteeship to be marred by the desire to shape the future of the
colonies moving towards independence in accordance with a
paternalistic philosophy of development which in the case of the
great Groundnuts fiasco had no relation to geographical realities
and in the case of the Central African and West Indian Federations
had no regard for local political realities. They seem to have been
almost completely unconscious of the strong desire for territorial
sovereignty that was developing parallel to the rise of black
nationalism, and of the impatience with any form of tutelage
that emerged among peoples who until after the Second World
War had accepted colonial government with little sign of discontent. The rulers of Britain hoped to avoid leaving behind them

a Balkanized Africa, or a Balkanized Caribbean, with their own single overriding authority replaced in each case by a score of separate and potentially conflicting powers. But, laudable though it may have been, this desire took no account of the extraordinary resurgence of local loyalties that has swept the world as a reaction to the specious unification created by the spread of communication. Pan-Africanism, even when preached by African leaders, has consistently failed.

If trusteeship and development, as practised in the 1950s by the rulers of the dwindling Empire, seem in retrospect like expensive versions of the old paternalism, there were also ways in which, though the word was now never used, the imperialist idea itself survived under altruistic guises proper to a world where the United Nations kept a sharper eye on overt exhibitions of colonial power, and where the emergence of the cold war enabled many things once done in the name of plain imperial defence to be attributed to a desire to preserve global freedom.

One of the most disastrously tactless expressions of such imperialism masked as crusade was made by a junior minister, Henry Hopkinson, in 1954. Cyprus was coming into the eye of the world. The British were planning to turn the island into a base to defend their interests in the Suez Canal as soon as, under treaty, they had withdrawn their troops from Egypt; at the same time the Enosis movement was gathering strength in Cyprus under the leadership of Archbishop Makarios, while Greece was raising the status of Cyprus in the United Nations and Turkey was showing an ominous interest. 'It has always been understood and agreed', said Hopkinson, 'that there are certain territories in the Commonwealth which, owing to their particular circumstances, can never expect to be fully independent.' Standing alone, that would have sounded like an old-fashioned assertion of bald imperial power. Hopkinson qualified it by adding: 'Nothing less than continued sovereignty over this island can enable Britain to carry out her strategic obligations to Europe, the Mediterranean and the Middle East.' Or, to put the matter more directly, Cyprus was needed, as it had been needed in 1878, to restrain the traditional Levantine enemy, Russia.

It was, in fact, under the guise of the Communist threat to freedom that Britain tried to carry out—even as the territorial empire was melting away from her grasp—the manœuvres that would allow her to retain the status of a world power. In reality that power had already been lost, for when Britain had it it depended on the command of the seas, and by the 1950s the command of the seas had not only passed out of Britain's hands but had become irrelevant, owing to the changes in the nature of warfare. Britain had never replaced in other fields the commanding position her navy had once conferred. In air power she had been deficient when war came in 1939, and by the time the deficiency had been remedied at great cost and effort, nuclear power took the place of ordinary air power. For a brief period Britain was second to the United States as an atomic power, but when Russia began to make nuclear weapons, Britain fell rapidly into the limping third place which she has retained ever since.

Yet one's actual strength can sometimes be inflated by bluff, as Britain knew, and many of the manœuvres undertaken by British politicians after the Second World War were linked not to a desire to retain the territorial possessions that had been the concrete substance of the Empire, but to sustain prestige that had followed from their possession. There were ways in which it was thought this might be done. One, of course, was the maintenance of the Commonwealth, with its parade of loyalties from former dependencies. Another was the establishment and maintenance of special spheres of influence which would emphasize that Britain was still more than a mere European country, that it was indeed a world presence that could defy the menace of Russia and—later—of China, on the strength of its imperial tradition, as a power centre separate from the United States.

This search for prestige as a world power sustained the structure of British influence in the Middle East, which remained intact, except for the loss of Palestine, for a whole decade after the end of the Second World War. It also inspired the formation of the so-called northern tier of Middle Eastern defence, by the negotiation in 1955 of the Baghdad Pact between Britain, Turkey, Iraq, Iran and Pakistan.

It was hoped that the Arab League, in which Britain retained a good deal of influence until the early 1950s, might become the basis for a second-tier alliance; this would make Britain the dominant power in the whole eastern half of the Muslim world, from Egypt to Pakistan. What British politicians had not taken into account were the hostilities that exist within the Muslim world between Arabs and non-Arabs, such as the Turks and the Iranians. The rapid rise of Arab nationalism not only made impossible a southern parallel to the Baghdad Pact; it also precipitated the astonishingly rapid collapse of British influence as soon as the 60,000 troops who had garrisoned the Suez Canal were withdrawn in accordance with the Anglo-Egyptian agreement of 1954.

Nasser had denounced the Baghdad Pact in 1955 and this prevented other Arab States from joining it, since they feared that this might result in internal disorders among their own nationalists. Early in 1956, under pressure from Egypt and the Palestinian refugees in his territory, the young King Hussein of Jordan abruptly dismissed Glubb Pasha, Commandant of the Arab Legion, and declared himself free of British influence. In July 1956 Nasser seized the Canal. There followed the Suez adventure, in which Britain, on the verge of military victory, was forced by diplomatic pressures to forgo a repetition of Gladstone's achievement.

The role of the United States in the Suez incident was at best equivocal. It was the refusal of an American loan for the Aswan Dam that originally provoked Nasser to seize the Canal, a consequence not likely to be unforeseen by a man as shrewd as Dulles. Yet when, as a result of his action, the Canal was seized, Dulles failed to give Eden effective diplomatic support. Given Eden's emotional reaction to the seizure (which in England was echoed in a last burst of jingoism that caught up even the working-class areas in a storm of anger), British military action was inevitable, as Dulles also must have foreseen. Yet at no time was the American position made clear enough for Britain to expect the United States to take the initiative in the crucial United Nations resolutions which had the ultimate effect of destroying Britain's position as a Levantine power. When one takes into account the fact that the State Department had disapproved of the Baghdad Pact (though it was completely in line with the Dulles policy of regional alliances aimed at restraining Russian penetration), it is hard to doubt that American action throughout the Suez crisis was aimed at terminating Britain's influence in the Middle East, partly out of traditional hostility towards the Empire, but partly also in the vain hope of adding the region to its own Far Eastern sphere of influence.

With the Suez fiasco, the position Britain had held since the Battle of the Nile more than a century and a half before as leading

arbiter of the Levant came finally to an end, its termination
marred by the international difficulties that attended the long
trauma of extrication from Cyprus. What the Cyprus crisis emphasized, with its accompaniment of difficulties within the NATO
alliance between Greece and Turkey, and of United Nations
interventions, was that imperial affairs were no longer private
affairs.

The loss of the Levantine sphere of influence in 1956 did not
mean the end of Britain's desire to retain the aura of a world
power. On the farther side of the Middle East, in southern
Arabia, where Aden remained a British strongpoint, and in the
Persian Gulf, British forces remained to control—even after
Suez was lost—the southern approaches to the Red Sea, and to
safeguard the oil supplies from the sheikdoms of the Gulf, more
vital than ever when, after a revolutionary coup in 1958, Iraq
moved out of the imperial orbit. In the Far East, the presence of
vital raw material—rubber and tin—kept the Singapore naval base
in British hands, and British regiments in Malaya. These two
regions were the last in which Britain still acted as a protecting
State and hence asserted her title to world power. By the later
'sixties the hollowness of that title had become evident to most
Britons, and in 1968 the fourth Labour Government ended the
long British adventure in Asia. At the beginning of that year
British forces finally left Aden and the sheikhdoms of Southern
Arabia. Later in the year it was announced that the other remaining British base in the East, Singapore, would be vacated, and
British forces would be withdrawn from Malaya and the Persian
Gulf, to be replaced by mutual defence agreements of dubious
utility. In all Asia there would remain only one British colony—
Hong Kong—and one British protected state—Brunei, which had
obstinately refused to be shed. The last manifestation of the imperial spirit, the last effort to impress upon the mind of the world
the knowledge that of all its tribes the greatest was the Anglo-
Saxon, had come to an end.

XVI Hustling to the End, Boys...

Britain emerged from the drama of the Second World War with all its dependencies intact and all its dominions left around it. To understand how it reached by the end of the 1960s that twilight in which even the word Empire had lost all resonance, we have to remember many circumstances, and some of them have already been delineated. The long fight of the settlement colonies for independence within the Commonwealth; the human and economic losses of two World Wars; the mounting and ultimately successful resistance to British rule within those two key territories with long memories of ancient civilizations, India and Ireland; the irreversible blow struck to imperial prestige by the Japanese destruction of British power in the Far East, and the less obvious but equally destructive efforts of the United States to erode the power of its ally in two great conflicts in order to assimilate the remnants of its prestige: all these and their effect on transforming and eventually eliminating the Empire have been sufficiently discussed.

But there remain two factors which came into especial prominence in the last days of the Empire. The first of these was the emergence into political self-consciousness of those peoples whom Europeans had for so long regarded condescendingly as primitives or, at best, noble savages. The other was the progressive and ultimately deliberate retraction of Britain into the European nexus from which the temptations of empire had temporarily abstracted her.

The alliance in revolt that developed in the Empire between peoples of ancient civilization and the peoples of primitive culture was one of the extraordinary effects of the European invasion of the unindustrialized world. In a traditional situation the gulf between a twice-born Brahmin and an untouchable member of an aboriginal Indian tribe was broader than anyone accustomed to the extremest rigours of the European class system could conceive. Even colour divisions in India were more subtle and harmful than anything a European society imposed. Apart from colour, and all its invidious hints of ancestry, there were extraordinary divergences of cultural experience within the Empire between, say, the Ceylonese Buddhist, the Sephardic Jew of Cochin, and the Solomon Islander who had hunted heads and ritually eaten human flesh.

The miracle was that the British Empire, which had performed the extraordinary feat of uniting an India that had never been united before, also performed the equally unprecedented feat of giving a common aim of liberation to all its subject peoples. In the past there had been revolts against other empires, against the Antiochids and the Romans, by the Quechuas against the Spaniards and the Tibetans against the Chinese and the Moors against the French. But these had all been the revolts of a single people, and even the great American wave of revolutions that destroyed the Spanish Empire was merely a rebellion of colonial Spaniards against metropolitan Spaniards spread over a number of different provinces from the Rio Grande down to Tierra del Fuego. What happened in the British Empire, and spread quickly to the other European Empires, was a simultaneous and sympathetic revolt—usually non-violent but occasionally extremely savage—of people of many languages and cultures against the colonial condition.

'My ambition is much higher than independence,' said Gandhi in 1928 when he was calling the peasants of Bardoli in western India to a tax strike which he designed as a model experiment in the effectiveness of *satyagraha* against the Government of the Raj. 'Through the deliverance of India I seek to deliver the so-called weaker races from the crushing heels of Western exploitation in which England is the greatest partner.' In South Africa, we have seen, Gandhi had made no effort to arouse or to help the native peoples of the country, though he felt a great deal of sympathy for them when he served as a volunteer ambulance worker with the British forces in the Zulu War. It was only away from Africa, and over a considerable period of time, that even Gandhi was able to apprehend that the struggle of the peoples who inhabited the lesser colonial dependencies was one with the struggle of India.

I suspect that he came to this realization through the same process of simplification in his way of life and thought that brought him close to the Indian peasant. He was a caste Hindu and a barrister of the Inner Temple, but—as Churchill never understood—he performed the feat of identifying himself with the disinherited without losing his own essential inheritance. By an extraordinary adaptability of mind that amounted to genius, Gandhi was able to attune himself to an untouchable cleaner of latrines as easily as to a European intellectual like Romain Rolland or an English aristocrat like Irwin or Mountbatten.

It was this special facility of rapport (which underlay the comprehension of the English mind he exploited so effectively in his strategy of Indian liberation) that enabled Gandhi's teachings to strike a responsive note among the leaders of the African liberation movements in the years immediately after the Second World War. But it is important to note that while it was the example of Indian liberation through Gandhian tactics that encouraged African leaders to persist in what at first seemed a hopeless struggle against the leading world power, and while on a small and temporally condensed scale the liberation of the Gold Coast resembled that of India, none of the classic leaders of the movement for the liberation of Africa were political saints (or saintly politicians) on the Gandhian model. There was no united religious tradition in Africa that might foster a leader of Gandhi's type who could make a universal appeal by the mere saintliness of his life. Every leader had to have his base in a local or a tribal constituency; Nkrumah had his early constituency among the people in Accra and the smaller towns of the Gold Coast littoral, and did not worry at first about the tribespeople upriver; Jomo Kenyatta had a solid base among the Kikuyu tribesmen who had been largely displaced to provide farms for the white settlers in the Kenya Highlands, and Julius Nyerere among the Zanski tribe of northern Tanganyika, of which his father was a chief; Kenneth Kaunda and Hastings Banda found their nucleus of support among the mission-educated and moved outward, just as the leaders of Congress in India moved outward from an immediate following of aspirants to university graduation.

Leaders of liberation movements in British Africa accepted Gandhi's methods of non-violent protest for a number of excellent reasons. They had just dramatically proved their efficacy in the liberation of India; they were much more practical than violent insurrection, which would have required the arms and organization Africans did not then possess; they fitted the prevailing mood among the British colonial administrators, who in most cases— Kenya was an exception because of the complex racial situation— were reconciled to the idea of giving out independence by easy instalments.

Nkrumah's later career as semi-dictator should not be allowed to cloud the sincerity of his early search for African liberation or the tactical skill and calculated moderation with which he carried out the first liberation of a colonial territory outside the immediate orbit of India. Nkrumah, like most of the first generation of African leaders, was Western-educated, and had spent a fair time in London, where he and Jomo Kenyatta came under the influence of one of the least known but most important figures in the dissolution of the Empire, the American-educated West Indian, George Padmore. During the 1930s, working among other exiles from colonialism who had gathered in England, Padmore often seemed to one a lost man, for he had abandoned his own islands, in whose liberation he played no direct part, and he had abandoned Communism, which he felt had no relevance in African terms. The socialist Left in Britain gave him some support, and he turned his interest to black Africa. With Kenyatta he founded the International African Services Bureau, and it was to this group that Nkrumah gravitated when, after graduating at an American University, he reached London in the 1940s.

In 1945 the Pan-African Rally was held in Manchester, to prepare for the post-war struggle for independence. Previous rallies of this kind had been dominated by non-African blacks—West Indians and Americans—but in 1945, except for Padmore, the dominant figures were African, including Nkrumah, Kenyatta, Wallace Johnson from Sierra Leone and Peter Abrahams from South Africa. They passed resolutions demanding complete independence for Black Africa, and specifically calling for a struggle to be based on Gandhian *satyagraha*—with the rider that violence must be accepted as a last resort. The men who passed this resolution were Westernized African intellectuals. They included none of the British-trained military caste who would play a significant role in the African countries after independence, and those who, like Akintola from Nigeria and Kenyatta, had retained their roots in tribal life were in the minority. Most of them were members of the emergent black middle class, and they appealed directly to the educated minority and to people of the towns, alienated from their tribal past—the classes on which the first stages of a colonial struggle have always been based.

Nkrumah stayed on in London to edit the *New African*, and did not return to the Gold Coast until 1947, when he was called back by Joseph Danquah, leader of a group of Westernized liberal intellectuals who had formed themselves into the United Gold Coast Convention. The Gold Coast had maintained its pre-war position as the most economically and educationally advanced part of British Africa, and in 1946 the Labour Government in Britain had granted it a reformed constitution in which the majority of the legislature would be unofficial. The franchise was narrow, the British administrators retained executive authority and were not responsible to the legislature, but the fact that an African majority could now pass laws relating to local matters was regarded as a major advance by the Colonial Office and accepted as such by Danquah and his group.

Nkrumah came from London with quite different ideas. He rejected the British official view, held even by the Labour Party, that the colonies must pass through a period of political education and economic development before they could be given independence. Instead, he argued that Africans must gain substantial political power as early as possible and plan their own economic development. His methods were quite different from the quiet constitutional co-operation envisaged by Danquah. He realized that, in order to attain rapid results, the struggle must be broadened to embrace the masses at least in Accra and the coastal regions, and he began by organizing the thousands of men who had fought with the British in the last war and had come back dissatisfied. He led protests against price increases and boycotts of western merchants, in which he was fervently supported by the market women. He organized ex-servicemen's parades, and it was at one of these, in February 1948, that the situation exploded into violence, when an inexperienced police officer ordered his men to open fire. The result was an outbreak of mob violence which lasted for three days, spread to the other towns, and left thirty people dead. The incident hastened drastically the end of British rule in the Gold Coast and, indeed, throughout the Empire.

The Labour Government immediately sent out a British lawyer on an investigatory commission. He condemned the rigidity of the colonial administration in failing to take account of the frustration felt by educated Africans kept in a condition of political tutelage. He also recommended an immediate increase in self-government; to advise on this point the Labour Government set up an all-African commission. The Coussey Commission called for a national assembly elected on universal suffrage, with eight of the ministers Africans responsible to the assembly. Only finance and law and order would remain in the hands of white colonial servants.

Nkrumah, who had seceded from the United Gold Coast Convention to form his more radical Convention Peoples Party, rejected the proposals as insufficient, and led a 'Positive Action' campaign of civil disobedience. He was imprisoned, and immediately became a martyr, his position as popular leader assured. The elections of 1951 under the new constitution gave the Convention Peoples Party a handsome lead in the new assembly, and Nkrumah—still in prison—was elected by a landslide vote. A pragmatic compromise was now effected. Nkrumah was let out of prison and abandoned his opposition to the new constitution. He became 'Leader of Government Business' and acted as virtual prime minister until, a year later, that title was officially accorded him. He sailed the Gold Coast through some troubled years of dissension until in 1957 its independence under the name of Ghana was granted. It was the first of the African colonies to fight its way to nationhood.

What had been given to the Gold Coast could hardly be denied to Nigeria, the other model colony of West Africa, and after difficulties between the northern and the southern peoples had been patched up (none too securely as events following independence were to show) Nigeria became a federation and in 1960 acquired its independence.

Already by this time the dismemberment of the Empire was drastically changing the world map. In 1956 Britain had gained a small revenge for its humiliation at Suez by unilaterally ending the Anglo-Egyptian Condominium in the Sudan, which it declared an independent nation, greatly to the annoyance of the Egyptians, who had been planning to annex it at some appropriate time. In 1960, when the United Nations gave independence to the former Italian territory in Somaliland, Britain rather gladly added her own portion of that troublesome country, and Somalia emerged as an independent State.

Unlike Ghana and Nigeria, neither Sudan nor Somaliland stayed in the Commonwealth; they abandoned all their links with Britain. This was not the case with Malaya, which became independent in 1957. Logically, the independence of Malaya should have come about in the general regional liberation which had set Ceylon and Burma free immediately after India, but once the Communist guerrilla war began the British had no intention of leaving until they made sure that the vital sources of rubber and tin were in friendly hands. Once that had been achieved, independence became, more than anywhere else, a matter of gentlemanly agreement. There had never been any important popular liberation movement, for the Malays were a feudal-minded people and left the matter to the native aristocracy, who established Malaya as a federation of the original sultanates, plus Penang and Malacca; it was the second independent kingdom in the Commonwealth, whose ruler was elected by the princes themselves.

By 1960, with the liberation of Nigeria, an important change had taken place in the character of the Commonwealth. In the periodic gatherings of prime ministers, the original grouping of Britain and the white dominions, reduced to five by the defection of Ireland, was outnumbered by a non-European combination of four Asians—India, Pakistan, Ceylon and Malaya—and two Africans—Ghana and Nigeria.

It was clear that the relationship of Britain to the rest of the Empire would have to be reconsidered. There were in fact two strongly opposing forces within the gatherings of the Commonwealth Prime Ministers. One was that of colonial liberation, represented by the six Afro-Asian leaders, who were inclined to press for the extension to other subject territories in the Empire of the independence which they had achieved. The other was that of unregenerate imperialism, represented in its most extreme form by South Africa, committed to a policy of *apartheid*, and supported in the background by the white regime of Southern Rhodesia.

The conflict of interests and philosophies came to a head between 1960 and 1961. They were the years when the compass of British policy shifted from the far lands of the Empire back to

Europe, the years dominated by the strange figure of Harold Macmillan, who came in Edwardian guise to bury the remnants of Britain's Edwardian glory. Macmillan represented the transformation of the Conservative Party, long the stronghold of imperialism, into a continentalist party. Eden, like his guru Churchill, had remained an imperialist to the end, and his last significant act had been the atavistic adventure at Suez. Macmillan, who had a great deal of the chameleon in his showy character, had also once been a convinced believer in the durability of the British Empire. 'The Empires of the past have died because they were rigid,' he said in 1942, when he briefly took over the Colonial Office. 'By contrast our Empire has had the great quality of adaptation.' He had gone on on that occasion to remark that the colonies were 'four or five centuries' behind in development. 'Our job is to move them, to hustle them across this great interval of time as rapidly as we can.' By 1960 Macmillan had become convinced that the policy must be to hustle them completely out of dependency, out of the Empire indeed, even if into the Commonwealth. He chose, so that his message should not be lost even on the most extreme imperialists, to make his celebrated speech at the South African Parliament:

> The most striking of all the impressions I have formed since I left London a month ago is of the strength of this African national consciousness. In different places it may take different forms, but it is happening everywhere. The wind of change is blowing through the continent. Whether we like it or not this growth of national consciousness is a political fact.

He went on deftly to indicate that the Afrikaners should understand other nationalists because theirs was 'the first of African nationalisms'. Macmillan did not on this occasion specifically attack *apartheid*, but the drift of his speech was clear enough, and shortly afterwards Britain joined in the United Nations votes that condemned South Africa.

The crucial incident that would reveal the future trends of the Commonwealth and of British policy occurred when in 1961 South Africa became a republic, a move that was the natural conclusion of the nationalism of Malan and Verwoerd and had no direct connection with recent events. Having changed its status, under the rules of the Commonwealth South Africa had to apply for readmission, as had happened in the case of India and Ghana under similar conditions. Usually the matter was a formality, but in the case of South Africa it provided an opportunity for the forces within the Commonwealth to show their strength and their alignment. South Africa wished to enjoy the advantages of continued Commonwealth membership. Macmillan wanted her to stay, but felt unable to throw Britain's influence in the balance on either side. The Afro-Asian countries formed a solid bloc, and much depended in the final count on the attitudes of the other white dominions.

Once again, as in the achievement of dominion status, as in the dissociation from British policy in the Suez crisis of 1956, it was Canada who took the lead. Her Conservative Prime Minister, John Diefenbaker, arrived fully prepared to demand the expulsion of South Africa unless she promised fundamental changes in policy. The debate narrowed down to a symbolic point. Was South Africa willing to accept black High Commissioners from Nigeria and Ghana in Pretoria? To have done so would have encouraged black nationalists within South Africa, and Verwoerd indicated that he would refuse. It was obvious that the feeling of the the conference was overwhelmingly against him, for only Australia showed any open regret at the prospect of South Africa's leaving the Commonwealth. Accordingly, rather than face the humiliation of being expelled by the six Afro-Asian nations supported by Canada, Verwoerd withdrew his country's application for readmission. The Commonwealth was no longer a congenial place for imperialists; that lesson was reinforced when in 1965 the racist white Government of Rhodesia unilaterally declared independence rather than accept the conditions regarding black suffrage which Britain, urged on by the Commonwealth, wished to impose.

These incidents coincided with Britain's shift towards continentalism, which became evident when in the summer of 1961 Macmillan and his Foreign Secretary, Lord Home, made it clear that Britain intended to apply for membership in the European Common Market. It was the end of a long process of largely unsuccessful dissociation from the continent. Ever since the Roman legions occupied Britain two thousand years ago, its links with Europe had been close and inevitable. Its island position had allowed England to become a nation long before most other European countries, and this fact had nurtured a sense of separation and superiority. Yet in religion until the Reformation, and culturally afterwards, it had remained a part of Europe, its flexible language a unique hybrid of the two great European linguistic strains, the Latin and the Germanic. Throughout the Middle Ages England had sought a continental empire, and even when the pursuit of territory and gain was shifted across the oceans, defence was still a matter of European politics, and Britain fought a whole series of wars across the channel from the sixteenth century down to 1815 to prevent any one power gaining the hegemony of Europe.

It was in these wars that Britain's navy was built up, to give her world sea power, and that many of her best colonial possessions were acquired as the extra prizes of war. ('The Empire has done very well out of sideshows,' as Lloyd George once remarked.) And it was the colonies, together with the absence of a threatening power on the continent, that enabled Britain to stay on the periphery of European affairs from 1815 to the end of the nineteenth century. But as soon as it became evident that there was a power— the new German Empire—that intended to establish a hegemony over Europe and threatened to outgun the Royal Navy on the high seas, Britain was forced to build Admiral Fisher's famous dreadnoughts, and to abandon its Victorian policy of non-alignment by establishing the Entente Cordiale with France, which led it fatally into the war of 1914 and the subsequent war of 1939, where its resources were wasted and its financial power destroyed in a European cause. Even after the threat of Germany was finally exorcized, Russia took its place as the spectral presence overshadowing Europe, and as a gauge of commitment to the continent Britain left an army of sixty thousand men in Germany to guard the confines of western Europe.

It was little wonder that when the countries of western Europe seemed to have discovered the secret of economic prosperity in co-operation, Britain should hope to share the benefits of a continent it was paying to defend. Leading members of the Commonwealth—Canada and even Australia—were withdrawing from the imperial trade system to become involved in its American rival; other members were exploring economic autarchy. Europe seemed to offer the greatest benefit in terms of better living, and, despite the humiliating rebuffs delivered by De Gaulle, Britain kept renewing its application for membership of the Common Market until at last, on January 22nd, 1972, it entered the European Economic Community, taking with it the Republic of Ireland, which ironically—of all the former imperial dependencies—was the only one that had remained a close economic satellite of the United Kingdom.

If any date can be taken as marking the end of the Empire, the day when Britain entered the Common Market seems more appropriate than any other, for on that day it made final its abandonment of a role and order that visibly belonged in the past. Through the 1960s the liberation of imperial dependencies had been steady and rapid. Gone were all the theories of trusteeship and development that as late as the previous decade had considered liberation as the end of a slow process of national maturation. The leisurely progress from autocratic Crown colony through an elected minority in a legislative council, thence to an elected assembly, to responsible local government and finally to complete independence, which in India's case had taken some twenty-eight years, from the Government of India Act of 1919 to liberation in 1947, was now so telescoped that a country would go through all the stages in a couple of years or even less. Gambia was a Crown colony with no semblance of democratic rule before she attained full self-government in October 1963. In February 1965, less than two years later, she became fully independent. Tanganyika's progress was even more spectacular: responsible government in 1960, and full independence in 1961.

It was now Britain, not the emergent nations, that was anxious to hustle the colonies. Curzon's vision of the pointlessness of the colonial empire without India had taken more than a decade to impress itself on later British rulers, but by 1960, when there was no presence in Suez to be sustained, the truth of it had become evident. Liberation proceeded apace and, since it suited the imperial power, normally without violence. The worst situation had occurred in the 1950s, and then only when there were particularly complex issues involved. In Kenya, for example, there was the question of land occupied by white settlers and needed by Kikuyu tribesmen; out of the Kikuyu grievances sprang the terrorist Mau Mau movement, and out of the suppression of Mau Mau the last authoritarian excesses of British imperialism, complete with concentration camps and gallows. Yet in the end, in 1963, thanks to the extraordinary political tact of Jomo

Kenyatta, whom the British had repeatedly imprisoned, Kenya gained independence in the atmosphere of good will that attended most British departures. Even Cyprus, where the strife between Greek and Turk had become a complicating factor in the general resentment felt over the British intent to turn the island into a Levantine citadel, elected on its liberation in 1960 to remain in the Commonwealth, to whose meetings Archbishop Makarios, Ethnarch and President of Cyprus, in his Orthodox robes, brings a fugitive flavour of an empire more ancient and even more lost in time than the British—the empire of Byzantium, the eastern Rome.

To talk in detail of the individual progressions towards independence would be mainly repetitious. Yet the roll should be called if only to illustrate the magnitude of the process of devolution. In Africa, Sierra Leone achieved nationhood in 1961, Uganda in 1962 and Zanzibar in 1963; the fugitive colonies of the Central African Federation, Nyasaland and Northern Rhodesia, became independent as Malawi and Zambia in 1964; in 1966, defying South African disapproval, Britain gave freedom as African-controlled states to Bechuanaland on the borders of the Union and Basutoland within its territory (as Botswana and Lesotho respectively), and in 1968 to Swaziland, the last British-controlled territory on the African continent.

In Asia the major territories had all been liberated by 1957. The principality of the Brookes in Sarawak and the realm of the North Borneo Company had been declared anachronisms and turned into Crown colonies in 1946, and in 1963, together with Singapore, which became a self-governing, territory in 1959, they were separated from British rule and incorporated in an expansionist Malaya (known henceforward as Malaysia). Singapore withdrew in 1965 to become a separate State. Mauritius and the Maldives became independent in 1968. By the time Britain joined the Common Market the Seychelles were self-governing and on the verge of independence.

In the Persian Gulf, Kuwait had attained independence in 1961; ten years later, in 1971, Bahrain, Qatar and the Trucial States (now the United Arab Emirates) shed British domination for treaties of friendship. Aden and the Hadhramaut, with the legendary island of Socotra, had already passed out of the Empire in 1967 as the Republic of Southern Yemen; that had been one of the few unpleasant partings, for Britain had clung to her historic base in Aden, in the face of mounting terrorist attacks, as long as the Suez Canal remained open; but when the Canal was closed by the Arab–Israeli war of 1967, the base became redundant and the British forces quietly slipped away. No one left the blistering rock of Aden with regret.

In the Mediterranean, Malta followed Cyprus into independence in 1964, but the historic British presence in the Middle Sea still remained, since by agreement bases were maintained on both Cyprus and Malta, and Gibraltar remained a dependency. Given Britain's return to the European fold, the Mediterranean is perhaps the last area outside the home seas in which she will completely relinquish her military power.

In the Americas, the break-up of the West Indian Federation was accompanied by the acquisition of independence by Jamaica and Trinidad, both in 1962. Barbados became independent in 1966; so did British Guiana, transformed into Guyana. The Bahamas and British Honduras (which became Belize) were liberated by 1972.

The last region in which the process of colonial independence began was Oceania, and this was in part because of the reluctance of Australia and New Zealand to abandon the prestige linked to the possession of even miniature empires. Nevertheless, the fact that Western Samoa was a mandate enabled it to apply pressure through the United Nations, so that independence was accorded in 1962. It was not until 1968 that the next South Pacific territory, Nauru, achieved its full liberation, followed in 1970 by Fiji and by Tonga, which, divesting itself of British protection, became the third independent kingdom in the Commonwealth.

The remnants of empire consist now of little more than rocks and islands. Every territory that is reasonably viable—politically, economically and culturally—has been allowed to go its way, and to remain in or leave the Commonwealth according to its will. Some of the dependencies that remain are held because of apparently insurmountable political difficulties. Gibraltar would certainly be forcibly occupied by Spain if the British departed, and the Falkland Islands by Argentina, and yet the inhabitants of these colonies have overwhelmingly expressed their repugnance towards any such annexation, so Britain stays to protect their wishes. In the New Hebrides the British stay because the French show no intention of departing. That St Helena and its attendant rocks, or the barren atolls of the Gilberts, will become economically viable is improbable, so that, however independent their forms of government, they are hardly likely to become completely detached from Britain. The small communities of the Leeward and the Windward Islands have reconciled themselves to this situation; they have become associated states, accepting British aid and allowing Britain to defend them and manage their external relations. Only two of the remaining fragments of the Empire seem destined to find their way to independence in the near future. One is Papua-New Guinea, which has already attained internal self-government; the other is the Solomon Islands Protectorate, which is about to attain responsible government. But the area and the population of all these territories that remain in some way under British control is a minute fraction—no more than 1 per cent, in each case, of the area and population of the Empire in that summit year of 1930 when all the paths began to run downward.

XVII Who Killed the Empire?

Who killed the Empire? The question reminds one of that curious play by Lope de Vega, *Fuenteovejuna*, in which the Extremaduran village which gives the play its name rises against the local feudal tyrant and kills him. The king's officers are sent in to investigate the murder, but when they ask the villagers to name the ring-leaders, to say who killed the Comendador, the unanimous cry is 'Fuenteovejuna!' And, indeed, the king decides on the evidence that the whole village is guilty, since it was an act of collective despair, and he pardons Fuenteovejuna because the provocation was great.

It would be easy to say that the British Empire was killed by its world and its time because it also offered great provocation. Fortunately, it is possible to make our diagnosis somewhat more exact than that of the king of Spain's investigators. The verdict should probably read that the British Empire died partly of natural causes, but that its end was precipitated by the acts of many identifiable individuals, though, as in Fuenteovejuna, no single individual assassin can be identified.

Let us deal first with the natural causes. The first was the very fact which made Britain unique as an imperial power: that it was subordinating vast areas of the earth to its arbitrary will while carrying on an internal evolution in political forms and philosophies that ran diametrically counter to its imperial policies and practices. Sooner or later, Englishmen would judge the conditions in their colonies by the freedoms they had demanded and won for themselves. And — though it turned out to be late rather than soon—the colonial peoples would ask to be given what their Western education had taught them were the rights of those who were ruled by the mother of parliaments. One cannot rule indefinitely according to Curzon and teach according to Milton and Shelley.

The second of the great natural causes of the decline of the Empire was the revolution in military techniques that began towards the end of the nineteenth century. It must be considered in connection with the third natural cause, which was the relative decline of Britain as an industrial and financial power.

Up to the end of the 1860s, because Britain was engaged in no major European wars, it could afford to be militarily obsolete with relative impunity. When European nations were rapidly changing over to modern types of rifled breech-loading artillery, the experts of the Horse Guards obstinately clung to smooth-bore muzzle-loading cannon, and since they were engaged merely in a long series of colonial wars against even worse-armed opponents, this did not matter greatly, at least until the South African War.

Later, when Britain was forced, in the early twentieth century, to rejoin Europe in a military sense it found difficulty in keeping up with Germany and later with the United States as a military power. This was due partly to the fact that Britain's head start in the industrial revolution of the early nineteenth century had left it with factories and techniques that were obsolete in comparison with the new industrial nations, while British financiers found overseas investments more attractive than sinking money into the modernizing of industrial equipment. While seapower remained important it was still possible for Britain to hold its own and thus to hold its Empire. But once the simple days of gunboats and cruisers came to an end and military equipment grew steadily more sophisticated and therefore more expensive, the cost of defending such great imperial routes as Britain had maintained up to 1939 became prohibitive even for the greatest power.

A pairing of figures, taking 1930 against 1972, will make the point more dramatically than any amount of description. In 1930, when the Empire was at its largest, the budget for all the military services of Great Britain—army, navy and air force—amounted to £110 million; the budget for the Indian army and marine, raised from local sources, amounted to £44 million, a total of £154 million to defend Britain and India, all the colonies, and all the imperial sea routes; the amounts which the dominions raised for local defence were negligible. In 1972, with modern equipment, modern rates of pay, and the obligations of European defence, the estimated cost of British military services, at a time when the legions had finally been called home from all the far corners of empire, was £2,852 million, or approximately seventeen times as much. Clearly, to have defended in 1972 the Empire as it stood in 1939, even if it had been politically feasible, would have been economically impossible for a country so relatively impoverished as Britain had become after the Second World War.

But even if such general and impersonal causes may explain why the Empire was predisposed to an early death, there still remain particular contributing causes that precipitated its demise, and here we can identify those individuals who conspired to make certain its end. For the Empire was like an ailing old woman, short of money but rich in jewels, with the relatives growing impatient for the estate, and not above hastening the funeral.

There was, as we have seen, the play of external influence. Britain had come by its Empire very largely by playing for high stakes in international conflicts, and it was not immune from the hazards out of which at times it made profit. During the later nineteenth century the rivalry of both France and Germany restricted and therefore shaped the final form of the British Empire, and shortly afterwards, by drawing Britain into their conflicts, these two countries contributed greatly to the financial weakness which in 1945 was one of the decisive motivations behind the desire to retreat from India.

In the long run the major external threat to the Empire came from the changing climate of world opinion, which small and frankly conservative countries like Portugal may successfully ignore for a period, but which a nation with Britain's professed political ideals cannot do. Imperialism has not vanished—all the three great powers, the United States, Russia and China, practise it in their own ways—but its form has changed, and the kind of patrician autocracy which Britain practised is no longer accepted.

Soviet Russia's disapproval has probably influenced the British Empire less than Tsarist Russia's military manœuvres did (for nobody took seriously Kruschev's threats of nuclear action at the time of the Suez crisis), and the main Chinese gains against the Empire were made under Chiang Kai-shek rather than under the Communists. But the United States has consistently applied pressure tending to the diminution of the Empire from the time of the Washington Treaty fifty years ago. Before then it played a potent indirect role in provoking the development of Canada into the increasingly independent nation that led the dominions and finally the colonies in their search for self-government. Nor can one underrate the United Nations, which has always been at its most effective as a forum for world opinion; as, one by one, the liberated colonial nations have entered that organization, it has become steadily more vigilant and influential in its detection of the remaining pockets of imperial power. Some of the former British dependencies, such as Tanganyika, undoubtedly owed their rapid liberation to the moral pressure of the United Nations.

A quite different influence on the fate of the British Empire was that of Japan, the only country that in war deprived Britain of a large portion of its possessions since the Thirteen Colonies fought themselves free a hundred and fifty years before. Everything that Japan took from Britain was returned, but Japan had irretrievably changed the image of Britain in the minds of colonial peoples; it had ended the voluntary acceptance of British pretensions at face value.

This brings us to individuals, and to Gandhi, for one of Gandhi's achievements was complementary to that of the Japanese. If the Japanese showed the colonial peoples the hollowness of British prestige, one of Gandhi's achievements was to show Britons the reality of their own consciences, to reveal to them the gulf between their religious pretensions and political ideals and their actual practice as imperialists. He also found the means to take the cause of liberation out of its narrow setting of the Westernized Indian middle class, and to recruit whole new armies of resisters—the women, the peasants, the pariahs—in a national fight for freedom and dignity. He devised what in the conditions of India was incomparably the best form of struggle. And he presented his achievements as an example to other colonial peoples. Undoubtedly, if one had to choose any individual as more responsible than others for the death of the Empire, it would be Gandhi.

But such tasks are not for one man to undertake or to accomplish, for just as the general circumstances of the times made the Empire increasingly vulnerable, so Indian circumstances, and particularly the unification of India by the British, contributed to Gandhi's success.

Moreover, Gandhi's task would have been immeasurably more difficult if the struggle he began in India in 1919 had not followed a century of Canadian work for colonial independence. In Canada the precedents of responsible government, dominion status and internationally recognized independence, were established over generations of endeavour, mostly non-violent, in which, after the pre-Durham rebels, such as Mackenzie, Papineau, Joseph Howe and Robert Baldwin, the chief roles were played by Sir Wilfrid Laurier and Mackenzie King in relentlessly extending the bounds of Canadian independence, and in the end by Lester Pearson, who during the Suez crisis showed that Commonwealth loyalties did not preclude independent judgment in international situations. Without the example of Canada's struggle and its development of the concept of dominion status, India would not have made that half-step to freedom she had already achieved in 1935 with provincial self-government, and without that half-step her liberation after the war would have been a longer and perhaps a much more violent process.

Among other individuals whose action was crucial, George Padmore should be remembered for his role as tutor to the young men who returned to lead free Africa, and Kwame Nkrumah for demonstrating that Africans were as capable as Indians of fighting shrewdly for their own freedom—though he failed to demonstrate, at least in his own behaviour, that they could use it well. That was left for wiser men like Jomo Kenyatta and Julius Nyerere.

Finally, there was the achievement of Gamel Abdel Nasser, who did more than any other individual to destroy that last important bastion of British imperial military power. From the takeover of Suez down to the loss of Aden, Nasser's hand could be seen directing every blow that contributed to the destruction of the long-standing British hegemony over the Levant and the sea coasts of Arabia.

One is constantly tempted to use the rhetoric of struggle, and a great struggle there indeed was in the long process by which the Empire worked towards its end, but the astonishing aspect of that progress remains its comparative peacefulness; compared with the winding-up of the French Empire, which involved two major colonial wars, it was remarkably lacking in bloodshed on either side. Partly, I think, this was due to the scattered nature of the Empire. It was not a territorially solid continental empire, where the tanks can be sent within a few days to any source of trouble. The logistics of British imperial warfare were always complicated,

and in many cases—that of Canada especially—a political solution
to a political problem was more practicable as well as more sen-
sible than a military one. This was particularly the case after
the South African War, whose cost in money and men robbed
the British of most of their Victorian taste for punitive
expeditions.

Yet I think we get even nearer to the heart of the matter when
we perceive that the mass of the British people, and even the
greater part of the ruling class, were not imperialists, though many
individuals were. Colonies had come with wars, and were kept,
and had somehow to be administered, but the early Victorian idea
that they were an expensive nuisance survived to join the later
radical criticisms of irresponsible administration, so that there
was always a great body of opinion in Britain which recognized
that the kind of rule over other men implied in the possession of
colonies was inconsistent with the broadening tradition of individual freedom that had existed longer than the Empire itself. And
here the individuals are too numerous to name, for one would
have to compile a roll-call of British liberal and radical thinkers
and propagandists.

Yet it remains problematical how far the arguments of intellectuals were more important in the dissolution of empire than the
pragmatic calculations of politicians. Attlee in 1947 was influenced
in his abandonment of India as much by the immense problems of
transferring Britain from a wartime to a peacetime economy as by
anti-imperialist ideals; the leading motivation of Macmillan's
actions in the 1960s was the desire to set Britain free to enter
Europe. Yet it is doubtful if any theoretician of liberty contributed
more than these two men to the dissolution of the Empire. And
where intellectuals did affect events profoundly it was usually in
more concrete ways than by writing books. Macaulay's educational
policy, as developed in India, with its eventual creation of a
Westernized and discontented intelligentsia, had vaster consequences than any of his celebrated books. And Allan Octavian
Hume, in calling the first meetings of the Indian National Congress, was a more potent eventual influence on the course of events
than either Forster or Orwell.

In the final resort, it was weariness as much as conviction that
made Britain decide to abandon the burden of empire. To have
sustained it after the Second World War would have meant austeri-

ties the British people was in no mood to endure; to have length-ened the process of parting beyond the 1960s would have deprived Britain of what—rightly or wrongly—its leaders believe is the only chance for economic regeneration: the entry into Europe, a setting in which the British hope they may recover something of the leadership, and respect in the eyes of the world, which they lost during the twilit period when they were trapped in the dilem-ma created by the incompatibility between their imperial preten-sions and their loss of genuine power.

Today the Empire is no more. The Commonwealth remains. It is a body without structure and without sanctions, with no unified political philosophy and no homogeneity of political aims. Its members have warred with each other, and it has not even acted as a court of arbitration, preferring to leave such tasks to the United Nations. There is no longer, since the British Nationality Act of 1948, a common citizenship, though Commonwealth citi-zens are usually allowed to travel without visas in each other's territories. There is no common legal system; some members still accept the judicial committee of the Privy Council in London as a final court of appeal, and some do not. There is no common defence system; some members belong to NATO and similar Western alliances, some have mutual assistance treaties with Com-munist countries, and some are completely neutral. There has never been a Commonwealth bloc in the United Nations, and there has been no attempt to establish a common approach in foreign affairs. The Commonwealth, indeed, has its Secretariat, it continues its regular meetings of Commonwealth Prime Ministers in Westminster, it bows to the past by accepting the Queen of England as its head (but not its sovereign), it operates certain com-mittees relating to common interests in economic matters and communications. It does little else that is concrete and tangible.

Its real functions, indeed, are probably the intangible ones. It recognizes that all the countries which adhere to it have shared a common experience of immersion in the Empire, that they have derived their common language from Britain, and with it some of the cultural attitudes which a language transmits. Most have shaped their political systems, their legal systems, their armed forces, their civil services and their educational systems on the British model, though each has made its own variations. The

Commonwealth, in so far as it is a formal organization, maintains contact among peoples whose problems, because of a common recent past, may be similar even if their aims are not always so. The fact that it demands no exclusive loyalty, that it seeks to establish no political orthodoxy, that it encourages its members to join in other associations of peoples, is an advantage, for today the world needs not rigid, all-inclusive international organizations, but a multiplicity of contacts, of circles of association to dissolve its antagonisms on many levels.

The Commonwealth will certainly be useless if it is regarded as a mere successor to the Empire. It continues certain bonds that were incorporated in the Empire, but it has become, by the 1970s, a quite distinct entity, and the test of its survival—and of the form it will eventually take if it does survive—will come as Britain becomes more deeply involved in the European Common Market. If the Commonwealth is merely a matter of sentimental loyalty to the past, and dependent on the centrality of Britain, it will certainly follow the Empire very quickly into oblivion. But if Britain moves out of the centre into the circle of equality in what becomes a genuine Commonwealth of Nations rather than a British Commonwealth, then it may survive as a common ground in which co-operation will eventually lead to concord. Its success in that form will demonstrate that even the ghost of the Empire has at last been laid.

Bibliography

Since this book is one of the results of an interest in the devolution of empires which I have nurtured ever since the liberation of India in 1947, it would be impossible for me to list all the books that have contributed information or stirred ideas. Indeed, a great deal in the way of fact and insight has come from direct observation or has been absorbed in meetings with people of many kinds during a quarter of a century spent in parts of the Empire outside Britain. Since 1949 I have been domiciled in Canada and have observed actively its political life. During that period I have made four long trips to India, and two to Malaya, Singapore, Hong Kong and Japan. I have travelled in Egypt, Pakistan, Bangladesh, Ceylon, Iran, Aden and New Zealand, and in the spring of 1972 I spent five months in the islands of the South Pacific, which include some of Britain's last colonies. All these journeys have contributed in terms of understanding to the texture of this book.

The books listed below are those which I have recently found useful or enlightening and from which I think readers may gather valuable background material. Except for two or three unusually important titles, I have not thought it necessary to duplicate the bibliographies included in the *Encyclopedia Britannica* under the article on the Commonwealth of Nations or under those relating to the various dominions and to India, though I have naturally consulted all the works listed there.

Afigbo, A. E.: *The Warrant Chiefs: Indirect Rule in Southeastern Nigeria 1891–1929* (1972).
Barber, Noel: *Sinister Twilight* (1969).
Barr, Pat: *The Deer Cry Pavilion* (1968).
Bastin, John (ed.): *The Emergence of Modern South-East Asia* (1967).

Beasley, W. G.: *Great Britain and the Opening of Japan* (1951).
Beloff, Max: *Imperial Sunset* (1970).
Bennett, George (ed.): *Concept of Empire, Burke to Attlee, 1774–1949* (1953).
Biggs-Davidson, John: *Africa—Hope Deferred* (1972).
Blake, Robert: *Disraeli* (1966).
Bondurant, Joan: *The Conquest of Violence* (1958).
Brecher, Michael: *Nehru: A Political Biography* (1959).
——: *The New States of Asia* (1963).
Burroughs, Peter: *The Canadian Crisis and British Colonial Policy, 1828–41* (1972).
Cambridge History of the British Empire (1929–63).
Campbell, Robert D.: *Pakistan* (1963).
Clark, Manning: *A Short History of Australia* (1963).
Clodd, H. P.: *Malaya's First Pioneer* (1948).
Coen, Terence Creagh: *The Indian Political Service* (1971).
Collier, Richard: *The Sound of Fury* (1963).
Collis, Maurice: *Foreign Mud* (1946).
——: *Raffles* (1966).
Creighton, Donald: *Canada's First Century* (1970).
——: *Dominion of the North* (1957).
——: *The Empire of the St Lawrence* (1956).
Cross, Colin: *The Fall of the British Empire* (1968).
Crozier, Brian: *South-East Asia in Turmoil* (1965).
Cumpston, I. M.: *The Growth of the British Commonwealth, 1880–1932* (1973).
Curtin, Philip D. (ed.): *Imperialism* (1971).
Dangerfield, George: *The Strange Death of Liberal England* (1935).
Das, M. N.: *India Under Morley and Minto* (1964).
Davidson, Basil (ed.): *The African Past* (1964).
Davidson-Houston, J. V.: *Yellow Creek* (1962).
Dhawan, Gopinath: *The Political Philosophy of M. K. Gandhi* (1946).
Dilke, Sir Charles: *Greater Britain* (1885).
Drage, Charles: *Servants of the Dragon Throne* (1966).
Duff, Charles: *Six Days to Shake an Empire* (1966).
Eayrs, James: *The Commonwealth and Suez* (1964).
Edwardes, Michael: *Bound to Exile* (1969).
——: *The British in India* (1967).
Endacott, G. B.: *An Eastern Entrepot* (1964).
——: *A History of Hong Kong* (1964).

Erikson, Erik H.: *Gandhi's Truth* (1969).
Farwell, Byron: *Queen Victoria's Little Wars* (1973).
Fieldhouse, D. K.: *The Colonial Empires* (1966).
Fischer, Louis: *Gandhi* (1954).
Fitzgerald, C. P.: *Revolution in China* (1952).
Fleming, Peter: *The Siege of Peking* (1959).
Gandhi, M. K.: *An Autobiography: The Story of My Experiments with Truth* (1927).
——: *Hindu Dharma* (1950).
——: *Non-Violent Resistance* (1951).
Greenberger, Allen J.: *The British Image of India: A Study in the Literature of Imperialism* (1969).
Grierson, Edward: *The Imperial Dream* (1972).
Griffiths, Sir Percival: *Empire into Commonwealth* (1969).
Hahn, Emily: *Raffles of Singapore* (1948).
Hitsman, J. Mackay: *The Incredible War of 1812* (1965).
Hobsbawm, Eric: *Industry and Empire* (1968).
Hobson, J. A.: *Imperialism: A Study* (1902).
Hutchins, Francis G.: *The Illusion of Permanence: British Imperialism in India* (1967).
Inglis, Brian: *Roger Casement* (1973).
Kincaid, Dennis: *British Social Life in India, 1608–1937* (1938).
Kirby, S. Woodburn: *Singapore* (1971).
Latourette, K. S.: *A History of Modern China* (1954)
Lenin, V. I.: *Imperialism: the Highest Stage of Capitalism* (1917).
Lewis, Martin D.: *The British in India: Imperialism or Trusteeship* (1962).
Ludowyck, E. F. C.: *The Modern History of Ceylon* (1966).
Lugard, Frederick D.: *The Dual Mandate in British Tropical Africa* (1929).
McNaught, Kenneth: *The History of Canada* (1970).
Magnus, Philip: *Gladstone* (1954).
——: *Kitchener: Portrait of an Imperialist* (1958).
Mansergh, Nicholas: *The Irish Question, 1840–1921* (1965).
Masani, R. P.: *Britain in India* (1960).
Meebolo, Henry S.: *Reaction to Colonialism* (1971).
Moon, Penderel: *Divide and Quit* (1961).
——: *Gandhi* (1968).
Moore, R. J.: *Liberalism and Indian Politics* (1966).
Moraes, Frank: *Jawaharlal Nehru* (1956).

Morris, James: *Pax Britannica* (1968).
Mosley, Leonard: *The Last Days of the British Raj* (1961).
Nehru, Jawaharlal: *The Discovery of India* (1956).
——: *India and the World* (1936).
——: *Towards Freedom* (1941).
Nutting, Anthony: *Lawrence of Arabia* (1961).
——: *Scramble for Africa* (1971).
Oliver, W. H.: *The Story of New Zealand* (1960).
Olivier, Sydney: *White Capital and Coloured Labour* (1929).
O'Malley, L. S. S.: *The Indian Civil Service, 1601–1930* (1931).
Owen, Frank: *The Fall of Singapore* (1960).
Pandey, B. N.: *The Break-up of British India* (1969).
Parkinson, Northcote: *Trade in the Eastern Seas* (1937).
——: *War in the Eastern Seas* (1954).
Parry, Benita: *Delusions and Discoveries: Studies of India in the British Imagination, 1890–1930* (1972).
Peffer, N.: *Transition and Tension in Southeast Asia* (1957).
Pelcovits, N. A.: *Old China Hands and the Foreign Office* (1948).
Roberts, P. E.: *History of British India* (1952).
Robertson, Terence: *Crisis: The Inside of the Suez Conspiracy* (1964).
Robinson, Ronald, and John Gallaher: *Africa and the Victorians* (1965).
Rose, Kenneth: *Superior Person: A Portrait of Curzon* (1969).
Rotberg, Robert I. (ed.): *Rebellion in Black Africa* (1971).
Runciman, Steven: *The White Rajas* (1960).
Sampson, Anthony: *Macmillan* (1967).
Searight, Sarah: *The British in the Middle East* (1969).
Seeley, J. R.: *The Expansion of England* (1883).
Smith, Goldwin: *The Empire* (1863).
Spear, Percival: *A History of India* (1965).
——: *The Nabobs* (1932).
Spencer-Chapman, F.: *The Jungle is Neutral* (1949).
Stephens, Ian: *Pakistan* (1963).
Strachey, John: *The End of Empire* (1959).
Thomas, Hugh: *The Suez Affair* (1967).
Thompson, Edward, and G. T. Garratt: *Rise and Fulfilment of British Rule in India* (1966).
Thornton, A. P.: *The Imperial Idea and its Enemies* (1959).
Tregonning, K. G.: *A History of Modern Sabah* (1965).
Wallbank, T. W.: *India in the New Era* (1951).

Winks, Robin W.: *The Historiography of the British Empire-Commonwealth* (1966).

Woodcock, George: *Canada and the Canadians* (1970).

——: *Gandhi* (1972).

——: *The British in the Far East* (1969).

Woodruff, Philip: *The Men who Ruled India* (1953–4).

Index

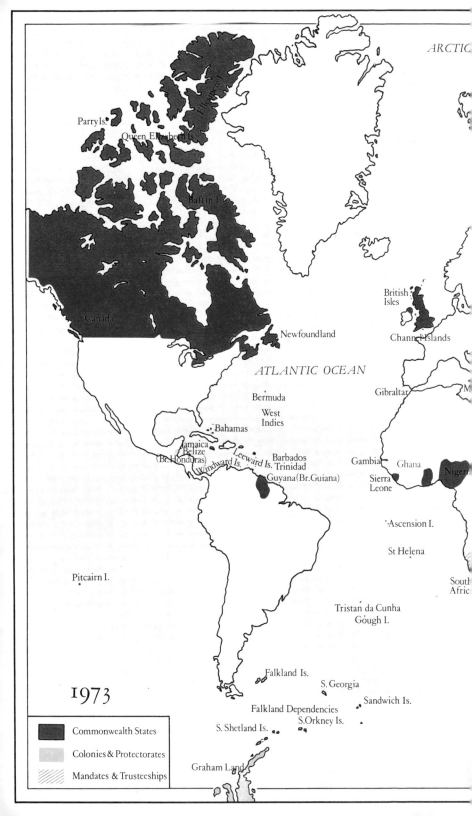

ARCTIC

Parry Is.
Queen Elizabeth Is.
Ellesmere I.

Baffin I.

Canada

Newfoundland

British
Isles

Channel Islands

ATLANTIC OCEAN

Bermuda

West
Indies

Gibraltar

M

Bahamas

Jamaica
Belize
(Br.Honduras)
Windward Is.
Leeward Is.
Barbados
Trinidad
Guyana(Br.Guiana)

Gambia

Ghana

Nigeri

Sierra
Leone

Ascension I.

St Helena

Pitcairn I.

South
Afric

Tristan da Cunha
Gough I.

Falkland Is.

S. Georgia

Sandwich Is.

1973

Falkland Dependencies
S. Shetland Is.

S.Orkney Is.

Graham Land

■	Commonwealth States
	Colonies & Protectorates
▨	Mandates & Trusteeships